THE VERNEY FAMILY DURING
THE CIVIL WAR

VOL. I.

SIR EDMUND VERNEY. K^t. M.
"Done in Spain. Very unlike"

Sir Edmund Verney, Kt.
from a picture painted in Spain, at Claydon House.

Ed: Verney

MEMOIRS OF THE VERNEY FAMILY
Vol. 1. DURING THE CIVIL WAR

COMPILED FROM THE LETTERS AND ILLUSTRATED BY
THE PORTRAITS AT CLAYDON HOUSE

BY

FRANCES PARTHENOPE VERNEY

'In winter's tedious nights sit by the fire
With good old folks, and let them tell thee tales
Of woeful ages long ago'

EAST CLAYDON CHURCH

VOL. I.

BARNES & NOBLE, Inc.
NEW YORK
PUBLISHERS & BOOKSELLERS SINCE 1873

Originally published 1892 by
Longmans, Green & Co., London
This edition published 1970 by
The Tabard Press Limited, London

First published in the United States, 1970
by Barnes & Noble, Inc.

ISBN 389 04032 0

Made and Printed in Great Britain by
Redwood Press Limited
Trowbridge & London

INTRODUCTORY NOTE

——◇——

In 1845 Mr. Bruce edited for the Camden Society 'Notes of Proceedings in the Long Parliament,' from the jottings of Sir Ralph Verney, and in 1853 he followed them up by a volume of 'Letters and Papers of the Verney Family' reaching down to the end of the year 1639, published by the same Society. The extraordinary value of the collection of MSS. preserved at Claydon House thus became sufficiently known, but though Mr. Bruce contemplated the preparation of another volume, he had not taken any steps towards it at the time of his death. The great mass of the papers was still in disorder, and much had to be done before progress could be made in this direction.

Not long after her marriage, which took place in 1858, the late Lady Verney's attention was attracted to the treasures contained in the house. Some of the numerous portraits were stacked in outhouses, one of them being fastened over a hole to keep out rats. These she arranged, and with the help of descriptions in old lists managed to identify most of the subjects.

No less care did she devote to the collection of papers, one bundle of which was endorsed by some fatuous person, 'Private letters of no interest.' She soon began to read them, all the more eagerly perhaps because she was even at that time somewhat of an invalid and compelled to pass a considerable part of her time on the sofa. The arrangement of the letters in chronological order was gradually completed, and many whole letters or extracts copied for easier reference.

Then the idea of writing the story of the family dawned on Lady Verney's mind. For this task she had admirable qualifications in addition to her extreme interest in the subject. She had received from her father, Mr. Nightingale, an excellent education, including a good knowledge of English literature. Her bright intelligence was quickened by her warm sympathy, and to her the personages of the seventeenth century, whose joys and sorrows are told in their writings, were as living as her own contemporaries. Gossip about the love affairs or the pecuniary embarrassments of Pen or Sue Verney, who lived during the Civil War and Commonwealth, flowed as readily from her lips when she found a fitting listener as tittle-tattle about the pictures in the London exhibitions or about the latest fashions flows from the lips of others. Nor was it only with the actions of these persons that she was familiar. She sounded their hearts, and came to know instinctively what each one of them was capable or incapable of doing.

No wonder, therefore, that the work which Lady Verney had undertaken fascinated her mind. Before she had proceeded far, she was attacked by the acutest form of rheumatism, arthritis, and. lived for years under the infliction of constant pain. Yet she never from this cause laid her work aside, which indeed to some extent alleviated her suffering by drawing her attention away from herself, the last object of which, in her days of health, she would have been likely to think. At first she was able to use a stylograph pen with difficulty, but at last the condition of her hands became such that not only did this become impossible, but she was unable to turn over the pages of the letters which she wished to consult. How great a difficulty was thereby thrown in the way of the composition of her narrative may be easily imagined. Mr. Bruce's books were of great assistance to Lady Verney in writing the first volume, and she has used them freely in the earlier part of the story, in some places adopting whole paragraphs.

What could be done for her by helpful friends was freely offered. Her own loving nature made helpful service easy. Her husband Sir Harry Verney cheered her by his constant interest in and sympathy with her work. Prominent amongst those who at this time rendered assistance were the Hon. Misses Frederica and Catherine Spring Rice, who were most energetic in collecting materials and verifying quotations, whilst much work in copying was entrusted to Lady Verney's faithful amanuensis, Mr. W. J. Morey.

After some hesitation Lady Verney decided on bringing down her work to 1650, the year of the death of Sir Ralph's wife, which formed an epoch in the domestic history of the family; the appearance on the scene of Sir Ralph's son, young Edmund, opening as it were a new chapter, and bringing a reader of the correspondence into the presence of the generation which took part in the overthrow of Puritan supremacy and the restoration of the monarchy. Lady Verney herself had almost completed the first, and had sketched out and partly written the second, of the two volumes now issued. What remained to be done by filling in gaps, by inserting quotations, and by some excisions where the narrative strayed too far into the domain of political history, has been accomplished by her daughter-in-law, Mrs. Verney, with the assistance of the Misses Spring Rice.

Mrs. Verney wishes me to add that she would be glad to receive any information from readers of the book who may have at their command any further evidence to offer on the history of the Verneys in the seventeenth century, or of other families connected with the Verneys, and that such communications should be addressed to her at Claydon House, Winslow, Bucks.

SAMUEL R. GARDINER.

February 20, 1892.

PREFACE

THE value of contemporary records, even of the purely private life of the letter-writers of bygone centuries, has only been acknowledged within very late years. It almost required an apology when such home-spun materials were presented to the public. Now, however, we are deluged by a mass of documents unearthed by the Historical Commission ; and it will be long before the information thus acquired can be worked into the common stock.

The period before and during the Civil Wars, to which the Verney letters so largely belong, must always be supremely interesting to us as the turning point in English History, especially when seen through the eyes of those who lived and wrote in those anxious times.

Though facts may have been misapprehended by them, though their opinions may have been mistaken, what cannot be wrong is the vivid record of the atmosphere in which these men and women lived, and of the beliefs and impressions that surrounded them and produced the overt acts which alone have been chronicled.

The 'dignity of history' has a great deal to answer for. It has been supposed to concern itself only with reigns of kings, conquests and defeats, alliances and treaties, and the intermarriages of rather uninteresting personages, while the great stream of life of common-place people, what they thought and what they felt, has till lately been only considered important when the mass of convictions became powerful enough to create an upheaval of some definite kind. History is indeed written in a different spirit at the present day.

The collection of original letters belonging to private families is probably larger in England than in any other country. The great houses in France, Germany and Italy have been ransacked by foreign armies ; millions of papers have been destroyed in political and religious persecutions, fire and the sword have made away with the owners and their homes, and what remains has generally been swallowed up in the national collections. In England the papers still exist in their original homes, but till now they have been a sealed book. The stories of the perils they have gone through are harrowing to an antiquary. At Wroxton some peculiar writing was noticed on the paper cap of a carpenter by an observant boy ; 'waste paper,' they said, 'taken out of those dirty old boxes'—in which were afterwards found the correspondence of a Chancellor of the days of Henry VIII. In another house some bags of rubbish were removed out of a closet to make way for jam and

soap, and a parchment of a Knight of the Garter of
Elizabeth's time dropped out. ' Oh, that's only the
old paper the housemaids have to light the fire with,'
said the housekeeper. When Sir R. Puleston of
Emral sold his goods and chattels, the Jews who were
carrying them away asked leave to pack the smaller
valuables in the piles of old papers which they said
they found in the garrets. Some wise man took the
trouble to look into them before they were removed,
and a number of letters of Margaret of Anjou were
found amongst them, of whose writing not a scrap
had previously been known to exist.

When the present possessor of Claydon, Sir Harry
Verney, came to live there, he found a wainscoted
gallery at the top of the house, forty feet long, full of
boxes on tressels containing bundles of letters, acres
of parchment, charters and pardons with the great seals
attached, early editions of plays, account books, terriers
and rent-rolls—these literally, as their name implies,
strips of paper stitched together, many feet in length,
and in this case dating from the time of Henry
VII.—' Mercuries,' diurnals of the period of the
Civil Wars, ' newes letters '—the early form of news-
paper before the printed manner of promulgating
news had been invented—all these were ' stacked '
round the room. Some few were touched by damp;
some, where the paper was at all greasy, gnawed by
rats ; but they were generally in very good condition.

The letters related to the private concerns of the
Verneys, who owned the Manor of Claydon for four-

teen generations, beginning with Sir Ralph, Lord
Mayor of London in 1465 and M.P. for London
in 1472, and going down to Mary Verney created
Baroness Fermanagh, who died unmarried in 1810.

These years include the most stirring periods of
English history. The Verney records are only those
of an ordinary gentleman's family of the higher class,
mixing a good deal in the politics of their times, with
considerable county and local influence ; Members
of Parliament, sheriffs, magistrates, soldiers—never
place-men—marrying in their own degree, with no
splendid talents or position to boast of, no crimes
either noble or ignoble to make them notorious, and,
for that very reason, good average specimens of
hundreds of men and women of their age. Their
actions, their opinions and beliefs, their thoughts
about public affairs and home perplexities, their joys
and sorrows, their habits of life and manners were
not too fair and good, or again too evil, to be shared
by households of their own class, so that we come
nearer to the ordinary public opinion and social
standards of their day than by reading of those
exceptionally great men who only partially represent
their age, and yet which history has brought before
us almost exclusively. Most of the work of the
world is done by average men and women, and the
personal records of the Verneys, touching on small
matters as they generally must, are not without a
very general interest in the great history of their
country. The materials are only too voluminous—

there are 30,000 letters up to the date of Sir Ralph's
death in 1696. Sometimes there is a letter for every
day in the year, with a copy of the reply subjoined
by Sir Ralph and carefully docketed by his son Lord
Fermanagh, with an interpretation of the ciphers,
initials, devices to conceal names of places and persons
which in these troublous times were frequently used.
The paper on which they write is coarse, with un-
trimmed edges, but is strong and lasting. The hand-
writing of the men is for the most part bold, clear
and good, but the education of the women in the
seventeenth century was evidently very inferior to
that of the time of Elizabeth ; their penmanship is
execrable, and their spelling purely phonetic. Lady
Sussex (a clever woman and very great lady, who
married three Earls in succession after the death of
her first husband, Sir Henry Lee) has considerable
doubts about her Hs—' Mr. Bakon,' half-nephew of
the Chancellor, ' his heer and is brother'—' will you
get me a Member of the hoper hose' (the upper
house). It requires some apprenticeship to recognise
Yorkshire, St. Alban's, and Lincoln's-inn-Fields
in ' Oyskescher,' ' Sentarbones,' and ' Lingeslinds
fildes.' ' Amazes me ' is written ' A maisis mee.'
And Lady Sussex was no exception. Lady Verney's
two sisters, clever women of the world and accus-
tomed to the best society of the day, write and spell
much after the same fashion.

The great mass of letters were preserved by Sir
Ralph Verney, the then head of the family. He was

one of those useful men who seem to regard every
scrap of written paper as sacred. He kept everything ; notes in answer to invitations, old bills,
broadsides, doggerel verses, foul copies of orders to
bailiffs, attorneys' accounts, tailors' bills, &c., leaving
it to posterity to select what was valuable. Posterity
however is very capricious, and is apt to cast aside all
sorts of grand things committed to its charge, and to
find interest in petty details supposed to be beneath
its notice.

The materials are so abundant that in two volumes
it has been only possible to reach the year 1649–50,
after the execution of the king and the death of some
of the principal actors in the family history. This
period includes the story of the chivalrous, high-
minded, honourable Knight Marshal, Sir Edmund
Verney, torn in pieces by his attachment for his
master Charles, whom he had served almost from
their common boyhood, and his belief that the party
of the Parliament was in the main right ; who chose
rather to lose his life in battle than to continue the
struggle to fulfil such conflicting duties.

His son, the painstaking, conscientious Sir Ralph,
somewhat formal and precise, most upright of men,
writer of ' Notes of the Long Parliament,' of which
he was a Member, who, when he considered that his
party was going too far, preferred exile for about
seven years rather than sign the Covenant in which
he did not believe, or agree to measures which he
thought to be wrong (for this his estate was se-

questered, and he himself ousted from Parliament); the gallant young Cavalier, Sir Edmund the younger, brother to Ralph, brave, loyal, affectionate, unswerving in his convictions and in what he believed to be his duty, who, when little more than thirty, was put to death in cold blood after the storming of Drogheda; the scapegrace Tom; the clever, shrewd, worldly, exacting Lady Sussex, and the two sisters Mrs. Eure and Mrs. Isham, Ralph's aunts, figure in the earlier part of these volumes. Later, especially after Ralph is exiled to Blois, are long letters, describing what is going on in London from 1643 to 1649, from Dr. Denton, a mild Royalist, kind-hearted, cynical, clever; from Sir Roger Burgoyne, M.P. for Bedfordshire, who had espoused the ultra side in Parliament; from Colonel Henry Verney, selfish, self-seeking, faithless, who changed from side to side according to his interests, and from the charming Mary, Ralph's wife, painted by Vandyck, who was sent by her husband to London to try and negotiate his return. Married to him as the heiress of Abingdon, &c., when only a child herself, most devoted of wives and most tender of mothers, she wore herself out by her exertions and her journeys, generally on horseback, and died when only thirty-three after her return to her husband at Blois, just as her efforts had been crowned with success.

The materials had to be collected painfully, a few lines here and a few words there, out of hundreds of letters otherwise perhaps quite uninteresting ; but in such a case as that of Sir Ralph, after reading again and again, in thousands of different forms, the most minute details of his thoughts, his feelings, his difficulties and anxieties on every possible subject, one grows almost more intimate with him than with any living friend of the present generation, and it becomes a work of conscience to attempt, with the best skill one can bring to bear on the subject, to piece together into a coherent whole the character and fortunes of men and women so mixed up with the political struggles and the Civil War in England during those momentous years from 1630 to 1650.

F. PARTHENOPE VERNEY.

CLAYDON HOUSE,
December 8, 1889.

CONTENTS

OF

THE FIRST VOLUME

———•◦•———

CHAPTER III.

THE EARLY HISTORY OF THE VERNEYS, 1456–1599.

CHAPTER IV.

THE VERNEYS OF THE SEVENTEENTH CENTURY—THE HALF-BROTHERS, SIR FRANCIS AND SIR EDMUND VERNEY.

CHAPTER XIV.

THE VERNEYS IN PARLIAMENT.

NOTES ON THE ILLUSTRATIONS

TO VOLUME I

AFTER the ruin of the owner of Claydon in the eighteenth century, pictures, papers, and books were exposed, misused, and destroyed ; one picture on panel had been used to stop the window of the apple-room, another was in the loft over the pigs, the rats had gnawed the corners of a third. The names and stories of some have been hope-lessly lost, and a whole series which were sent up to ' Lundun to be cleand and vernist,' were literally flayed alive, while at least one Vandyck and two Jansens have disappeared altogether. Happily among the letters were several old lists of the seventeenth and eighteenth centuries which, together with some dates and inscriptions on the pictures themselves, have led to the identification of all the portraits here given. The illustrations are photo-intaglio copper plates, carefully reproduced from photographs taken of the original pictures at Claydon ; the autographs are facsimiles of signatures from old letters and deeds. We are greatly indebted to Messrs. Walker and Boutall for the infinite pains they have bestowed in producing such artistic and beautiful engravings. The descriptions of the pictures, given with quotation marks, are from old lists.

MEMOIRS OF THE VERNEY FAMILY

DURING

THE CIVIL WAR

CHAPTER I.

THE HOUSE AND THE HOUSE-KEEPING AT CLAYDON.

'. . . . an English home gray twilight pour'd
On dewy pastures, dewy trees,
. . . . all things in order stored,
A haunt of ancient peace.'—TENNYSON.

THE house at Claydon is spoken of as having been rebuilt in the reign of Henry VII., but there had been an 'ancient seat' on the spot in the days of the De la Zouchs and Cantelupes, from whose descendants Sir Ralph Verney, the Lord Mayor in 1465, acquired the property. A pencil sketch exists, of uncertain date, which represents one phase of the old building, with gables in 'corbel steps.' Its lines were framed on the initial letter of the king's name, H during the reign of the Henries, E during that of Edward and Elizabeth, and the fashion seems to have lasted into the reign of James I.

Although altered, added to, almost transmogrified, the form of the ancient manor house may still be

VOL. I.

traced at the core of the present building. The central narrow part, joining the two blocks, consisted, until thirty years ago, of two rows of rooms back to back, so that the ends of the house could only be reached by passing through a whole suite ; passages were unknown at that period of architecture. None of the walls were at right angles ; the floors rose and fell again in the same room to a difference of three or four inches in level ; it was like walking over a ridge in a ploughed field ; and a ceiling would vary in height as much as six inches in a length of thirty feet. A great chimney, with chimney corners on the ground floor, ran up the centre of the house, belonging probably to the hall-kitchen ; another was in what was called the ' Tenants' Hall.' These were probably the only two which the house contained at the time it was built. As late as the reign of Elizabeth, Harrison, quoted by Holinshed, observes, ' Old men have noted three things marvellously altered in England within their sound remembrance. One is the multitude of chimneys—in their younger days there were not above two or three, if so many, in most uplandish " towns " in the realm (the religious houses and manor places of the lords excepted), but each made his fire against a reredosse in the hall, where he dined and dressed his meat. . . .' ' Now we have many chimneys and yet our tenderlings complain of rheums, catarrhs and poses. Then had we none but reredosses ; and our heads did never ache.'

Originally the fire was made in a hole in the

earth or hearth,[1] shut down by a cover when the family went to bed—the ' couvrefeu' (curfew) of William the Conqueror's edict. The reredos was a movable back to the fire, which was in time transferred to the wall, the chimney formed a small chamber with settles on each side, and 'dog irons' or ' andirons'[2] in front to support the logs of wood. Three 'reredosses' with the family crest of the Phœnix in flames, were found in the outhouses at Claydon (one dated 1664, belonging to Sir Ralph), and several pair of andirons.

In the central chimney at Claydon, a small chamber of concealment was found (when the house was repaired thirty years ago), in which ten men could stand upright, a 'priest's hole or conveyance,' the secret of which had been so well kept as to be altogether forgotten ; such hiding-places were known only to the owner of a house and his eldest son, and were handed down with solemn secrecy to the next generation. At Claydon it was ingeniously masked by a blind passage in the middle storey, and was completely dark. It must have been entered by a trap-door in the muniment room, at the top of the house ; where, too, was a concealed door leading to a small private stair, long since destroyed, but of which the stone heads of the steps could still be traced. If enemies forced their way into the house, a man might

---

[1] Hearth is defined by Dryden as the 'pavement of a room where a fire is made.'

[2] ' Her andirons I had forgot, two winking Cupids done in silver.' — *Cymbeline.*

escape up the public stair, *down* the secret stair, and out by a door less likely to be strictly guarded than the other issues. A similar stair still exists at Mancetter, near Atherstone, with a break half way, where a man must let himself down several feet.

It is an illustration of the probable origin of half the ghost stories *de rigueur* in old houses, that this room where the trap-door and stairhead required that all prying investigations should be discouraged, was the haunted chamber of the place. The particular apparition most likely varied with the period ; at Claydon the ghost of Sir Edmund Verney, the Knight Marshal, as the most marked man of the family, was the one whose appearance had survived up to the present. He was supposed to be always looking for his hand, severed from his body at the battle of Edgehill, which, according to tradition, had been found still holding the king's standard, though the body itself was lost.

There was probably little or no glass in the house of Henry VII.'s time ; linen steeped in oil was the substitute, or wooden shutters closed only at night, still to be seen in Spain and South Italy. The glazed casements of the Dukes of Northumberland were removed for safety when the family left Alnwick, and Sir Thomas More in his ' Utopia ' mentions that ' there were glass windows in most of the houses ' of his ideal country, as a proof of its advanced civilisation.

The rough walls of the rooms were covered with

tapestry or wainscot. The tapestry at Claydon, mentioned in the old lists, has all disappeared, but much of the wainscot remained in garrets and out-houses. The 'use of the wainscot' was esteemed so important that it is specifically granted to Sir Edmund in 1634, in the lease of the house which he took in Covent Garden, and all the separate pieces are enumerated. 'Stock-locks' on the doors were also a luxury ; they were kept loose 'in the closet,' says the Claydon inventory ; and in 1650, when this same London house was let, it is mentioned as quite a new idea that, as the doors are so badly injured by the continual pulling off and on of the locks, they might as well be left on permanently. All classes were content to endure an amount of cold which we should find unbearable, from the absence of fires and the extreme airiness of houses, where no windows or doors ever fitted.

In 1620, when Sir Edmund took possession of Claydon, after buying back from the Giffards the end of a hundred years' lease, he was so hampered by the expense thus incurred, and by the bad condition in which the estate was left by his tenants, that he could do little to improve the house.

There are three inventories and descriptions of it, the first ordered by Sir Ralph soon after his father's death in 1645, the next about eighty years later, and the third quite at the end of the last century, which together give some idea of the growth of a country house.

Sir Ralph, then an exile in France, tells his brother that ' since the beginning of the Civil Wars, the best goods have been removed from ye right places to bee more saifly layed upp, and noates must be taken of what by my order are stored up, lent, sould or given away.' He mentions ' ye studdy over the greate porch,' Sir Edmund Verney's closet. Most of the rooms seem to have had an inner dressing-room with no separate access. Wheat had been stored on the oak floor of the dining-room when threshed, but it must be seen that ' the cullor of the boards be not hurt.' ' The odd things in the roome my mother keept herself, the iron closet, the little roome betweene her beds head and the backstairs '— evidently a secret place—' the little and greate Frip-peries [i.e. hanging closets for gowns] your owne greene wrought velvet furniture, the red velvet fur-niture, the looking-glasses (there should bee at least four), leather carpets for the dininge and drawinge rooms, the stooles with nailes guilt, the great cabanet like yours, the tapestry, the great branch candlestick, all such wrought worke as my mother had from London and was not finished, the booke of martirs and other bookes in the withdrawing-room, the pre-serving-room, the spicery with furnaces and brewing vessels, plat left for the children's use, all the lockes that are loose in the closet '—such was the interior of the old house in 1645.

The house is situated on a gentle slope sheltered from the east and north—our ancestors showed a

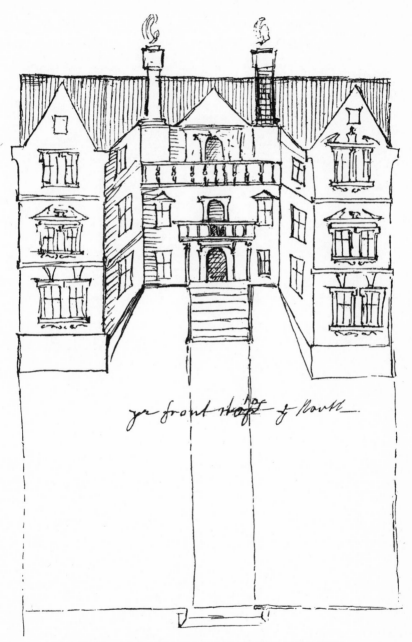

ye front ~~roff~~ of Rovll

CLAYDON HOUSE IN THE SEVENTEENTH CENTURY—NORTH FRONT
(From an old Pencil Drawing.)

strange dislike to wind in the positions they chose for their dwellings (as opposed to castles intended for defence), and none at all to damp, which is to us more objectionable ; the difficulty of obtaining fuel may account for their preference of what seemed to them warm—and to us low situations. To the east of the courtyard and stables which bear the modern date of 1764, lies a straggling mass of buildings of every possible description. A great house provisioned itself, with little help from the outer world ; the inhabitants brewed and baked, they churned and ground their meal, they bred up, fed and slew their beeves and sheep, and brought up their pigeons and poultry at their own doors. Their horses were shod at home, their planks were sawn, their rough iron work was forged and mended. Accordingly the mill-house, the slaughter-house, the blacksmiths', carpenters' and painters' shops, the malting and brewhouse, the wood-yard full of large and small timber, the sawpit, the outhouses full of all sorts of odds and ends of stone, iron, bits of marble, carved woodwork, and logs cut for burning—the riding-house, the laundry, the dairy with a large churn turned by a horse, the stalls and styes for all manner of cattle and pigs, the apple and root chambers, show how complete was the idea of self-supply and inde-pendence of trade of any kind at Claydon as in other country houses. Of the ' Dove Cotts,' we read continually in the letters, as a dozen pigeons were an acceptable present to friends in London, almost preferred indeed to the venison, which Sir Ralph is very generous in distributing.

In a series of graduated little pools in the garden called 'the Stews,' belonging to the Old Roman Catholic days, the fish caught in the larger ponds below was kept for immediate use. A supply of wild fowl was obtained from a Decoy 'celebrated in the neighbourhood,' observes Browne Willis, leading by a long watercourse from a great pool about a mile away into the heart of the 'Charndon and great sea woods.' The difficulty of keeping cattle and sheep alive in winter on the scanty stores of hay was so great that until the middle of the 17th century they were killed and salted down early in the autumn. In the Northumberland household book of the reign of Henry VII., it appears that fresh meat was eaten only between Midsummer and Michaelmas. The frequent mention of skin diseases in the Verney letters shows how the salt diet, almost unrelieved by vegetables for many months, told upon the health particularly of the women and children ; any little relief from fish and game was valuable.

Matters were however improving in the days of James and Charles I. Salt meat was now only used after Martinmas, potatoes had been introduced by Sir Walter Raleigh, and Sir Ralph is intent upon many sorts of salad and vegetables which he sends from France between 1644 and 1653. That they were not altogether new, however, is evident from the cynical remarks of his uncle, Dr. Denton. On receiving the presents of seeds and plants from his nephew, he often declares that he ' cannot see they are much better than the sallats he has already.' Ralph on his return is very anxious for the welfare of the vines and fig trees, the roots, seeds, flowers, and

THE GARDEN.
(From a sketch by Lady Verney.)

ornamental trees, which he gets over from Holland and France, and in spite of Lord Macaulay's state-ment to the contrary, it is clear that great attention was beginning to be paid to gardens and pleasure grounds. We hear of the ' Persian tulips and ranon-

cules' sent him by his son John at his particular
request, apparently from Holland ; the pinks, gilli-
flowers, melon seeds and pear-grafts, and 'the exact
fine gardens' at Claydon are mentioned in 1694 by
Cecilia Fiennes.   The woods were always a great
feature of the Claydon Estate, and the arts of wood-
craft and forestry amongst the constant interests of
its owners.   Sir Ralph desires his steward to go and
see 'Cozen Smith's hedges at Akeley,' which are
grown in a west-country fashion, and to give him
his opinion of them.

Within doors the activity of the family and household was as great and as multifarious as without.
The spinning of wool and flax (so universal that an
unmarried woman of any class was called 'a spinster'),
the fine and coarse needlework, the embroidery, the
fine cooking, the curing, the preserving, the distillery
that went on, were incessant.   The excellent linen
spun at home and woven in the cottage handlooms
(well described in 'Silas Marner'), was so valuable
that it was left by will with great particularity.
Margaret, Lady Verney, is as careful to which of her
daughters she will leave her 'best sheets,' and to
whom 'the second best,' and the 'table clothes,' as
about the destination of her diamonds, and though
her children are a loving family, there is nearly a
disagreeable quarrel between Sir Ralph and his sister
Pen, when she prefers money, and he allows her only
8*l.* for the sheets in question.   As 10*l.* at the time is the
price of a good horse, this sounds a quite sufficient sum.

The work with the needle and the wheel was a very necessary part of a lady's education, and as some of the poorer relations of the family resided in great houses as 'lady helps' (the equivalents of the pages of the other sex), they were useful and welcome in carrying out these important household labours. There are letters from five or six of these ladies, connected with the Verneys, well born, well bred, and as well educated as their neighbours, who seem to have been treated with great consideration. 'Sir George Strickland's daughter is my lady's gentlewoman' to Lady Sussex, and Sir Ralph's cousin, Lady Hobart, is very anxious when she becomes poor and a widow, that he should obtain the place for her daughter 'Frank.' Doll Leake, another cousin, is living with Lady Vere Gaudy and her daughter-in-law, Lady Mary Fielding, who are both warmly attached to her. She is busy embroidering a bed on one occasion, and writes to Sir Ralph in London to help her with the silks and crewels required for it.

Lace-making had been introduced into Bucks by Catherine of Aragon, whose dowry was derived from the revenues of Steeple Claydon. She was visiting at a house in Buckingham, still standing in Sir Ralph's days, when she received the news of the victory at Flodden Field. 'St. Katern's day' was held as a festival in her honour until not long ago, by the makers of pillow-lace in Buckinghamshire ; and the allusion to

'The spinsters and the knitters in the sun,
And the free maids who weave their thread with bones,'

whom Viola quotes as her authority for a song, shows that pillow-lace was commonly made in England in Shakespeare's time.

The work of the still-room, the 'preserving, conserving, candying, making syrupes, jellies, beautifying washes, pomatum essences, and other such secrets,' the making of vinegar and pickles, must have been held by the family to be quite as important a part of their business.

Accordingly in the fruit season the ladies are very fully occupied. Lady Gardiner is excused by her husband from writing to Sir Ralph—'being almost melted with the double heat of the weather and her hotter employment, because the fruit is suddenly ripe and she is so busy preserving,' and this though their household is very large, consisting of thirty persons. Mrs. Isham sends word to Lady Verney, through Sir Ralph, 'I praye tell yore mother (in London) I will doe oup hur sugar if she hath corrantes a nowe, for this last wicke of windes hath bine so bige that most of them was bloed off the treeses.'

The remains of queer tin vessels of many shapes with spouts at all angles, in the ancient cupboards of the Claydon still-room, and the endless recipes amongst the papers, show how the 'decoctions, infusions and essences of herbs and simples' were prepared. When a doctor wrote a prescription, he directed how the medicine was to be made. 'The snail water, the hiera picra, the mithridates, orbiculi, Bezoartis,' and the like, are all thus explained.

The fruit syrups, raspberry vinegar, home-made wines, currant, cowslip, and elder, were important drinks when tea, coffee, and chocolate were unknown. All three were introduced about the time of the Restoration. When Sir Ralph was young, the health of his bride was drunk by Sir Nathaniel Hobart 'in ale and cake, my wife and aunt will do the like,' showing it was the beverage for women as well as for men.[1] Some twenty years later, in 1650, Sir Ralph, in exile at Blois, writes anxiously to London for 'the quite new drink chocolate,' for his dying wife ; his uncle sends directions how to make it, because 'the thing itselfe is not knowne in France.' The fashion however spread quickly, for a few months after another exile sends the invalid a still better kind from Paris. The next year Sir Ralph, travelling after his wife's death with his little boy through Lyons, mentions 'coffee, a berry out of Turkey, ground for a drink,' as a curious novelty, and Pepys, as is well known, partakes of 'the new China drink, tea,' for the first time in 1660, after which the use of it became common.

Claydon must have looked melancholy enough to Sir Ralph, on his return from exile in the autumn of 1653, 'to keepe company with the ghostes,' a widower and alone in the deserted house. The estate had been so long without a head, under the management of

---

[1] The bitter and sweet do not sound pleasant to our taste, but that it was a favourite combination is evident from Sir Toby's speech in *Twelfth Night* : ' Dost thou think because thou art virtuous, there shall be no more cakes and ale ? '

the steward, that, as Sir Ralph wrote to a friend, 'In
these times our old servants are become our new
masters ; ' but after the Restoration his finances were
once more set in order ; the pictures, which had been
rolled up for safety, or carried abroad, were hung
again in their places, and there is much told of
rebuilding in the house and of improvements in
the gardens. Claydon is once more a centre of
hospitality.

Sir Ralph's aunt, Margaret Sherard, laments that
' my ill helth prevented me of com͞ing to Sweet
Claydon this som͞er for thers noe company nor plas
y^t I like better than what I had found ther.'

' My wife and I are thinking what new peice of
plate we shall find next time we come to Claydon,'
writes Sir Roger Burgoyne in 1671.   Sir Ralph
delights to share his plants with his friends. ' I have
received your presant,' says Lady Vere Gaudy in
March of the same year, ' and I shall indeavour to
make them grow, but our soile is not for raritys,
thorns and thistles is my portion in it, but now you
are goeing to your parradise, may it afford you all
the pleasure can bee injoyed on earth.'   Little as Sir
Ralph sympathised with Charles II., he found that
they had one taste in common, for he sends him
more than once some young trees from his nursery at
Claydon.   Sir William Boreman writes to Sir Ralph
from ' Whitehall this 12th of May 1671 ' :—

' So I begg y^r pardon that I have bin soe long
before I return'd y^u the king's kind acceptance of &

thankes for the Quickenbury trees [1] y^u sent his Ma^{ty} to whome I deliver'd them in yor name & told him howe bountifull y^u had bin before in furnishing, or rather beautifying Greenw^{ch} park wth plants of that kind ; they thrive exceeding well, & I should bee very happy to see y^u there, that y^u may see howe well they florish upon a piece of as barren ground as is in England. However, yor kindnes is not barren, wch upon all occasions I have receaved the fruite of, wch is most thankfully acknowledg'd by,' &c.

We hear of 'the spicery with a brass skillett,' of 'the fir walk' where the old man totters along, of 'the orange chamber' where he sits coughing and reading during his last illness, and where his meals are brought when 'he is too ill to get up for supper or prayers during his last week of life,' as his faithful factotum observes sadly ; of the brick parlour and of the great hall opening out of the porch into the best court, which were hung with black cloth when he died 'loved and honoured by all the country round,' as his niece writes.

Next comes a catalogue of the eighteenth century. 'The damask room,' the 'Lying in Room,' the 'velvet room with velvet curtains and squab ;' 'three pieces of superfine hangings, Tapstry ; one poeker

---

[1] Quicken-tree is a mountain ash or service-tree, some kinds of which were grown for their large berries. Miller says : 'In Italy they have many varieties from seed, but I have not observed in the English gardens more than three, and those are very scarce. . . . There was one in the garden of John Tradescant at South Lambeth (Charles I.'s Italian gardener) near 40 feet high, which produced a great quantity of fruit annually, shaped like pears.'

with brass head,' in my lady's chamber; chairs
covered with gilt leather are in the matted gallery;
chairs with walnut-tree frames, covered with yellow
silk flowered with silver, are in the white drawing-
room, while the 'middle brown lodgings' have 'iron
dogges, tapstry hangings, a silk quilt and Modena
window curtains.' There are new pictures of my
lord and my lady, but, alas! by Walker and Lenthall,
instead of the Vandycks and Cornelius Jansens of
the former generation.

The last account is quite at the end of the century,
when the last Verney of the old blood, Lady Fermanagh, inherited from her uncle, Ralph Earl
Verney.

He was a second son, and his elder brother died
leaving a widow with an unborn child, so that for
five months he did not know whether he should ever
possess the large estates which he dissipated so
unwisely. He was a man of magnificent instincts,
great artistic taste and knowledge, and boundless
extravagance. He began to build soon after his
father's death in 1752, the architect Adams, of the
Adelphi, giving the plans. Three large rooms, a
great central hall with marble pillars, and a ball room
120 feet long, were filled with carved woodwork,
doors inlaid with ebony, ivory, and satin wood, and
plaister mouldings on the ceilings done by Italian
artists of great beauty and variety. A central stair-
case, with steps like marqueterie, is a beautiful
feature; the wrought-iron scrolls and wreaths of

wheatears forming the banisters are of such delicacy and finish as to rustle at the tread of a passer-by. The proportion of the new rooms is very fine ; the library is nearly a double cube, 50 feet long and 25 feet high ; the pink parlour or summer dining-room, a single cube of 25 feet with lovely carvings, gives the impression of being much higher. Lord Houghton, sitting down to dinner there, exclaimed, ' I like a room where one feels one can stand upright.' The pictures, the books, the furniture were all on the same scale of lavish expenditure and taste ; one bedroom was ' furnisht all with silver,' of which only a lovely little mirror now remains.

Lord Verney fought the county in the Liberal interest against his rivals, the Temples of Stowe, and finally came to utter ruin. Before the house was finished the creditors rushed in and carried off every-thing, even to a marble chimneypiece for the library which had not yet been put into its place ; the pic-tures were happily heirlooms. His wife died in the crisis of their troubles, and he himself was said to have escaped in the empty hearse which had removed her body. After a while he returned, probably to get a little money, and hid in the desolate house, ' to keep company with the ghosts ' in a still sadder fashion than his ancestor. An old man used to describe, within living memory, how, as a boy of fourteen, he had ' seen the old lord a lookin' out of a window, and a beckonin' to me.' The house was perfectly bare, but the boy and a neighbour got him a table, a chair, and some food, and later a bed. The secret of his presence was carefully kept by the poor people at Claydon, lest his creditors should hear of it, and he remained hidden for a month. Half his estates had been sold, and he died soon after, forlorn and childless, in 1792. His niece and heiress, Lady Fermanagh, pulled down nearly two-thirds of his new building, but still left a large house standing; she was made a Baroness by Pitt, in right of her borough influence, and seems to have lived a cheerful pleasant life, chiefly at a villa near London; she remained a spinster, and with her the old race died out *en quenouille* in 1810.

ISABELLE GIFFARD.
(From a Brass in Middle Claydon Church.)

CHAPTER II.

THE MANORS AND CHURCHES OF THE FOUR CLAYDONS.

> Beneath those rugged elms, that yew-tree's shade,
> Where heaves the turf in many a mouldering heap,
> Each in his narrow cell for ever laid,
> The rude forefathers of the hamlet sleep.—GRAY.

THE estate now comprises the chief part of the manors of the four Claydons, Middel, Est, Botyl, and Steppel, as they are termed in the old deeds, but it was only gradually that the Verneys obtained possession of them, parting sometimes with land in other parts of Bucks and the adjoining counties of Oxford and Herts —Fleet Marston near Aylesbury, Penley near Tring, &c.—to consolidate their property.

The home chapel of Middle Claydon, which is much the oldest and the smallest of the three, stands within a few yards of the house, with the 'priest's door' at the top of a flight of stone steps overshadowed by yew trees, close to the library windows. It was during the long lease of 100 years granted by the Verneys to the Giffards, with whom they had twice intermarried, that the chancel was built, over the high narrow door of which is carved ' Rogerus Giffard et Maria uxor ejus hanc cancellam fieri fecerunt an'o D'ni 1519,' the work beginning in 1509. The body of the church was pronounced by Sir Gilbert Scott to be 'good fourteenth-century work.' It is set at such a different angle from the house which it so nearly adjoins that the dwelling was

MIDDLE CLAYDON CHURCH.
(From a sketch by Lady Verney.)

probably first on the ground.   Even with the utter disregard of symmetry evinced by our ancestors, which is one secret of the picturesqueness of their groups of buildings, it is almost impossible to fancy that the house should, without any reason of space or lie of ground, have been built askew with the church; whereas when ' St. Michael and all angels ' was the patron chosen from some unknown associations of affection, the line from east to west, settled as usual

THE PRIEST'S DOOR, MIDDLE CLAYDON CHURCH.
(From a sketch by Lady Verney.)

according as the sun rose on the morning of the saint's day, would be carried out quite regardless of the bearings of the mansion.

Within its walls are monuments of the Verneys and the Giffards intermixed, of every variety of size

and material. Close to the chancel step lies a large
brass of a knight in armour, Roger Giffard, builder
of the chancel and first holder of the lease of Claydon,
with Mary (Verney) [1] his wife in coif and wimple by
his side, thirteen little sons in gowns kneeling at his
feet, seven little daughters in coifs at hers, small as
befitted their inferior status to their parents (dignity
was denoted by size, as in the reliefs on an Egyptian
tomb), 'On whose sowlls Jh'u have m'cy, 1543,' says
the inscription. The brass of the last Roman Catholic
vicar, another Giffard, is at the foot of the pulpit,
with a label proceeding out of the mouth of his
portrait, ' Miserere mei Deus,' and ' orate pro a'i'a
D'ni Alesandri Anne p'sbiteri ' below. He bequeathed
a great bell and a legacy to the high altar of Middle
Claydon and for the repairs of the church. ' Also
5 p^{ds} in the hands of his right well beloved cosyn
Roger Giffard and Mary his wife, his executors, to
find an honest prest to synge and pray for his soul
and the souls of his father, mother, and all Christians,'
who is to have for his prayers—wages, meat and
drink, £5. 5s. 8d.

There is, however, a still older will by a previous
owner of Claydon concerning the two great wax
candles of 12 lbs. weight, to be burnt before the high
altar of the church, which is extremely curious.
William de Cantelupe gives these ' for the health of
his soul and the souls of his ancestors and heirs for

---

[1] Related to Thomas de Cantelupe, Bishop of Hereford, canonised
in 1306, ' after great importunity at Rome.'

BRASSES OF ROGER GIFFARD AND MARY VERNEY HIS WIFE.
(In Middle Claydon Church.)

ever ' (he looks both before and after), ' King Edward
I., son of King Henry, giving licence.'

The extreme anxiety of the dying man for his
candles and the ' remains' of his candles is half
touching, half ludicrous ; he gives a ' toft' of about
24½ acres of arable land of his own occupation in
satisfaction of a mark, 13s. 4d. (the mark was only
money of account, not a coin, and represented about
£8 of present money in 1390), to supply the torches
which were to be newly furnished on the vigil of
Easter, ' and to be kept burning for ever.' ' Whatsoever remains is to be made into other candles before
the Holy Cross, the Blessed Virgin, and elsewhere in
the Church, as the Bailiff of the Lords of Middle
Claydon and the Churchwardens shall think most
meet.' They are also to be witnesses of the weight
of wax, and the provisions for the execution of his
wishes are many and stringent. ' Thomas the prest'
is bound very straitly ' not to embezzle or fail in
finding, renewing, or sustaining the torches, or de-
livering the remains' (the holy candle-ends are much
on Cantelupe's mind!). ' The Lords of Middel
Claydon are to distrain for any deficiencies either in
torches or remains ;' he has evidently little faith
either in the clergy or his heirs ; each are set to watch
the other. ' These are to have no power to release
Thomas ; and if it should happen, which God forbid,'
he adds passionately, ' that my heirs should be remiss
in demanding the service of the torches, or making
distress for the arrears, any parishioner shall do it in

our name!' 'For ever,' repeats the poor man at every clause with pathetic reiteration, thinking he had provided for his soul's wealth and that of his family satisfactorily, even to the end of time, and little foreseeing how short that 'ever' would prove, either for his candles or his memory.

Urian Verney and his wife Lettice (Giffard) have secured a place for themselves as close to the altar and the candles as possible, which seems to have been considered a position of great comfort and honour to the souls of the occupants.   They kneel one on each side of a sort of altar, their hands joined in prayer, and between them is a small son who lived to be ' oon prest.' The epitaph contains a most inextricable confusion of pronouns and relationships.   ' I Urian, the sixt of seaven sonnes and daughters of Sir Ralph Verney Kt. at his death made this monument for myself and my wife Lettice daughter of Sir George Giffard, issue one sonne and I the survivore of my six brothers and twoe daughters [meaning sisters], the one married to Sir Francis Hynde Kt., and the other to Sir Nicholas Pointz,[1] &c., &c. A.D. 1608.'

The south side of the chancel is almost filled by an immense monument which Sir Ralph caused to be designed and executed at Rome when he went there in 1652, to the memory of his father and mother, his wife and himself.   Four fine busts in niches are surmounted by Faith and Hope, cherubs, skulls, and

---

[1] There is a fine chalk head by Holbein of Sir Nicholas in the Queen's collection.

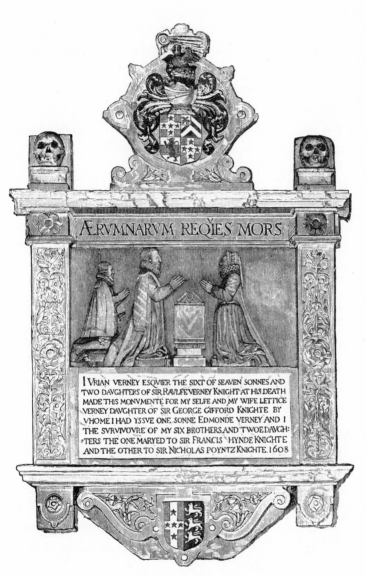

ÆRVMNARVM REQIES MORS

I VRIAN VERNEY ESQVIER THE SIXT OF SEAVEN SONNES AND
TWO DAVGHTERS OF SIR RAVLFE VERNEY KNIGHT AT HIS DEATH
MADE THIS MONVMENTE FOR MY SELFE AND MY WIFE LETTICE
VERNEY DAVGHTER OF SIR GEORGE GIFFORD KNIGHTE BY
VHOME I HAD YSSVE ONE SONNE EDMONDE VERNEY AND I
THE SVRVIVOVRE OF MY SIX BROTHERS AND TWOE DAVGH:
=TERS THE ONE MARYED TO SIR FRANCIS HYNDE KNIGHTE
AND THE OTHER TO SIR NICHOLAS POYNTZ KNIGHTE. 1608

MONUMENT OF URIAN AND LETTICE VERNEY.
(*In Middle Claydon Church.*)

vases, &c. Sir Edmund Verney, says the inscription,
'killed at the memorable batayle of Edgehill, father
of 6 sonns and 6 daughters,' is a fine soldierly-looking
man in armour; the sweet-faced Dame Margaret with

INTERIOR OF MIDDLE CLAYDON CHURCH.
(From a sketch by Lady Verney.)

a veil over her head by his side. Below is the bust of
Sir Ralph of the Long Parliament, quiet, sedentary,
reflective, cautious, and conscientious, and the 'Lady

Mary,' his charming wife, whom he loved and reverenced so fondly in life, and after her death, during his forty-six years of widowhood.

The churchyard was altered by the last Lord Verney, and the tradition still exists in the village that ' he never prospered arter that, ye know, for why, he moved the dead. But they was all back again next marnin! safe in their graves !' 'What, some-one carried them back, you mean ?' said the hearer. ' Nay, none knew how, but there they all was,' replied the narrator solemnly, as befitted her super-natural history. The respect for the last home of those who can no longer defend it, is very deep-seated in this country.

' Est' Claydon is the type of an old English village ; a number of half-timbered black and white houses, with an occasional date from 1650, inter-spersed with great elms, stand in and out of narrow twisting lanes at every sort of picturesque angle, leading up to an old manor house, now a farm, where Mr. Abel, sheriff in 1658, kept four horses, ' the 'Sizes being then held at Buckingham.' In 1662 his only child Mary married Edmund Verney, the eldest son of Sir Ralph, and both he and his wife lived and died in the White House, which has hardly been touched since. It is now a farmhouse, but preserves the dignity of ' keeping a ghost.' The un-fortunate Mary, who went out of her mind shortly after her marriage and often wandered at night about the churchyard and gardens in a weird manner, is probably the unquiet spirit. The story, as told in the cottages, is that the white lady, who had been much beloved by her husband, haunted the house and especially her former room so persistently after her death that the unhappy widower got no rest. He removed the boarded floor, but without avail; the

COTTAGES AT EAST CLAYDON.

ghost walked along the joists; then in despair he drove nails into the joists, and filed their projecting heads into sharp points; the poor wounded ghost appeared no more! A brutal tradition to be associated with the memory of one who 'was very pious and gentle,' notwithstanding her sad state, with occasional respites of sanity, and who, in defiance of the

legend, survived her husband several years. The
inn, 'the half-way house,' belonging to her was rebuilt by Edmund Verney with their joint arms and
initials over the door. It stood by what was once
the high road from Buckingham to London, diverted
to its present course in the reign of Queen Anne ; it
can still be traced as a mere track across the fields ;
it is probably quite as good now as it was then ; the
ruts were so deep that Sir Ralph describes his coach as
sticking fast near Aylesbury, and only to be dragged
out by cart horses.

The church dedicated to St. Margaret stands on
a little eminence surrounded by high elms and over-
looking the vale of Aylesbury. The distant Chiltern
range bounds the view, with the chalk hills above
Hampden and Chequers still in possession of a
descendant of Oliver Cromwell, beyond which lies
Chalfont, where Milton took refuge at the time of the
plague. Two bells, inscribed ' in melodiæ nomen
Magdalenæ,' and a ' Mary bell,' with ' ora pro nobis '
on it, still remain.

' Botyl ' Claydon, from a word meaning a hamlet
or place enclosed from the waste, belongs to the
same church. Botolph and East Claydon, after
belonging to the De Mandevilles and De Greys, were
owned, like Steeple Claydon, by Lionel, Duke of
Clarence, and passed from him to the crown in the
time of Edward IV. They were connected with the
order of St. John of Jerusalem, and a well approached
by steps, called St. Botolph's well (a corruption of

Botyl), and the name of an adjacent farm, Muxwell
(Monk's well), probably refer to some old monastic
establishment, of which all trace is lost. A number of
small parchment deeds, measuring two or three inches
deep by seven or eight wide (the more ancient the

EAST CLAYDON CHURCH.

deed, the smaller are its dimensions), still remaining
in the muniment room, concern little purchases and
arrangements between the rector or the owner of
Claydon and the inhabitants, small parcels of land,
'tofts,' 'crofts,' and 'pickels,' which passed into the
hands of the Verneys at different times. The earliest

in date are generally witnessed on Sundays, as
learned men, able to write their names, were always
rare in the country, and it was convenient to get a
deed signed at the church door where there would
be a greater choice of 'clerks' in the congregation.

A deed of 16 Edward II. concerns the 'toft of
Alice Avenel of Est Claydone,' and is witnessed by
'John called the monck, Roger le prest, and John le
Bonde,' showing that either he or his fathers had
been bondsmen.[1]

Botolph House, a substantial brick and stone
manor house, stands at the east end of the village
shaded by an old cedar, and a magnificent sycamore,
the largest in the neighbourhood. The tradition is
that the last Lord Verney gave his steward seven
acres of land and 3,000l. to build a house on it, and
that the money was all spent in the foundations and
the ground floor.

In a distant part of the estate, in the midst of
lonely meadows and woods, far removed from any
road or even footpath, is a spur of land called
Finmere, standing out into the flat plain towards
Oxford, with a far-reaching view over fields, copses,
hill and dale, arable and grass, stretching for thirty
miles or more, to Edge Hill in one direction to the
north-west, and to Cumnor Hurst, the home of Amy
Robsart, in another to the south-west. In this most
appropriate situation there was a tiny hermitage,

[1] 'Dom' (Dominus) 'John, Rector of the Church of Middele
Claydone,' signs another.

which with ' meadow pasture and wood for repairing
fences and houses ' and ' passage for swine ' was given
by Henry II. to a religious house of the ascetic
order of Augustines, who allowed the hermit 13s. 4d.
a year. If the holy man did not live on acorns and
the beauty of the position, it is difficult to see on
what he fed, unless he condescended to a goat and
perhaps a garden of herbs, for the distance from
human help in the way of alms must have been
great indeed in the thirteenth century, as it can
hardly be reached now in bad and muddy weather.

Steppul or Steeple Claydon is much the largest
village of the four. In the days of William the
Conqueror ' it was considered the most populous
town' (indeed, a sort of capital) of the Lamua
hundred ; when ' Alric the cook holds of the King,
Claydon,' it is described in Domesday Book as
possessing fifty copyholders or villeins, and three
cottagers having nineteen ploughs, mast for 100
hogs, and as being worth 16l. a year, a sort of gauge
of the inhabited state of the country round.

In 1120 Henry I. granted the manor to Edith,
' amasiam suam,' as a portion, when he caused her to
marry Robert de Olleyo (de Oily or Doyley), son of
the Lord of Oxford. After this she is called ' an
eminent and devout matron,' and was buried in the
Abbey of Oseney ' in the abbite of a vowess ' on the
north side of the high altar, in the church she had
built in expiation of her misdeeds ; being miraculously
directed to the spot by chattering pyes, who were

painted over her tomb. She bestowed much land at Claydon on the Priory, and bequeathed 'one of the villeins of Claydon, with his wife, children, and cattle in perpetual alms,' as slaves, in fact !

A curious little deed in the muniment room concerns the granting of a piece of ground in order to build a ' common house,' a sort of village town-hall, where business might be transacted which was otherwise done in the church, greatly to the distress of the clerics. This house is to be 56 feet long and 18 feet broad, to the north side of the rectory threshing floor. ' The religious man John by divine permission Abbot of Oseney grants it to the proctors and parishioners of the Ville of Steppul Claydon to have and to hold.' They are to pay fourpence rent at the feast of the Blessed Virgin for ever, but if they do not 'pay up,' the convent, after three demands, may distrain and impound ; and if the house go to ruin without hope of restoration they may resume the ground. The deed is signed and sealed by an official of Buckingham, ' because the seals of the churchwardens are not known to many.' Probably, indeed, they had none ! The whole transaction shows an interesting little bit of village government, the tiny parliament of Steeple Claydon holding business transactions with the great Abbot. The Mote or Court for the meeting of the Hundred of Lamua was anciently held in the park meadow below the church (where are a number of ditches and earthworks)—another link in the intricate series of little local assemblies culminating in the Witenagemot,[1] the parent of our present Parliaments, which our ancestors had devised with that curious instinct of self-government inherent in the English race.

Steeple Claydon has been the dowry of a great number of royal ladies since William the Conqueror first granted it to his niece Judith, Countess of Huntingdon. ' Edith, King Edward's Queen [query Isabella], held this Manor,' says Brown Willis. It was afterwards held by Philippa, granddaughter of Edward III., wife of Edmund Mortimer, Earl of March ; then by Cecily, Duchess of York, and was given by Henry VII. to his wife, Elizabeth of York, Duchess Cecily's granddaughter. In 1508 Henry VII. granted it to Catherine of Aragon, Princess of Wales, on her marriage with Prince Arthur, and she held it again as the wife of Henry VIII. Queen Elizabeth made a grant of some land charged with a ' maintenance of lamps in the Church of Steeple Claydon.'

At the time of the Civil War the Chaloners were lords of the manor.[2] Sir Thomas Chaloner was tutor and chamberlain to Prince Henry, eldest son of James I. ; his nearest neighbour, Sir Edmund Verney, being also of the prince's household ; ' which Sir

---

[1] ' Our present Parliament is the true and lawful representative, by true and lawful succession, of the ancient "Meetings of the Wise." '—*Freeman*.

[2] For a fuller account of Sir Thomas Chaloner and his duties, moral, ceremonial and sanitary, in Prince Henry's household, see Birch's *Life of Henry, Prince of Wales*, where the discovery of the alum mine is attributed to him and not to his son.

Thomas,' as the monument in the church records,
' was son of the famous Sir Thomas Chaloner, a great
soldier and scholar, knighted by the Protector of
Edward VI.   He was by Queen Elizabeth for his
bravery and learning sent ambassador to the Emperor
Ferdinand and to Philip II., King of Spain.'

Another Thomas Chaloner, grandson of the
ambassador, described as ' a well-bred gentleman, of
very good naturall parts and of an agreeable humour,'
had a strange career.   He discovered while hunting
in Yorkshire that there was alum in a certain kind
of soil, such as he had seen in Germany, and he got
a patent from Charles I. for the first alum works in
England.   The profits proving considerable, the
king did his best to deprive Chaloner of the fruits of
his discovery, which so incensed him that he threw
himself into the Parliament cause, and was one of
the king's judges.   He was a man with a good deal
of cynical wit.   He would spread a false rumour in
the morning in Westminster Hall for the sake of
seeing how the scandal would have grown by the
afternoon ; and he greatly exercised his friends the
Puritan ministers, for whom he had scant sympathy,
by publishing an anonymous pamphlet on ' The
Discovery of Moyses' Tomb,' which they long
thought to be genuine.

At the Restoration ' the Regicide Chaloner ' was
attainted and his estates forfeited.   They were bought
back by another member of the family, and then sold
in 1705 to Sir John Verney, Lord Fermanagh.   There

is a monument in the church to Edward Chaloner, who died in 1766, 'a Lieutenant in the Navy above

STEEPLE CLAYDON CHURCH.

30 years; he showed his courage in 10 expeditions in Eastern, Western, Northern, and Southern Seas.'

The church dedicated to St. Michael is the largest and the least interesting of the Claydon churches.

The vicarage has an oak-panelled parlour, with an elaborate plaister ceiling richly and grotesquely ornamented, said to be of the time of Henry VII.

An old stone barn close to the church, on a ridge commanding a very extensive view, bears this inscription, written by Mr. Bruce:—

'The Camp Barn.

'Around this spot, the Army of the Parliament, under the command of Cromwell, was encamped March 1644, and on the 3rd of that month, advanced from hence to the attack on Hillesdon House.'

A school-house was built by the Chaloners, and furnished with a clock; but so far had that ancient seat of learning decayed, that when Sir Harry Verney first came to Claydon, the school was in ruins and the yard was used for bull-baiting. The name, still existing, of Bull Lane, shows the route by which the bulls entered Steeple Claydon.

The lower part of the village belongs, as seems to have been the case for at least 300 years, to a number of small proprietors, from the owner of an acre to 'King Dodge, a farmer.' Some of these cottages are wretched, small, and insanitary, mostly built on the waste—i.e. the space which, before hard roads were made, it was necessary to leave on each side the muddy track, amounting sometimes to 60 or 80 feet in a clay country.

The old letters show how much the aspect of the country has been altered by cultivation. Sir Ralph, writing to his steward, mentions a piece of moorland and rushy, boggy swamp between Bottel Claydon and the rectory, now part of the park and excellent pasture. Colonel Henry Verney complains that his horses are 'fleeted'—i.e. tethered—which injures them, and Sir Ralph, who is keeping them for him, replies that as all the meadows are unenclosed they would otherwise escape.

Quainton Seech, about five miles from the outer border of the estate, was a swamp given up to bittern and woodcock. Cromwell on his return from Bicester was met there by the mayor and aldermen of Aylesbury, and had a day's hawking on the wild marshy plain, now all cultivated fields.

Not far from Thornborough is a public-house still called ' The Lone Tree,' showing that there was once a wild treeless common here, though it now stands in the midst of hedgerow timber.

CHAPTER III.

THE EARLY HISTORY OF THE VERNEYS, 1456–1599.

> Thronging through the cloud rift, whose are they, the faces
> Faint revealed yet sure divined, the famous ones of old ?
> ' What '—they smile—' our names, our deeds, so soon erases
> Time upon his tablet where Life's glory lies enrolled ? '
> BROWNING.

ALTHOUGH there are different mentions of Verneys from the time of King John, Sir Ralph Verney, Lord Mayor of London, is the first of the family of whom we gain a distinct notion.   He was a successful merchant living near the Great Market, or Cheap, where was the hall of his Company of Mercers, close to ' Paul's Walk, the general resort for business and gossip ; ' he was chosen sheriff in 1456.

The contest of York and Lancaster had lasted eighteen years, and cost the lives of 100,000 of the people ; it was ended by the battle of Tewkesbury, and Edward IV., representing the White Rose, which was considered the party of progress, was popular in London ; he testified his gratitude by knighting twelve citizens, of whom Sir Ralph stands first, on the very day that the dead body of Henry VI. was exposed to public view in St. Paul's.

The year after, Sir Ralph was elected one of the members for London in the Parliament which finally settled the succession.

Edward, 'considering the good and gratuitous service rendered by Sir Ralph,' granted him several forfeited lands in Buckinghamshire ; he bought back the old family property at Fleet Marston, and purchased the manor and advowson of Middle Claydon, on which he had advanced money.   He did not however live there, but leased it for a hundred years to the Giffards, and died in 1478, when he was buried in the church of ' St. Martin's Pomary,' so called from the many orchards which, as 'large void places,' were to be found even in the reign of Elizabeth, in what is now the very heart of that wilderness of houses called the City.   He ordered his tomb to be placed ' between the quire and our Lady's Chapel ; ' both church and tomb were destroyed by the great fire in 1666.   His will is in English.   He bequeaths his ' soule vnto Allmyghty God in trinite, fardir, and sone, and holy gost, to the moost glorious virgyn, our lady saint Marie, modir to the ij^{de} person in trinite, our blissed Lord Crist Jesu my redemer and saviour.'   After providing for his widow Emme, his daughters Dame Margaret Raleghe and Beatrice Danvers, and his two sons, he gives legacies for the ' reperacione ' of the church of St. Martin : ' 100 marks to fynde an honest and convenable preest to syng for my soule, and the soules of my fadir and modir, my brothrene, my sustren, my children, and

the soules of my speciall frendes Thomas Fauconere,'
&c. To the 'oolde werks of the Cathedrall Chirche
of saint Paule' he gives 'xx^s.' He does not forget
'poure and nedy prisinors' in Newgate and Ludgate,
Marshalsea and King's Bench, and other prisons.
For the 'reparacione' of the church at Fleet Marston,
his country home, he gives 'cs.' A bequest for
'thamending of foule and ruynous weies about the
citee of London, and nere aboute Aylesbury and
Flete Merston,' shows the state of the roads at that
time. To his twelve servants he gives liberally : 'xs
to John Jakke, child of my kichen.' To his 'trewe
lover,' John Brown, alderman of London, he bequeaths one of his 'cuppes covred of silver gilt.'
Gifts for 'good dedes and werks of charite and pitee'
are to be added ' to profite unto the helthe of my soule.'

His eldest son, Sir John, married the great-grand-
daughter of Sir Robert Whittingham, stated in the
pedigrees to have been Sheriff of London in 1419,
often confounded with Whittington of good cat
memory ('who was certainly neither sheriff nor lord
mayor'). Sir Robert's son was 'Squier of household
and servant' to King Henry VI., and his grandson,
another Sir Robert, was a staunch Lancastrian, who
held several important offices and stood by Queen
Margaret against the offer of Parliament that Edward
should succeed instead of the infant prince. After
the disastrous battle of Wakefield, in which he fought,
a price of 100l. (equal to 1,500l. of our present
money) was put on his head, as one of her most dis-

tinguished adherents.   When Margaret, the only
child of so loyal a Lancastrian house and named
after the queen, married John Verney, son of an
equally strong partisan on the Yorkist side, there
was probably much opposition in both families.
Whether it was some old-world story of Capulets and
Montagus, the hatred of the parents staunched by
the loves of the children, or only a ' canny ' political
alliance, cannot now be found out.   Sir Robert the
father was, however, attainted of treason after the
defeat of his party, and all his possessions and lordships, his rights of fairs and markets, his houses and
advowsons in London, &c., were forfeited, and Margaret was left penniless.

But again the tide turned in favour of the Red
Rose ; Sir Robert took the field for the queen, while
Sir Ralph was as strenuous as ever for Edward IV.
in the city.   The Yorkists soon regained their
ascendency, however, and at the battle of Tewkesbury Sir Robert died an honourable death.   Sir
Ralph was returned to Parliament, and brought all
his influence to bear with the king in favour of his
son's wife.   In consideration of his own humble
and faithful service, the lands of her father were
restored to Margaret : unfortunately, however, the
king had given them for life to Sir Thomas Mont-
gomery, and to his brother the Duke of Gloucester
(Richard III.), and for years the struggle with them
went on unsuccessfully, even after the death of Sir
Ralph.

After the battle of Bosworth and the death of
Richard III., everything, however, was changed, and
Sir John Verney changed his tack also ; he sank all
mention of his father's services to the House of York,
and brought prominently forward the sufferings and
losses of his wife's father to the House of Lancaster—
' it is contrary to all reason and conscience ' that the
land should be taken away because of the service ' he
did and owed to the blessed Prince Henry VI.'
There must have been a great deal of such tergiver-
sation where one party succeeded another so quickly
on the throne. Sir John Verney now took possession
of the different estates of his wife, and they lived a
quiet, secluded life at Penley Hall, which he rebuilt.
He served as sheriff for Bucks in 1494, and for Hertford
and Essex, where he had property, in 1499, and was
much occupied with a number of lawsuits entailed by
the difficulties concerning his wife's estates. Just
before his death in 1505, aged only fifty-five, he
renewed the lease of Claydon to the Giffards for eighty
years, at a rental of 13*l.* 6*s.* 8*d.*, with the important
exception of the great woods, which were leased soon
after to Sir Harry Lee of Ditchley. Only once he is
mentioned as joining in the court ceremonials, when
he was present at the coronation of Elizabeth of
York. He was buried at the beautiful convent at
Ashridge, near Penley, with his wife's relations, and
four years after, at her particular wish, she was laid
by the body of her husband. She had sold in her
husband's lifetime, 1501, the advowson of St. Stephen

Walbrook, bought by the Whittinghams in 1432 ; the sale of livings is no new or Protestant institution.

In these early days when there are few or no letters, more can be learnt from the wills concerning family life than from any other source. Lady Verney leaves her lands, manors, lordships, and tenements among her three sons, but her ' horses, oxon, shepe, and other catell' at Salden go to her son John ; to her daughter Cecilia and her husband ' on fader bed, on bolster, on payre off blanketts, and a hanging for a chamber as shalbe thought convenient by my executor and broder sir Rauffe Verney ; also I beqweth to my doughter Anne Dame on kyrtyll off blake damaske, and on gowne of blake cloth, purfeld [bordered] with tawney velvet.' . . . ' The resydew of all my goodds and catall, my detts and beqwests fully content,' she gives to her brother Sir Ralph Verney, executor of her last will, ' he to dysposse for the well off my soule and all my frynds soulls as he shall thynke most expedient.'

Among the ' certen detts ' due from Dame Margaret Verney, ' wedewe late wyfe to sir John Verney knyght, the Lady Colett claymeth xxxvj li ' : she was mother of Colet, Dean of St. Paul's, one of the most marked among the Oxford reformers, celebrated by Erasmus—' when I listen to him it seems like listening to Plato himself.' He was the first to attempt the reform of English education, and his good work may still be seen in St. Paul's school, which he founded.

The younger brother of Sir John, a second Sir Ralph, passed his life at Court. At the coronation procession of Elizabeth of York, in 1487, he rode as one of ' two esquiers of honor, well-horsed, in gowns of crimson velvet, having mantles of ermine . . . on their heads hats of red cloth of gold, ermines, the beaks forward.' They came with the lord mayor, next before the queen. Soon after Sir Ralph Verney married Eleanor Pole, a lady-in-waiting to the queen, and related to Henry VII. Her grandmother secondly married John, Duke of Somerset, and became the mother of Margaret, ' the good Countess of Richmond,' whose memory was long held dear, and whose beautiful altar-tomb is to be found on the south side of the royal chapel in Westminster Abbey, erected by her son Henry VII. ; the king thus had the same grandmother as Lady Verney. When young Prince Arthur had a separate household arranged for him, his cousin Sir Richard Pole was made chief gentleman of the bedchamber. He married the last of the Plantagenets, the Lady Margaret, niece to Edward IV., who was afterwards created Countess of Salisbury. She was barbarously beheaded by Henry VIII. in her old age, nominally for receiving letters from her son, Cardinal Pole, then conspiring against the king as a heretic, but really for the crime of having blood royal in her veins ; the Cardinal was one of Lady Verney's nephews. Eleanor, Lady Verney, in right of her cousinhood to the king, had a considerable position in the household of the queen, with whom she seems to have lived in familiar

intercourse ; she has a salary of 20*l.* a year, equal to
more than 200*l.* now.   An account of a year's expenses of the privy purse of Elizabeth of York exists,
and during that time Lady Verney lends the queen
' fifteen shillings suddenly,' and is repaid ; again she
supplies ' 3*s.* 4*d.* as her Majesty's alms to a poor person,' the same to the ferryman at Datchet when the
queen crossed the Thames, twice as much to 'an old
servant of her Majesty's father,' and 17*s.* on St. Peter's
Eve, when there was always much jollification in the
streets of London, bonfires, pageants, &c., indeed the
city carnival was one of the sights of London ; 3*s.* 4*d.*
to Robert Fyll, ' the king's painter,' and 10*s.* ' to
John Reynolds,' another artist, for ' making of divers
beasts and other pleasures for the Queen at Windsor,'
shows that there was entertainment going on.   Then
comes 20*d.* to a man who brought a present of cherries
to her majesty, to ' Carvenelle for his costs, riding
to the Princess [Catherine of Aragon], 5*s.*,' ' for
making and lining a kirtle and other gear 2*s.*,' ' an
offering at the altar of St. Frideswyde at Oxford on
the Queen's progress into Wales in the summer of
1502, 20*d.*'   Another item, the keep of the horse of
Margaret Yone, a servant of the queen's household
apparently in attendance on Lady Verney, 4*d.* a day
for 125 days, shows how all the ladies with their
attendants went on horseback, as did the queen herself on the ' summer progress,' and reads like a page
out of the idyl ' Guinevere.'

When the Princess Margaret, Henry VIII.'s

sister, was betrothed to James IV. of Scotland, through whose blood the Stuarts claimed the throne of England, her chamberlain, Sir Ralph Verney, was present. In the following year he and his wife accompanied his mistress on her brilliant progress through England to join her husband, ' the dresses, the viands, the pageants, even the many kisses of the bridegroom to the impetuous bride—a true sister of Henry VIII.— are minutely chronicled by the English herald.' ' With the said Queen was deputed Sir Ralph Verney, her chamberlain, the which well and nobly exercised his office in the said voyage.' As Chief Commissioner appointed to look after Margaret's dowry he was present at a meeting of the Scottish Parliament, where King James's engagements were solemnly ratified.

On his return Sir Ralph was appointed to the same post in the household of the king's other sister, the Princess Mary, and in 1514 was present at the high ceremonies of her betrothal to the aged King of France, Louis XII., who died a few months after ; two of the other witnesses were Wolsey, not yet a cardinal, and Brandon, Duke of Suffolk, whom she married almost immediately after her return from France.

The eldest son of Eleanor and Ralph soon after married Dorothy, a ward of the Duke of Suffolk. Meantime at Penley Sir John had been succeeded by his son the third Sir Ralph, who was sheriff for Bucks and Beds in 1511 and 1524. In 1525 he

was one of a goodly band of knights who attended
Queen Catherine to the 'Field of the Cloth of Gold,
having twelve men and horses eche in the Queen's
Trayne, which consisted of 1,158 persons and 910
horses.' A bas-relief of the meeting of the two kings
is still in existence, and shows the dress and appearance of the queen's knights. We hardly realise, when
we speak of the Field of the Cloth of Gold, the
enormous expense and difficulty there must have been
in transporting such an immense crowd as attended
the king and the queen—'persons 5,696, horses
4,325 '—but apparently it was done without any
national or individual murmur.

Sir Ralph was three times married; his first wife,
Margaret Iwardby, brought him the manor of Quainton, where she lies buried; her brass, with the effigies
of one son and three daughters, has been removed
from its place near the altar in the old church, which
has lately been cruelly defaced by a restoring, or
rather destroying, rector. Ralph's second wife was
Anne Weston ; she and her brother Richard were in
the household of Elizabeth of York at the same time
as Eleanor, Lady Verney. After the death of the
queen she became maid-of-honour to Catherine of
Aragon, who was already connected with Steeple
Claydon, and when she married Sir Ralph Queen
Catherine gave her a marriage portion of 200 marks
and the custody of the lands and person of John
Ganers, a minor, always a lucrative charge. The
wardships of lunatics and minors were in the hands

of the king, and the grievance was one against which the Commons complained ineffectually for the next hundred years. Sir Francis Weston, Lady Verney's nephew, was afterwards beheaded for treason with Anne Boleyn in 1536.

Sir Ralph was for the second time serving as sheriff for Bucks and Beds in 1525, when his death occurred very suddenly ; he made his will and died the same day. The list of his estates comprises seven manors in the county of Bucks, and many elsewhere. His children were all under age ; each daughter was to have 500 marks, but 'if anny of my foresaid daughters wolle not be advised nor ruled in the preferrement of hir mariage, by my executours and supervisoures, it shall be at their liberty to mynishe parte of the somme bequethid until she wil be refourmed.' His third wife, Elizabeth Broughton, was to have all his moveable goods and a large jointure ; his sons Francis and Rauffe take his 'manours and landes'; for the 'reparacion of the churche of Albury' he gives 3*l.* 6*s.* 8*d.*, and there is a curious bequest of the gowns of his second wife (and gowns were then magnificent garments, lasting more than one generation) 'to make vestiments [i.e. priests' robes] according to the discrecion of myn executours. . . . Myn uncle Sir Raaf Verney thelder knight' is to have 'my blacke gowne of satten, furrid with marternes ;' while his cousin John is to have his ' gowne of tawny velvit, fore parte lind with damaske.' The robe of a man of a certain age was a sort of dressing-gown at home, as distinguished from his armour and riding-gear when he went abroad. ' My cowsen Paule Darrell,' who is ' debutye and under-sherif,' is to have an annuity of 6*l*. 13*s*. 4*d*. for keeping the courts and receiving the rents of the testator. ' Item, that Richard Verney my servaunte have the house and lande he dwellith in during his life naturall, for keping of my woddes in Claydon ; . . . also that Richard Verney's wife have a cowe. Also, that my servauntes have deliverid to theim every man his hole yeres wages. Also, that parte of them have certaine of my gildinges geven them at the discrecion of myne executours, and to each a blacke gowne.' As a sort of afterthought comes twenty shillings to ' Sir Thomas, Chauntry preest of Albery, to pray for my soule.' He has begun his will ' in the name of God, our blissid Lady, and all the holly company of heven : ' there is no trace as yet of the Reformation.

His courtier uncle, who had been rewarded for his services to the late king and queen by a valuable manor given by Henry VIII., died soon after. He was buried at King's Langley in 1528, in a splendid altar-tomb with coats of arms of the Verneys and Poles, which also ornament the surcoat of the ' recumbent figure of the knight and are reversed on the magnificent mantle of the lady.' This tomb has been lately torn from its place within the altar rails by an innovating clergyman.

The fourth Sir Ralph, his son, was only fifteen when he inherited his father's large property ; he

married when he was nineteen, and took up his abode
at Penley.   Soon after we hear of a dispute concerning the estate at Claydon, with his tenant, Sir George
Giffard.   The house and church had been suffered
to fall into ruinous decay, and Giffard at last agreed
to pay 200 marks and to repair both, if Sir Ralph
would renew his lease for 100 years instead of eighty,
' to which Verney said he would not doe it for
nothing.'   So Giffard said he would give him a
hunting-horse which he valued at 30*l.* (probably an
exceedingly fine one, for the sum is now equivalent
to 300*l.* or more), ' so Verney consented to it.'   The
church was repaired and the house rebuilt, ' but the
Verneys paid dear for the hunter,' Lord Fermanagh
adds significantly.   The new lease is dated 1535.

Sir Ralph's marriage was supposed to be an
excellent one, to Elizabeth, one of the six heiress
daughters of Lord Bray, inheritor of the estates of
Sir Reginald Bray, who had stood by Henry VII. in
perilous times, and had been rewarded by the king
with many grants of land ; he was said to have found
the crown in a bush after the battle of Bosworth, and
set it on ' Richmond's ' head.

For some time there was no male heir to the great
Bray estates, but at last a boy was born to Lady
Bray—'a youth of great promise, a paragon in court,
and of sweet entertainment.'   Sir Ralph seems to
have been in bad health, and to have lived, like his
grandfather, a secluded life at Penley.   In 1537,
however, we find him specially noted as one of the

gentlemen present at the christening of Edward VI.;
and in 1539 he was appointed to help in receiving
Anne of Cleves, so that he must have been considered
a man of mark. In 1543 he was sent by Henry VIII.
with the army which inflicted terrible ravages upon
Scotland. It was considered a hazardous expedition,
and he made his will before starting ; shortly after his
return, ill and perhaps wounded, he died, aged only
thirty-seven years, and was buried with his ancestors
at Ashridge.   His will shows the progress of the
Reformation ; [1] there is no mention of our lady St.
Mary ; he 'beqweths his soul to Almighty God, his
Saviour and Redeemer,' but still he must have thought
it would do no harm to add ' I wyll that oon honest
prist shall synge for the sowlles of me, my father and
mother, of Rauff Verney, etc., etc., etc., and of all
Crystens ;' this, however, is only to go on 'for oon
holl year.'   He is to have a ' stypend of syx pounds
sterlyng, and to fynd himself wyne and waye to
celebrate withal, and is to say every Wednysday and
Fryday diriche and commendacions for the sowlles
aforesaid.'   The value of his manors and lands is
called 330l. a year, to be multiplied by about twelve
to give modern value.   In the translations of the
Bible about this time, the master of the vineyard

---

[1] ' In this year the miracle of the liquifaction of Christ's blood was
exhibited at St. Paul's Cross for devotion and adoration by the Bishop
of Rochester,' and shown to be only honey clarified and coloured with
saffron.   It is curious to find the blood of St. Januarius still in vigour
at Naples in the present day.

agrees with the labourers for a penny, considered to be about a shilling, a day.

The marriage portions of his daughters are fixed at 400 marks each, and if they are obstinate and wilful, or behave in any way improperly (the clause is very crudely expressed), their portions are to be 'rated and apporcioned' by their mother. Lands are left to the six younger sons, of the value of 10*l.* a year each ; and a bequest to his heir of a flock of 500 ewes, or an equivalent of threescore pounds in ready money (about 2*s.* 4½*d.* apiece), gives a certain standard of value. The price of ewes of the present day is from 50*s.* to 60*s.* ; the size of the sheep in 1546 was certainly, however, very small. Soon after there is a mention of 3 lbs. of beef for a penny.

Sir Ralph left nine young children, and makes an earnest appeal to the 'overseers' of his will to 'maintain them in erudition and learning, and advance their welfare by good marriages and other promotion ;' liberal legacies are left to his servants, and fourpence to each of his god-children 'if they require it.' His death was a great loss to his family, for his wife married again and again—four times in all—and had other matters on hand than the care of her first husband's children.

The seven sons and two daughters were thus left to their own guidance, the eldest, Edmund, being only 18 years old ; he soon after married Dorothy Peckham, daughter of a Bucks squire, cofferer to Henry VIII. and subsequently one of the Council

appointed to assist his 'executours.' He was afterwards executor to Anne of Cleves, who left him 'a
jugge of gold with a cover, or a crystal glass
garnyshed with gold and sett with stones.' Dorothy
died in 1547, and was buried at Bittlesden Abbey,
the brass to her memory showing a label coming out
of her mouth with 'Sancta Trinitas Unus Deus
Miserere Nobis,' and the words 'Jesu have mercy,'
with her name below.

Sir Edmund was chosen knight of the shire a few
years after he came of age, and sat with his brother
Francis who represented the borough of Buckingham.

The times were difficult for members of Parliament ; the sudden changes in religion and politics,
as the different monarchs succeeded each other, must
have been perplexing in the extreme ; the Reformation had advanced in the latter years of Henry VIII.
and had gone back after Thomas Cromwell was
ruined ; its progress became rapid under Edward
VI. and the revulsion was violent when Mary came
to the throne. The influence of France, Spain, and
Germany rose and fell in the same way. After
Mary's unpopular marriage with Philip, the Parliament, which had been subservient in her father's
reign, showed signs of opposition which greatly
incensed her.

At the end of two years the crowds of the much
hated Spaniards in England, and the deep animosity
arising from the executions, imprisonments, and
punishments of the other party, aroused such a

feeling that a plot for transferring the crown to
the Princess Elizabeth, commonly called ' Dudley's
Conspiracy,' was attempted.   Mary was to be sent to
Spain to her husband, Elizabeth was to be set on the
throne and married to the Earl of Devon ; the
conspirators hoped to be assisted by the Protestant
exiles on the Continent, who in many of the free
towns had received protection in spite of the remonstrances of Mary and even of the Emperor.   The
sympathy in England with the exiles was so deep
that the House of Commons in 1553 rejected a Bill
brought in by Government to confiscate their property.

There had been a very remarkable scene in the
Commons when Sir Anthony Kingston ' took the
keys of the House from the Serjeant-at-Arms in
order to compel attention to the grievances of the
nation in the matters of religion,' the foreshadow of
the more famous day in 1629, when Sir Miles Hobart
also locked the doors of the House during a protest
against the Government.   Sir Anthony and the
Serjeant were both sent to the Tower, but upon their
humble submission they were released after a fortnight's imprisonment.

It was among the younger members that the
Government looked out for men likely to have joined
the conspiracy.   Edmund Verney was arrested with
his brother Francis and his brother-in-law Henry
Peckham ; Sir Anthony Kingston, ' head of the late
contemptuous behaviour of the Commons ; ' Throg-

morton, a Bucks Squire, and some others were also taken. All these belonged to a company of ' young heads,' who used during the sitting of Parliament to meet at a sort of club called Arundel's, and avowed themselves ' right Protestants,' declaring ' that they intended to resist the proceedings which the Queen and all Catholic men went about.'

Several of the prisoners were put to the torture, others threatened with it, and all confessed excepting Throgmorton. The Verneys were not charged with treason, but for having ' given in their adhesion.' Edmund was not put on his trial, and received his pardon—now in the muniment room at Claydon, dated July 1556—under the great seal of Philip and Mary. Francis Verney was tried and found guilty, but his punishment was afterwards remitted ; it was given in evidence that he and Peckham had plighted their troth in a way still practised in the north. Peckham took a ' demi-sovereign and broke it in two parts, one part thereof he traitorously delivered to Francis for an undoubted sign of their common consent to perform the said treason, which the said Francis traitorously received with the consent of the said Edmund then and there, and so the death and final destruction of their supreme lady the Queen and subversion of the Kingdom of England imagined and compassed ; ' the inversion of the sentences, the verb coming at the end, is curiously like the German construction.

Throgmorton must have been a very noble

fellow ; when put to the torture he would give no
information to implicate any one, and when told that
unless he did so it would be repeated, he replied with
simple heroism, ' Then I fear I shall be put to it
again, and I will assure you it is very terrible pain.'
He was convicted and told that ' he must die unless
he gave just occasion for mercy ; ' he replied that ' if
his life stood therein he was a dead man,' signifying,
as the Dean of St. Paul's, who was urging upon him
that other men had spoken, understood, ' that he
would rather die than reveal or detect any man : '
after which he was ' drawn to Tyburn in the accus-
tomed manner, and so hanged, and afterwards cut
down and quartered.' Several others were executed at
the same time, ' and the morrow after their heads set
on London Bridge, after the barbarous fashion of the
day.'

The young uncle of the Verneys, Lord Bray, did
not get off so easily as they did ; he was imprisoned
in the Tower, and though his friends were allowed to
relieve him with meat and drink, little of it seems to
have reached him, and he was in a pitiable state.
His poor wife, with whom he had quarrelled, but
who had returned to help him in his trouble, was
treated with no gentleness in her efforts to assist him.
The queen would not receive her or old Lady Bray,
having shut herself up, ' sad and heavy,' for two
months at the news that Philip, whom she was
expecting, had put off his coming. When, however,
Mary heard that the forsaken wife had come to inter-

cede for her husband, she 'gave her great praise and
said God sent oftimes to good women evil husbands.'
One of the principal accusations against Lord Bray
was that he had said 'yf my neighbour at Hatfield
might once reign,' meaning the Lady Elizabeth, 'he
shold have his landes and debtes given him again,
which he bothe wished and trusted to see.' The
violent jealousy of the queen against her sister made
this a very sore point ; after twelve months' imprisonment, however, he obtained his liberty. Parliament was about to meet, and Mary may have
been glad to release the prisoners.

The Government does not appear to have been
severe in dealing with the plot, but in its ramifications
among persons of all ranks who took part in it, Queen
Mary must have felt how slight was her hold on the
affections of the people. Lord Bray went abroad,
distinguished himself at the battle of St. Quentin
on her behalf, and came home to die in 1557, aged
only 30, and childless. He had a splendid funeral,
and Edmund Verney—his nephew, although of the
same age—was one of the chief mourners, and placed
the 'mass penny' and his coat of arms on the altar
as part of the ceremony ; after which a Black Friar
preached a sermon, showing 'how Christ raised
Lazarus from the dead, seeing how he was a gentleman given to chivalry for the wealth of his country,
and so,' he said, 'was that nobleman which there lay
dead,' which was not exactly relevant.

By the death of her brother, Edmund Verney's

mother became once more a co-heiress of the Brays ;
there was no estate remaining, but the title was
revived in favour of one of her descendants in the
female line in 1839.   Edmund Verney died in 1558,
having witnessed the accession of Elizabeth (for
which he had risked so much), and the triumph of
Protestantism ; he left no will, but had settled his
land on his brothers, and was succeeded by one of
them, another Edmund, a name which, with that of
Ralph, is found henceforward in every generation of
Verneys.   Edmund, aged 23, took up his abode at
Penley, served as sheriff twice for Herts and once for
Bucks, and was very active in the public business of
both counties during the reign of Elizabeth.   At the
time of the Spanish Armada he was appointed one
of five captains who were to command the musters of
the county ; he was bound to bring in 300 men for
the defence of the kingdom, and his contribution in
money was large, 50*l.*   He married three times ; by
his second wife, Dame Awdreye Carew, a widow, he
had one son, Francis, who was only five years old
when his mother died.   Sir Edmund's third wife, Mary
Blakeney, though probably not above 40 years of age,
was marrying also for the third time ; her daughter
by her first husband, Geoffrey Turville of New Park
Hall, married Sir John Leeke, of whom we hear
much subsequently ; her second husband, St. Barbe,
belonged to Broadlands in Hants, which descended to
Lord Palmerston ; she had also one daughter, Ursula,
who when about 12 years old was married, with Sir

Sir Edmund Verney, Kt.
from a picture at Claydon House.

Edmund's consent, to his son Francis Verney, aged 14. Sir Edmund and his wife lived occasionally in a house in Drury Lane which belonged to her, where a boy was born, afterwards the standard bearer to Charles I. The last years of Sir Edmund, the elder, were spent on his different estates, and in arrangements to divide his property equally between his two sons, four manors to each. His widow was to have possession of Claydon until Edmund came of age. Sir Edmund only succeeded in effecting this by means of a private Act of Parliament, Elizabeth xxxix. ; and soon after, in 1599, he died at Chalfont St. Giles, in the house called the Stone House which was afterwards sold to the Hampdens. His funeral was a very grand one, performed more than a month after his death, with ' great pompt of streamers, heralds, &c. ; ' he was buried in the beautiful little Verney Chapel, within a handsome stone screen, in the very ancient church of Albury.

Sir Edmund's health was probably delicate, for a licence from the Archbishop in 1581, confirmed by letters patent under the great seal, permits him ' to eat flesh on days forbidden with a good conscience for the term of his life, because that the eating of fish was injurious to his health by reason of the great weakness of his stomach.' This luxury of permissions shows how strictly fasts were enforced to the end of the century.

Sir Edmund's portrait, in the ruff and doublet of Elizabeth's day and a heavy gold chain, is at Claydon.

CHAPTER IV.

THE HALF BROTHERS, SIR FRANCIS AND
SIR EDMUND VERNEY.

'A little more than kin, and less than kind.'—*Hamlet*.

THE change in manners and modes of thought is very great when once we have buried the last Tudor and entered on the reigns of the Stuarts. We are almost beginning upon the spirit of modern politics, and the habits of modern life. The reign of James I. is still, however, a period of transition. Penetrated as he was with the old despotic spirit of government by divine right, yet he was soon made to feel that high-handed acts, which had been submitted to under Henry VIII. and his daughter, would not be endured from the wavering, garrulous, clever pedant who had succeeded the strong-minded Elizabeth, grasping firmly whatever power she could keep, and yielding in a politic and graceful way whenever she saw that resistance was useless.

Sir Francis Verney, eldest son of Sir Edmund, was only sixteen when his father died ; he had lost his mother when he was but five years old, and seems never to have been under any control either from

affection or education. His wild life was short and
unhappy : in 1604, when not above twenty, he was
living in St. Dunstan's-in-the-East, in the neighbourhood of Alsatia (showing the haunts he preferred),
when one of his servants was slain, apparently in
a drunken brawl, such as often disturbed that very
unsavoury region.[1] He seems to have quarrelled
with his stepmother at the earliest possible moment
after he came of age : his brother was too young to
have aggrieved him, but he petitioned Parliament to
set aside the settlement made by his father of part of
his estates on Edmund and of Lady Verney's jointure,
which the Act of Elizabeth's reign had confirmed. A
Bill for this object was brought in, and Sir Randal
Crewe (afterwards Parliamentarian Chief Justice)
pleaded before the House on behalf of Sir Edmund's
widow. Several members who had sat on the Committee to which the former Bill had been referred,
gave evidence that ' Sir Edmund Verney the elder
did follow the Bill himself, and laboured divers
friends in it, and the repeal would overthrow many
purchasers, sixty at least.' After ' much dispute and
argument' the Bill was rejected. Sir Francis had
claimed as eldest son under a former settlement by
his uncle Edmund, which had been annulled in the
Elizabethan Act, and his claim had a certain appearance of equity. There was said to be some hardship
at least in being deprived by his father of his rights

---

[1] The graphic and unpleasant account of Alsatia in the *Fortunes of
Nigel* is borne out by this story.

during his minority. This was probably urged on his stepmother, for she resigned her dower house at Quainton to him in 1606. The rejection of his Bill had, however, stung the young man to desperation ; the dissensions and heart-burnings with his family, the keen sense of what he thought injustice, and probably the debts with which he was overwhelmed, at last determined him to sell everything and 'forsake the friends who had injured him, and the country which had refused him redress.'

Quainton was sold first : it consisted of about 800 acres with the advowson, and brought only 500*l.* Fleet Marston, where his ancestors had lived, went next ; Penley, where his father died, followed, and the furniture was sold with it, as if to show that the break-up was final.

At this time Francis seems to have taken a journey to the Holy Land, for a letter exists from George Carew, English ambassador at Paris, ' to my very good Lord the Earle of Salisbury, principal Secretary of Estate at Court,' telling how ' the bearer hereof, Sir Francis Verney, hath entreated me to accompany him with my letter, in which I can do no less than gratifie him, for his readinesse and respective offices used to me his Majesty's minister, whereof your L[ppe] may be pleased to take notice. Since his retourne hither from Jherusalem, he hath frequented at my house and other where (as I understand) the exercises of our religion [at that time no English Protestant worship was allowed except at the embassy], which hath the rather moved me to give him this commendation to your Lordshippe. And so with my humble duty I leave the same to the good protection of the Almighty.'

Lord Fermanagh's notes observe 'that this Francis was a great traveller and fought severall Duellos.'

He certainly was in England for some time in the summer and autumn of 1608, when he disposed of his other estates and of everything saleable, gave a general irrevocable authority to his uncle, Urian Verney, to act for him in all business concerned with the wreck of his property, and assigned his title deeds to another uncle, Ralph, described as ' of High Holborn, gentleman,' and then disappeared from all knowledge of his friends.   His wife is not mentioned at this period, but as she was the daughter of his stepmother, and he had been married to her when only a boy, she was probably mixed up in his mind with the rest of his ' enemies.'

There is no doubt that he left England, and rumour and tradition declare that he went to Algiers, where it is reported that he ' turned Turk,' but this part of the story perhaps may be understood politically, not religiously (or irreligiously).   A war of succession was going on in Morocco between the three sons of the Emperor Muley Hamet, who had lately died.   One of these, Muley Sidan, obtained the services of a body of Englishmen, who were highly paid and well treated.   They were under the com-

mand of Captain John Giffard, a near relation of
Lettice, wife of Urian Verney, and daughter of Sir
George Giffard who held the lease of Claydon.   He
was ' a gentleman of a worthy spirit, of the auncient
stemme of the Giffards,' on whom ' Sidan bestowed a
rich sword and a scarlet cloake, richly embrodered
with pearle, sent to his father by our late sovereigne
of famous memorie, Queene Elizabeth.'   On one occasion the Moors during a battle ran shamefully away,
and Muley Sidan sent to Captain Giffard and the other
Englishmen to save themselves.   ' The English returned word that they came not thither to run, but
rather die an honourable death. . . .   Giffard being
charged by eight Abdelians, one behinde him shot him
throw and so was he slaine.   Few of al the English
nation were left alive.'   As Francis Verney is known
to have gone to Barbary, he probably joined these
desperadoes for a time.   It was an age of somewhat
lawless adventure both by sea and land ; during the
war with Spain the English cruisers were employed
as privateers with commissions from the queen herself.   Sir Walter Ralegh's exploits were often little
better than piracy, and the adventures of Elizabeth's
famous Devonshire captains hovered perilously near
to buccaneering.   When James I. ascended the
throne and made peace with Spain these commissions
were recalled, but in the eyes of the public ' to spoil
the Spaniard ' continued to be considered good service, and they were ' slow to condemn such gallant
fellows.'   If the French and Venetians suffered also,

it was no great harm in their opinion.   When the
English ports were closed to them, the pirates took
refuge on the coast of Barbary.   The great tide of
European commerce passed up the Mediterranean
almost within sight of Tunis and Algiers, and here
piracy was a recognised institution.   Every man who
could procure means to fit out a ship and collect a
crew could, under the protection of the Dey, put out
to sea and lie in wait for the richly freighted mer-
chantmen.   The prisoners were kept in slavery of
the most cruel and hopeless description, and but few
lived to be released on ransom like Cervantes, or to
escape by the help of their captor's family like St.
Vincent de Paul.   It is clear that Sir Francis was in
command of one of these ships and was the terror of
even English merchant vessels, for in 1609 Cottington,
attached to the embassy in Spain, writes word that
' Verney had taken three or four Poole shipps and
one of Plymouth.'   Another of the Giffards was also
captain of the ' Fortune,' a buccaneering vessel, and
the proceeds of successful piracy were such that it is
said ' no English nobleman kept such state as Captain
John Ward, who is called their chief, with whom
were associated Sir Francis Verney, Granvile, and
others.'   In vain did King James endeavour to put
them down.   In one year nineteen of the pirates,
some of them persons of note, were executed at
Wapping.   In another year a pardon for life and
goods was offered upon their promise to give up free-
booting, but ' the greater number still adhered to

their wild and desperate life.' Above twenty sail were at one time plundering the commerce of the Mediterranean, and in return, whenever a Barbary vessel was taken, the captive Moors and Turks were made slaves, and were to be found serving in most great houses in Spain. 'The multitude of them was very great,' says Cottington.

Of Sir Francis' exploits we know nothing further, and the chroniclers admit that the pirates did not all turn Turks, though they 'submitted themselves under the protection of the Turks or Barbarians, . . . exercising all manner of despites, and speaking of blasphemy against God, their king, and country.' Above all, their greatest crime was that 'they taught the infidels the use of navigation, to the great hurt of Europe.'

There is an extremely fine portrait of Sir Francis at Claydon, called a Velasquez, but of too early a date for this to be probable, as the painter was only born in 1599. It is the very beau ideal of a gallant gentleman of the time: his tawny silk Spanish jerkin and trunk hose slashed and lined with dull red, his large loose boots of yellow Cordovan leather and gilt spurs, his embroidered gauntlet gloves and the plume of many-coloured ostrich feathers in the hat that lies on the table beside him, are all in the best taste of the best fashion of the period. He is immensely tall, and carries his fine clothes with the grace and dignity of a thorough gentleman; his face is handsome, with a small pointed beard, and set in a little

Sir Francis Verney, Kt.
from a picture done in Spain at Claydon House.

quilted ruff which is very becoming.   In his hand is
a gilt cane, the two ends painted black, the original
of which has been preserved and now hangs under
the picture.   He looks older than the twenty-three
years which was his age when he left England for
ever, yet it is difficult to imagine how it can have
been done in Spain at any later period, after his life
as a pirate captain had fairly begun.   The expression
is full of spirit and intelligence, without a trace in
it of the desperate, wild manner of man which he
afterwards became ; and it makes one the more
regret the sad fate of one evidently born for better
things in life than to command a crew of Algerine
desperadoes.

His reckless career went on for three or four
more years of which we have no notice, till in 'the
most delectable and true discours of an admirid and
painful peregrination by William Lithgow,' published
in 1623, we come on him once again.   'Here in
Missina [in 1615] I found the sometime great English
gallant, Sir Francis Verney, lying sick in a Hospital,
whom six weeks before I had met at Palermo, who
after many misfortunes, exhausting his large patri-
mony, abandoning his country and turning Turk in
Tunisis, was taken at sea by the Sicialian galleys, in
one of which he was two years a slave, whence he
was redeemed by an English Jesuit upon a promise
of conversion to the Christian faith.   When set at
liberty he turned common soldier, and here in the
extremest calamity of extream miseries entreated

death. Whose dead corps I charitably interred in
the best manner time would afford me strength.'
The chief authority of the great Hospital of St. Mary
of Pity, Don Peter Garsia, 'pater magni Xenodochei,'
certifies only that Sir Francis Verney, 'Anglum,'
came to hospital sick, and that they took him in.
Also that on September 6, 1615, he died there.
This certificate was obtained for his family in England
by John Watchin, an English merchant, and with it
he sent home a turban, two fine silk pelisses, two
pair of slippers, the cane, and a curious pilgrim's
staff inlaid with mother-of-pearl crosses, belonging
to Sir Francis, all still preserved ; the last 'seems to
show that he did not commit the unnecessary and
improbable offence of becoming a renegade,' and
also shows that he was not quite in such 'extream '
poverty as Lithgow represents when he performed his
'pious offices.'   A sadder story cannot be imagined ;
that in his misery he should never have applied for
help to any of his friends at home—neither to his
wife, the uncles in whom he trusted, nor to the
brother who was too young when they parted to
have had any real quarrel with, and who was now
old enough to assist him—shows how desperate he
must have considered his condition in the eyes of his
country, and was probably also due to the wayward
pride which had ruined his fair career in England.
'There, victor of his health, of fortune, friends, and
fame,' ended poor Francis, aged thirty-one years
only

His widow, Ursula, married about four years
after the son of Sir W. Clark, 'without his father's
privity. . . . Though there be no great inequality
between them, either for wealth or years (he being
four or five and forty, and she two or three and
thirty), yet the old knight is so much offended that
he threatens to disinherit him, and hath vowed they
shall never come within his doors.' Parental authority was severe at that period and exercised unspar-
ingly.

Ursula, Lady Verney, re-married a third time to
John Chichely, Esq., and her long life continued
until 1670, when her great-nephew Edmund writes
to his brother John at Aleppo that 'old Aunt Ursula
is deceased,' aged eighty-three.

The career of Sir Edmund Verney, who was now
the head of the family, was in every respect, save
that of courage, the greatest possible contrast to that
of poor Francis—a high-minded, conscientious, chivalrous man, a most affectionate father and husband,
devoted to his duties, ' both public and private, both
of peace and war,' to fit a man for which Milton
sums up as the ideal of education. After his father's
death he lived in Drury Lane with his mother, who
had no home in the country for some time when she
had given up her house at Quainton to Francis.
'Dame Mary' received the rents of Claydon and
Muresley during her son's minority for the purposes
of his education, which was provided in the form
then considered most becoming for a young man

intended for the army and the Court. 'After some time spent with my Lord Goring to see the armies in the wars in the Low Countries, and some sallies out with my Lord Herbert and Sir Henry Wotton to see the Courts of France and Italy, he goeth with my Lord of Bristol into Spain,' says old Lloyd. On his return in 1616, 'an accomplished gentleman,' he was taken into the household of Prince Henry as chief sewer, where his Uncle Francis was one of the falconers, and Mr. Bruce remarks that it was evidently an additional recommendation to the prince, that he found sympathy in Sir Edmund's religious principles, which inclined to simplicity in worship and to the reformed Protestantism not in favour at James's Court, and beginning to be called Puritanism. In January 1611, he was knighted when just of age, and in the same year he visited Madrid, where Lord Digby was then the ambassador, apparently on some public business. It must have been shortly after his return to England that Prince Henry gave him his picture, a three-quarters, which hangs at Claydon ; it represents a handsome, gentle, and somewhat sickly young man, sitting in a chair of state with a sort of sceptre in his hand. He and his brother ' were under the pedagogy of Mr. T. Murray, and Prince Charles was so studious that Prince Henry took Archbishop Abbot's cap one day, and clapt it on his head, saying that if he followed his book well he would make him Archbishop of Canterbury,' a better fate for Charles, and for which he was more fitted, than to be king of England.

Henry, Prince of Wales,
from a picture attributed to Mireveldt at Claydon House.

In 1612 Prince Henry died, not yet nineteen ; Sir Edmund felt his loss acutely, and twenty-seven years after alluded to it as having occasioned him the greatest sorrow of any he had ever known. Indeed the grief was general, and in a tract dated 1687 it is said : ' When women in England do lament the death of their dearest children, to comfort them it is ordinarily said, and is past into a proverbe, " Did not good Prince Henry die ? " '

It is difficult to judge of heirs-apparent who have not had time to carry out the hopeful expectations which they so often inspire, but there is no doubt that Henry was a young man of much promise, and that his prolonged life might not improbably have changed the fortunes of England.[1]

In the next year a household was formed for Prince Charles, aged thirteen, and Sir Edmund was placed in it as one of the gentlemen of the privy

[1] There is an interesting letter from him to his father, the more remarkable as coming from so young a man : 'touching my marriage to the second daughter of France.' She is only nine years old, but the prince thinks 'by bringing her over sooner there will be a greater chance of converting her to our religion.' He entreats his father ' never to agree that he will give her greater liberty for the exercise of her religion than privatamente, as Sir Henry Wotton did expound it, in her most private and secret chamber.' In comparing the different proposals for brides that have been made for him, ' the sister of France,' ' the daughter of Savoy,' he hopes ' that the King will respect that which will give the greater contentment and satisfaction to the general body of protestants abroad '—(a wise policy to which James never could attain)—and thinks that he will ' incline sooner to France.' He winds up with a little joke ' craving pardon ' for his advice, and saying the king is fitter to resolve what course is most convenient, ' Besides your Majesty may think that my part to play, which is to be in love with any of them, is not yet at hand ! '

chamber.   He was barely twenty-three himself, and
in later and more difficult years the fact that they
had been together almost from boyhood, singularly
complicated the feeling with which Sir Edmund
regarded the proceedings of his master, while Charles
after his rather cold fashion seems to have respected
and liked the chivalrous and warm-hearted gentleman—' A man,' says Clarendon, ' of great courage
and of a very cheerful and generous nature and con-
fessedly valiant,' who served his king faithfully, but
with the same sort of misgiving that beset Falkland
and so many other loyal gentlemen who looked ahead
and saw the danger of the course which their ill-fated
master pursued with obstinate blindness to the bitter
end.

In the interval before his second appointment, Sir
Edmund, aged twenty-two, married the daughter of
a neighbouring proprietor ' of birth and estate,' Sir
Thomas Denton,[1] whose ancient house at Hillesden,
with a large and beautiful old church close by, and
an elm avenue leading to it along the crest of the hill,
could be seen from the higher part of the Claydon
estate.   ' Two black trumpeters in red used to sound
a reveille, answered by two trumpeters from the other
hill,' says an unwritten tradition.

Margaret Denton was one of a very numerous
family, but she had what must have been considered
a good fortune—2,300*l.*—equal to four or five times

---

[1] The last of the Dentons married Mr. Coke of Norfolk, whose son
was made Earl of Leicester.

MARGARET, LADY VERNEY. BORN DENTON.

Dame Margaret Verney.
dau: of Sir Thomas Denton.
from a picture at Claydon House.

Margaret Verney

the sum at present. The question of settlements
was therefore serious. Dame Mary was a managing
woman and had bought a home at Langley Marsh
'with the Verneys' money, which she after sold away
for 200*l.* more than her grandson Sir Ralph offered,
a matter he took very ill,' writes Lord Fermanagh in
an angry note, but at this time she did her best
for her son. Sir Thomas demanded a jointure of
400*l.* a year, which Sir Edmund at that time was
unable to secure. His mother, however, gave up a
recognisance for 1,000*l.*, upon receiving an annuity of
100*l.* a year, and the marriage took place in December
1612. Margaret Verney was a good and clever
woman, devoted to her husband and children, gentle
and retiring : 'the heart of her husband trusted in
her,' and obliged as he was to be very often away
from his home when in attendance at Court, much of
the business of the family fortunes devolved upon
her.

There is an interesting picture of her, with a
tender sad face full of feeling and intelligence, in an
undress white 'smock' trimmed with lace, and a
large 'jewel' hung round her neck : she is leaning on
her left arm, held so as to show the marks of a burn,
with which there is evidently some honourable story
connected, but which has been vainly sought for
among the papers.

She was much attached to her own family, the
Dentons, whose portraits still hang all round her
own at Claydon. One of her father with a high bald

head ; of her mother, Susan Temple of Stowe, great-
aunt of Sir Richard who built the first splendid house
and laid out the gardens there ; he was a godson of
Sir Edmund, an unscrupulous, violent man, but one
of the few who had the courage to resist Charles II.
in the earlier Parliaments of his reign, and a member
of the very small party of ' Whigs ' who succeeded in
getting seats.   A panel picture of Margaret's brother,
Sir Alexander, who held the house at Hillesden for
several days against ' Colonel Cromwell ; ' and a portrait of his wife, a cousin of John Hampden's, and of
Dr. Denton, the king's physician, are still at Claydon,
none of them first-rate, but all interesting.

Margaret was only eighteen, Claydon was still let
to the Giffards, and it must have been a material and
pleasant help to the young couple when the Dentons
agreed to give their daughter and her husband ' four
yeares boarde.'   Sir Edmund seems to have vibrated
between the house in Drury Lane, then a very
fashionable part of the town, his chamber at Prince
Charles's Court, and Hillesden, where his wife chiefly
lived and where eight of their twelve children were
born, the four eldest being boys, Ralph, Thomas,
Edmund, and Henry.   The Dentons were among the
chief people in the county of Bucks, one or other of
them serving in Parliament for Buckingham or the
county for a couple of hundred years, and Sir
Edmund took part as a magistrate in all the county
business, together with his father-in-law, his wife's
uncle, Sir Peter Temple, Sir W. Fleetwood, the father

of Cromwell's son-in-law, &c. In 1622 he was appointed Lieutenant of Whaddon Chase by Villiers, then Marquis of Buckingham, who had been made its keeper by James I. and occasionally resided at the manor house, where an old oak in the garden was long shown as that under which Spenser used to sit when he was writing the 'Fairy Queen.' A letter to Sir Edmund from Sir R. Graham, one of the marquis's gentlemen, says, 'You moved it [the lieutenancy] to the Marquess on Newmarkett heath when I was by, myself. There are many suters for the said place, but my Lord thought you had a minde to itt. He wishes the imployment be worth your desserveing, and grants you the leevetennancy with all his hart. . . . For the venison hee will not lymmitt you by the allowance of a warrant, but gives you free leaue to kill what you will, both in the parke and chase. You need not be spareing to pleasure yourselfe and your friendes also, for there are to many in the parke. . . . Sir I would have seene you before the progress, but I have had so much busines in furnishing my lorde for the progress, and my lady for the country, that I protest I have had no spare tyme to doe anythinge.'

'Buckingham, who had formerly behaved with ill-bred insolence to Charles,' had now changed his tone ; the old king was failing, and he desired to stand well with the coming sovereign and was therefore glad to do a pleasure to his friends.

A curious petition three years after this time

from a number of cottagers, only able to sign their
mark, ' to the wor^ppful Sir Edward Varney Kt., to
be delivered at Hillesden,' complains of the injury
done by the Whaddon deer to the common land.
They ask for help as against Villiers, now Duke, and
speak out in a fearless way creditable to both Sir
Edmund and themselves. ' Worthie S^r, We heare
that M^r· Sandys did latelie write to you about your
deere lying in o^r corn and grasse, and that Robert
Heiward being told of it should answer that none but
M^r· Sandys and Arthur Smyth would say it.   These
are therefore to certefie that it is most true that the
deere doe much oppresse us in most places of o^r feeld
[i.e. common land], and we are continuallie damni-
fyed by them.   Soe that we had a purpose to petition
to the Lord Duke his grace, rather then to endure the
injuryes that we suffer.   Yet first we thought fitt to
acquaint your worship with o^r grievances, humblie
entreating that you would be pleased to thinke of
some course whereby they may be remedyed.   We
have ancientlie used to cutte and fetch furzes from
offe o^r sheep-com̄on for o^r own uses.   But now of
late we have been forbidden and discharged as from
you.   We hope o^r gracious Lord will suffer us to
enjoy o^r ancient rights and therefore we desire that
you would not goe about to take them from us.
And thus craving pardon for this our boldnesse we
take leave, resting your worshipp's in all duty.
Little Horwood, June 25, 1625 ' ; and then follow
eight signatures, five of them marks.

The estate at Claydon had all this time been a great source of annoyance to Sir Edmund. The lease which had been renewed to the Giffards for 100 years in 1535, had still fifteen years to run. It had been sublet to a tenant who cut the timber, ploughed up the pastures (a great crime in Buckinghamshire, where they are exceptionally good), and made himself otherwise disagreeable. Sir Edmund in 1620, to put an end to the continual disputes, agreed to pay 4,000*l.* for the surrender of the remainder of the lease. If he had had the money it would have been an excellent investment, but as he had to borrow it he was only involving himself in more serious trouble. He writes :—' Heretofore my means being small I did, to my great charge, attend the late most renowned Prince Henry and my ever most honoured and famous Prince Charles, my loving master, and for my better maintenance and supporting myself to do my best service to the said Prince, I did buy in a lease of my landes, and thereby I became much in depte.' He had ' made knowne the same to his highness, and it pleased him to promise to pay unto mee 4,000*l.*, by a thousand pounds yearely for fower yeares. According to his princely woord and promis he hath paid unto me one thousand pounds of the same, and the said most worthy prince hath ever been so just of his word and promise that he will no doubt give order for payment thereof.' Charles, however, was in much too great trouble for money himself to fulfil any such engagement ; the remainder of the money never was paid, and Sir Edmund continued in more or less pecuniary difficulties to the end of his life.

The year 1623 was memorable for the strange and foolish episode of the journey of Charles to Spain in search of the Infanta. The Spanish alliance was most unpopular in England, and the prince and Buckingham started on their reckless enterprise very privately, with only three attendants ; even these were afterwards left on the road, partly as it appears from want of funds, so that ' the sweet boys and dear venturous knights, worthy to be put into a new romance,' as James calls them, arrived in Madrid quite alone.

The prince's household was sent after him by sea, sixty in number, among whom was Sir Edmund Verney. In about six days they reached Santander, ' a very poor thing, having neither glass windows, nor chimneys,' says Sir Richard Wynne of Gwedir, one of the party. The English were shocked at the treatment of the Spanish women : ' they make their wives their slaves, who till the ground and carry the luggage. . . . We have seen when these women have come with great trunks upon their heads from the shore, and ready to sink under the burthen, their own husbands standing by, their pride was such they scorned to put their helping hands to help their wives, and suffered our people to help them, when they stood by and laughed.'

After waiting a week for orders, the party set

forth for Madrid, 'on sorry mules' which would only go at a walk and 'kicked backwards' when the spur was used, every man with a cloakbag before him—'the young gallants' wondering what their friends in England would say if they 'had but seen them in these postures.' The road over the mountains 'was terrible stony ; the hills we climbed and the steep downfalls we descended are not to be believed ;' for two leagues it was made like a stair, a narrow passage two feet broad. At night they rested at 'a lodging without windows, the floors without a foot that wanted holes, it was so much decayed, but they said that King Philip and his Queen had both layn in the house : the night very cold and sharp : there was no table nor stool for supper, but with much adoe wee got a piece of timber, about which we stood and gave God thanks for what we had.' The people came and stood round, 'handling one thing and feeling another, not leaving till they saw us abed.' And now arrived a letter from the prince desiring that they should all return to England by the ships they came in. The sadness and perplexity were general ; they did not know what to do, fearing for their master's safety. Most of them resolved to obey the order, but Sir Edmund Verney, Sir William Howard, and a few of the most determined, declared that the prince might be under duress, and that they would go on and see for themselves.

Before starting afresh they went to church and heard a sermon in Latin by a Jesuit, wherein he

called Elizabeth ' the daughter of lust and adultery,
whose mother was begot by none but Satan,' said that
' King Henry's soul lyes chained in the bottomlesse
pit of Hell' (not very promising for the prince's suit),
and ended with a declaration ' that the Prince of
England had doubtless come with the resolution to be
a Catholick, and leave the damnable way he and his
people were in.'

When the suite at length reached the king's
palace at Madrid where the prince was lodged, ' we
found him and the Marquess [Buckingham] in
Spanish habits, such as will make the handsomest
man living look another thing. . . . He had
only two little rooms, with a garden so nasty and so
ill-favouredly kept, that a farmer in England would
be ashamed of such another ; ' in this he must walk or
' mew himself up all day long.' Howard and Verney
were in attendance ; the others who had followed,
after many delays and counter-orders, were lodged in
the Duke de Monteleo's palace, a long way off, and
had nothing to do but play at cards. The dirt in the
streets and houses ' did almost poison us. . . .
The ladies are painted thick and palpable, you would
think they rather wore vizards then their own faces.
The boldest women in the world, numbers call'd and
becon'd to me as I passed.' The general want of
civilisation in Spain, which was then considered the
first country in the world, compared to what they
were used to in England, is remarkable.

Most of the suite were sent home after this, some

by sea, some by land, with scant regard for their convenience ; Sir Edmund, however, remained with the prince.

Although Charles had arrived at Madrid in March it was not till October 3 that he made up his mind to depart, wearied by the delays and deceits of all concerned, Olivarez, the Spanish Minister,[1] 'playing with him as an angler plays with a salmon.' He had fallen deeply in love with the Infanta, and not being troubled with scruples about the fulfilment of promises, he was ready to agree to all the stipulations made by the wily Spaniard, whose real object was to get rid of him. In the end he proved himself, however, as great in dissimulation as Olivarez himself. After having given way on one condition after another, having obtained *carte blanche* from his father for anything he chose to sign, so that the Spaniards believed that even his conversion was only a matter of time, he finally went off swearing in the most solemn manner to the marriage treaty, and leaving a proxy to Lord Bristol to 'despatch it,' while he privately arranged that it should be broken off as soon as he could get out of Spain. Philip had refused all the requests of James I. for help to his son-in-law in the Palatinate, and never for a moment yielded in his demand for privileges to the Catholics in England, which should in the end lead to their supremacy. Charles, instead of declaring that the condition was one which the English nation would never endure,

[1] Gardiner's *Spanish Marriages.*

and that he must therefore break off the marriage
treaty, with which he was thoroughly disgusted,
went off with a lie in his mouth.   On August 28
he took a solemn oath binding himself to the marriage, and wrote afterwards ' that even if all the
world conjoined were to oppose itself and seek to
trouble our friendship it would have no effect upon
my father or myself.'   The only time when he allowed
his real feeling to appear was when starting from the
Escurial on his way home.   Cardinal Zapata inquired
whether he would like the carriage open which was
to convey him to the coast.   ' I should not dare,'
replied Charles, ' to give my assent without sending
first to Madrid to consult the Junta of Theologians,'
to whom every point in the marriage treaty had been
referred to his great annoyance.

During these long months the chief knowledge we
have of Sir Edmund's doings is from Howell's letters,
who mentions that ' the Prince his page Mr. Washington, is lately dead of a calenture.   A little before
his death one Ballard, an English priest, went to
tamper with him, and Sir Edmund Verney meeting
him coming down the stairs out of Washington's
chamber, they fell from words to blowes, but they
were parted.   The business was like to gather very
ill blood, com to a great height, had not Gondomar
quash't it.'   The little company of Englishmen were
terribly excited ; gathering in a knot about the door
they barred the entrance, as they said by the prince's
orders, and Sir Edmund struck the priest in the face

with his fist.   The poor boy was from Buckinghamshire, so that his strong feeling against Catholicism
was stimulated by his interest in his compatriot.   It
must have been with a feeling of relief at having at
least saved his friend from further molestation, that
he, with all the English company, attended his burial
' under a fig-tree in Lord of Bristol's ' garden, the
only resting-place allowed him by the bigotry of the
Spaniards.

The King, much annoyed, sent Gondomar to
desire that Sir Edmund should be rigorously punished ; on the other hand, Charles, deeply offended,
demanded that an Alcalde, who had laid hands upon
his servant, should suffer.   At last Philip cut the
matter short by telling the prince that if he wished
to spend the winter in Madrid he must dismiss his
Protestant attendants.   This was probably one of
the smaller affronts which at last determined the
wavering resolution of Charles to leave Madrid.   Sir
Edmund was not sent away, and twelve days after
Charles himself took his departure.

It is mentioned how at the last moment, when the
prince was scattering presents on all sides, he found
that his stock had run short, and he bought ' a cross
of ten thick table diamonds from his servant Sir
Edmund Verney as a gift to Don Maria de Lande.'
This was probably one of the jewels belonging to his
great-grandmother, the splendid maid of honour,
Anne Weston, which he had taken with him into
Spain.

A picture of Sir Edmund,[1] marked at the back 'done in Spain, very unlike,' represents him as a smart young gentleman with a ring in his ear, a pointed beard, an exceedingly rich lace collar and ruffles, and a crimson sash over his breastplate, curiously unlike the serious, statesmanlike, soldierly look of the picture of him by Vandyke painted in later years.

The prince and his attendants returned by sea, and only reached England on October 5th. Sir Edmund hurried off to Buckinghamshire, where a little daughter Margaret had been born to him at Hillesden during the anxious time which the poor mother had passed on his account, for the season was a stormy one, and the voyage across the Bay of Biscay protracted and dangerous. In the following year Sir Edmund was returned for the borough of Buckingham in the Parliament which met in February 1624, the last having been dissolved by James 'in great heat' after the memorable protestation of December 1621, which asserted that ' the liberties of Parliament are the ancient and undoubted birthright of the subjects of England '—and again, 'that the Commons of England have freedom to treat of the defence of the realm, the making of laws, and redress of grievances . . . .; that every member hath, and of right ought to have, freedom of speech.' It is a noble and temperate assertion of their liberties, and of rights which nothing could induce them to

[1] See frontispiece.

abandon.   The king's answer had been to tear out
with his own hands the pages of the journals of the
House containing the protest.

The borough of Buckingham had never received
a summons until the reign of Henry VIII. ; many
towns indeed refused the honour of a member in
order to avoid being saddled with the costs of the
election—an excellent provision against bribery.   In
the first year of Mary Tudor the choice of a member
was ' limited to the Corporation, consisting only of a
Bailiff and twelve capital burghesses '—(a state of
things which continued to the time of the Reform
Bill in 1832).   Sir Edmund had seen the world and
was a man used to business ; he took his turn on
Committees, but does not appear to have joined in the
debates.

In the following year King James died, aged
fifty-nine ; the failure of his negotiations to get his
daughter and her husband restored to the Palatinate,
which they had lost in their vain pursuit of that
shadow, the crown of Bohemia, had gone to his heart.
The breaking up of the alliance with Spain, which he
had carried out against the will of the nation, brought
on him an infinity of troubles, peculiarly distressing
to one so proud of his statecraft and powers of negotiation.   He was suffering severely from gout, and
anxiety probably hastened his end.

The accession of the new king brought with it an
improvement in Sir Edmund's position.   He was
made Knight-Marshal of the Palace, a very ancient

office which had been held by such men as Baron
Hunsdon and Sir Ralph Hopton.   It was a troublesome post, and the duty of preserving order about
the Court was no easy task.   During the reign of
James it had been beset by a ' crowd of idle rascals
and poor miserable bodies ' from Scotland, against
whom the king issued many vain proclamations.   ' A
multitude of idle and masterless persons' kept the
place in an uproar with their quarrels, and the danger
of infection was not slight in such gatherings at that
very unsanitary period.   A kind of market was held
at the Court gate, where the 'beefs, muttons, veales,
chickins,' &c., were bought, which had of old been
supplied to the sovereign at certain low prices with
or without the consent of the owner.   The precincts
of the palace must have been a scene of confusion,
noise, dirt, and squalor, such as we can hardly conceive as surrounding a Court.   The state officers and
the royal tradespeople lived in the palace, with a
number of workmen and hangers on ; while innumerable petitioners, beggars of all classes and every
description, hung about trying to obtain notice.

Many papers concerning the redress of these
grievances are to be found at Claydon—one wherein
the king gave orders that ' the Knight Marshal shall
continually ride both in the daytime and in the night
about our Court,' arresting and punishing the offen-
ders : fortunately he was allowed a deputy and from
four to six officers under him, which relieved him of
many of these very distasteful duties.   ' The great

and excessive number of landers and landresses that
follow our court, without order or limitation,' next
oppresses the royal mind. ' Wee, intending the reformation thereof, doe hereby lymitt and apoint '
such a number ' of good reputation, not to ouer
burden our court with vagabonds. . . . Wee allow
for our bodie, one landres, 2 maides ; the same for
ye Lord Admiral, ye Lord Chamberlain &c. Mil-
layners 1, glovers 1 &c.' A paper of the previous
reign expresses ' our highe displeasure and offence at
the bolde and barbarous insolency of multitudes of
vulgar people, who pressing vpon vs in our sportes,
doe ride over our dogges, not without sometime perill
both of our owne person and to our dearest sonne
the prince.' These too 'it is our will and pleasure
that the Knight-Marshall shall presently apprehend
. . . in all places of our removes this progresse and
ells where . . . : Given at the Castle of Belvoir,' 1619.

In 1625 Charles changed a pension of 200*l.* during
pleasure, which he had previously given to Sir
Edmund, ' considering his many faithful and acceptable services,' into one for life, and added another of
the same amount to him as part of the emoluments
of the Knight-Marshal, who seems to have otherwise
been paid by the fees of his court, which ' took cogni-
zance of all causes arising in the King's household,
or within the verge '—i.e. twelve miles from Court.

The Parliament of 1625 had granted the king two
subsidies as ' the first fruits of their love,' but when
they proceeded to insist on the redress of grievances

as a preliminary condition to any more grants they were summarily dismissed. Charles, however, required money immediately, and could now raise it only by prerogative ; the Verney papers during 1625 and 1626 are full of orders for the levying of money upon privy seals, and for ' coat and conduct money,' as it was termed—that is, for the outfit of men pressed for an expedition to Cadiz against Spain, and for their expenses in going to the place of rendezvous.

As soon as the Buckinghamshire proportion of the subsidy—3,052*l.*—had been assessed, a demand was made for an additional loan of half the amount. A letter from the Duke of Buckingham to Sir Edmund and the other deputy-lieutenants of Bucks adds a direction to ' disarm the Roman Catholiques,' who were at this time in bad odour, in consequence of the favour they were believed to receive at Court, and the queen's vehement partisanship : this order was apparently a wretched attempt to obtain popularity at their expense. The duty seems, however, to have been regarded as a very unpalatable one, and in a letter from Sir Thomas Tyringham to ' Sir Thomas Deynton [Denton] at Hilsden,' he mentions that magistrates feared ' being lawffed at ' for their pains. ' I mett the Kynge but last nyghte, so that as yett I have had noe speeches with him mysealfe. . . . He hath resowlved of some stricktter coursses.'

The assessment of the loan was a source of much dissatisfaction, and created much ill-blood, each man esteeming that his proportion was set too high. There is a curious item in a letter from Sir W. Borlace to Sir Thomas Denton in January 1626 : 'I do think Mr. John Hampden to be £13. 6. 8 and his mother £10 is a harder rate then I finde upon any other.' The protest was unattended to at the time, but the point appears to have been yielded, for in the official list Hampden is set down at ten pounds, though his mother's tax continued as before.   The deputy-lieutenants of the county of Bucks sent up a very earnest remonstrance to the Duke of Buckingham as to the grievances of the county ; the ' coat and conduct money' of the last year they said had never been repaid ; also that the ' multiplicitie of payments in maynetayninge of soldiers is very greevious . . . fallinge out in these times of affliction and dearth,' and never made good.

In 1627 fresh men were pressed in Bucks to be sent to the Low Countries and the Isle of Rhé ; the continual calls for payments of all kinds brought on disputes between the ' hill districts ' and those of the ' vale,' each considering the other favoured by the assessors.   Again, each hundred had to provide its levy of men, and pay 14 shillings for the coats and other money for their ' conduct' on their way, which could rarely be got back from the ' Council of War.' Whole pages of remonstrances and orders to constables and magistrates follow.

For the two Parliaments of 1625 and 1626 Sir Edmund did not stand, but in that summoned in 1627–8 he was returned for Aylesbury.   It lasted

barely a year, but the work done was more important
for the liberties of England than at any other period,
except perhaps during the first years of the Long
Parliament, and it was performed at a much greater
risk to the members themselves.

The Parliament of 1626 had been violently dismissed by the king to save the Duke of Buckingham
from the gathering wrath of the Commons ; and Sir
John Eliot, who led the attack, was illegally sent to
the Tower, although the session was not yet ended :
the House, however, refused to go on with any business, and Eliot was released after a ten days' imprisonment.   Charles had next proceeded to levy a
forced loan in place of the subsidies which the Parliament refused to grant until their grievances were
redressed.   Soldiers were quartered on recalcitrant
towns, Commissioners were sent to overawe the
counties, men were pressed into the army and navy,
and some of those who would not pay towards the
loan were thrown into prison.   But the spirit of the
country had risen : fifteen peers, headed by Lord
Essex and Lord Warwick (who afterwards married
Lady Sussex, the friend of Sir Edmund), refused to
lend, the judges having made objections on the score
of legality.   Hundreds of country gentlemen, many
of whom had suffered imprisonment, were summoned
before the Council.   John Hampden was one of the
earliest to appear at the Board.   ' I could be content
to lend,' he is reported to have said, ' but fear to draw
on myself that curse from Magna Charta.'   He was

imprisoned for his protest in the Gatehouse with such
severity 'that he never afterwards did looke like the
same man he was before.'   Buckingham attempted to
retrieve the king's position by a military success, and
sailed at the head of 6,000 men to the Isle of Rhé
for the relief of Rochelle.   Nothing, however, could
be worse than his conduct of the war, and he was
ignominiously beaten.

Charles, now overwhelmed with debt and defeat, at war with France and Spain, and without
money, was obliged to summon another Parliament,
which met in March 1628 : the elections had gone
against the king, and the spirit in which the members
came together was more resolute than ever for the
redress of grievances.   'We must vindicate our
ancient sober and vital liberties by reinforcing of the
laws made by our ancestors,' said Strafford (then
Wentworth), still among the patriots.   In spite of
sharp messages from the king and demands that they
would first grant supplies, and 'take his royal word'
for the maintenance of 'just freedom,' the House
betook itself to its great work, the drawing up of the
Petition of Right.   Nothing is more remarkable in
their discussions than the conservative tone of the
great leaders.   An appeal to the old statutes, to the
liberties of earlier days, is the foundation on which
they all rest.   No new privileges are demanded by
the most advanced.   When they declared that ' No
man was hereafter to be compelled to make any gift
or benevolence without consent of Parliament,' the

statutes which protected the subject against arbitrary taxation were formally recited.

After a vain attempt at conciliation by the Lords, and an evasive reply of Charles to the Petition, Sir John Eliot again took the lead in the debate which ensued.   He was evidently about to declare that the removal of Buckingham was the real necessity of the time, when he was silenced by the Speaker, 'by command laid upon him to interrupt any that should lay an aspersion on the Ministers of State.'   This breach of the privilege of free speech produced a scene of passion such as never had been witnessed, 'men weeping, expostulating, prophesying the ruin of their country.'   Pym rose, but his emotion was such that he could not speak : Sir Edward Coke, M.P. for Bucks, formerly Attorney-General, 'one of the toughest men ever made, melting into tears like a girl.'   It was resolved to go into Committee, and Coke then made a speech, blaming himself for the timid counsels which had checked Eliot at the beginning of the session, and protesting that the Duke of Buckingham was the 'author and cause of all those miseries ;' his name was inserted in the Remonstrance then drawn up to be presented to the king, amidst shouts of 'Aye, aye!' 'Well spoken!' 'Well moved!' 'Aye, aye!' which resounded through the House.

The danger to his favourite now induced the king to sign the Petition of Right, which had been drawn up by the old lawyer Coke : it was not the first time that he had thus distinguished himself.   In 1616 he had been deprived of the office of Chief Justice for opposing King James, in 1621 he had been committed to the Tower for supporting the privileges of Parliament, and on the accession of Charles he had been named High Sheriff of Bucks to prevent his being chosen member for the county.

The Parliament was soon after prorogued ; in the interval before it met again, Buckingham, about to start on a fresh expedition to Rochelle, was assassinated, and hopes that a better time was at hand rose high.   When, however, Charles had granted the Petition of Right he had no intention of parting with his power of arbitrary arrest, or of levying customs, and the illegal demands for tonnage and poundage, as appears in the Verney Papers, went on as vigorously as before.

The Commons met again in January, '29, but their first care was not, as might have been expected, with questions concerning taxation, but with those of religion.   The fall of Rochelle, leaving the Huguenots in France at the mercy of Richelieu, the triumphs of the Imperialists over Lutherans and Calvinists alike— made it seem as if the cause of Protestantism was almost lost on the Continent ; while at home Laud, who might now be termed the chief minister of Charles, was preaching passive obedience, and enforcing a scheme of ritual and dogma dangerous and odious in the eyes of the nation, for the mass of the clergy as well as their flocks were at this time Puritan.   With these views Sir Edmund most

warmly sympathised ; his earnest Protestantism was
well known, and he shortly after was the chief mover
in bringing over Archbishop Usher from Ireland to
preach ' right doctrine ' at St. Paul's Church in
Covent Garden.   Out of his scanty income he sub-
scribed most liberally to the fund required, and
received the archbishop into his house.   When therefore Eliot, the most eloquent and earnest of the
parliamentary leaders, declared in his place that ' the
Gospel is that Truth in which this kingdom hath
been happy through a long and rare prosperity ; this
ground let us lay as a foundation, not with words
but with actions,' we know how warmly Sir Edmund
must have sympathised with the speaker.   ' There is
a ceremony,' Eliot went on, ' used in the Eastern
Churches of standing at the repetition of the Creed to
testify their purpose to maintain it, not only with
their bodies upright, but with their swords drawn.
Give me leave to call that custom very commendable.'
To the declaration of Charles that ' the interpretation
of articles of religion only appertaineth to the clergy
and Convocation,' in fact to himself as Head of the
Church, the Parliament replied by asserting that the
right to determine its belief and settle its own forms
of faith lay with the nation itself.   ' The religious
question indeed,' observes Mr. Gardiner, ' was more
precious in the eyes of these men than even the
securities for free speech, for the liberty of person,
and the safety of their property.'   That right
doctrine should be preached, that good principles of

Church government should be enforced, appeared to them matters of life and death, and the welfare of their souls had a more living interest for them than any merely political affairs.

These, however, came again to the front by a sudden move of the king's. The Commons had deferred all grants of customs till the illegal levy of taxes had been relinquished, and as a first step to enforcing their rights they summoned the Custom House officers before the bar of the House to account for having seized the goods of a member of Parliament. The officers pleaded the king's commands, but the House, determined to grapple with the whole question of privilege, debated the matter for several days. A set of resolutions, including the religious grievances, was drawn up, but on March 2, before it was formally adopted, the Speaker signified that he had received the king's order to adjourn. It was clear that Charles was about to dissolve the Parliament before any vote had been carried, which would have been fatal to the cause of reform, and Sir Miles Hobart (cousin of Sir Nathaniel) locked the door of the House and put the key in his pocket, while the king's messenger was knocking for entrance. The Speaker was held down in his chair, and a stormy discussion ensued, Eliot declaring, amidst the gathering tumult, that ' none had gone about to break Parliaments but in the end Parliaments have broken them,' words which it is said were remembered afterwards as of terrible significance.

By successive resolutions ' whoever should bring
in innovations in religion or endorse the levy of
subsidies not granted by Parliament,' was declared
' a capital enemy of the kingdom and commonwealth ;
and every subject voluntarily complying with illegal
exactions, a betrayer of the liberty of England and an
enemy to the same.' The loud ' aye, ayes ' of the
chief part of the members resounded before they
broke up in great excitement. It was the last effort
Eliot was allowed to make in the great cause. He
was imprisoned as soon as the House was dissolved,
and never again left the Tower, the king refusing
even to allow his dead body to be removed to his own
county.

This was the last Parliament that met in England until the summoning of the Short and then
the Long Parliament, to which Charles was only
driven by sheer want of money to carry on his
government. It was impossible that Sir Edmund,
belonging as he did to the king's household, could
have joined actively in the late proceedings ; but that
he did show a very uncourtly sympathy with at least
the religious side of the patriot opposition, and risked
unpopularity with the king, is evident from a hint in
a letter about this time of Sir John Leeke's, who,
seeking as usual for some advancement for his Irish
son-in-law, begs Sir Edmund to obtain ' a copyhowld
in Lemsterre of the Queen's jointure.' ' Good Sr, I
pray that you may countinance Badnage in this
preferment. It hath bine formerly in yor power to

gette such a thing effected, I knowe not how things stand now.'

Though somewhat out of favour, Sir Edmund belonged to the class of powerful country gentlemen, whose influence was great, and whom it was important to conciliate, and Charles seems to have felt that the presence in Parliament of one so respected and so independent, who yet had a strong personal feeling for his sovereign, was a help to his cause.

The number of gentlemen out of Buckinghamshire who distinguished themselves at this time in the struggle for the liberties of England, is indeed very remarkable, and may well make those who dwell there proud of their county. Beginning with Sir Miles Hobart, M.P. for Marlow, imprisoned in 1629 in the Tower for his conduct in the last Parliament— Sir Edward Coke, M.P. for the county, who had been the legal adviser of the constitutional resistance of so many years, and who lived at Stoke Pogiss [1] near Slough—we have also Sir Peter Temple, uncle of Lady Verney, who 'was kept a prisoner in his own house at Stowe, to answer for arrears of ship money,' which he refused to pay ; Whitelocke ; Fortescue of Salden ; Ralph Verney, the writer of the ' Notes of the Long Parliament ' ; and last and greatest of all, Hampden, the chief gentleman of England at that period, whose old house on the Chilterns was about 17 miles from Claydon, with

[1] The scene of Gray's *Long Story* — ' long windows that exclude the light, and passages that lead to nothing.'

many others of inferior note, but all taking the same line.   The 5,000 freeholders, who rode up to London for the protection of Parliament in 1641, were follow-ing in a path wherein the gentlemen of the county had long been leading the way.

' An influence had been growing up,' says Mr. Green, ' that of the gentry, the squires—as they were soon to be called, which told more and more upon English politics.'   Their wealth and position had risen greatly in the last few years, and 'in political consequence the merchants and country gentlemen who formed the bulk of the members of the Lower House now stood far above the mass of the peers.'   ' The nobility and gentry of England,' says Carlyle, ' were then a very strange body of men. The English Squire of the Seventeenth Century clearly appears to have believed in God, not as a figure of speech, but as a very fact, very awful to the heart of the English Squire.   " He wore his Bible-doctrine round him," says one, " as our squire wears his shot-belt," and went abroad with it, nothing doubting.'   The prominent interest in religious over political questions, even the most absorbing, is extremely remarkable both in Sir Edmund and Sir Ralph : it was not only that the liberties of England at this time were believed by them to hang as much on one as on the other, but that being men of the world, living the ordinary life, at Court, in Parlia-ment, in business, in war, sharing in the pleasures and the occupations of the world, whether in town or country, they were among those (and there were many) who truly cared to carry out their ideal of a higher life above all things, although without the smallest pretence at sanctity over and above their neighbours.   Mr. Green mentions how different was the Puritan gentleman of this period to the stern fanatics who bore the name a few years later.   Men of the stamp of Colonel Hutchinson could not be distinguished in appearance from such royalists as Lord Falkland in their dress and manners.   They were neither fanatics nor bigots, they mixed in the pleasures of the world without abusing them.   The close-cropped hair, which is commonly supposed to have been a badge of the Puritan party, was unknown at this time ; it will be seen how young Edmund Verney clung to his long hair in 1636, when the college statutes at Oxford forbade it.   Sir Ralph's hair in Cornelius Jansen's picture falls to his neck ; Sir Edmund's is as long in his picture by Vandyke : it was not by such signs that their faith was signified. The deep interest in religion as more important than any mere earthly concerns, the purity of life and respect for women which was part of their creed—(so ' that home, as we conceive it, was the creation of the Puritans as contrasted with the larger geniality of the age that was passing away ')—are all strikingly illustrated in Sir Edmund and his two sons, Ralph and Edmund.   Their pleasure in 'jest and youthful jollity,' wit and mirth and innocent enjoyments such as dancing, music, fencing, hawking, and ' in all liberal arts,' was entirely without the grossness which degraded the following reign, or the rigidity and narrowness of the time of the Commonwealth : their wives were as high-minded and pure-hearted as themselves, as might be seen in the case of Margaret, the wife of Sir Edmund, and Mary, the wife of Ralph Verney. 'It was a period,' as has been remarked, 'more eminent for steady and scrupulous conscientiousness in private life, than any perhaps that had gone before or has followed after.'

Sir Edmund, too, as is said of Colonel Hutchinson, 'had a loving and sweet courtesy to the poorest,' which was already felt to be part of the demeanour of English gentlemen. His care for the people at Claydon comes out in his orders, which are always both wise and considerate. Writing very kindly to his steward, Will. Roades, about his father, he says, ' He hath sent to mee about that ashwood. The poore old man offers to pay for it ; tell him I cannot wright to him now, but that I have sent to you to lett him have that wood or any other wood to keepe him from coulde. Trewly I am much greived to see that I cannott prevail with him for his own good, but because he understands it not, and has foolish jealousys in his head, I will saye noe more of it,' referring to some trouble which the ' ould man ' has taken to heart, but which is not explained. A shed has tumbled down in a great storm ; 'I am glad my hovell fell upon noe Christian creature,' writes Sir Edmund, and in his anxiety to ascertain that neither man nor beast has

suffered by the accident he quite omits inquiries concerning the money lost. The letters he receives show
the pains he takes in favour of the huntsman who has
left him, and the servants for whom he desires places.
His cottagers, his farmers, are all spoken of with a
degree of goodwill and friendly interest which show
the kindly intercourse between him and his depen-
dants and neighbours.   Indeed the traces of his kind
acts, and the help which he rendered to small and
great in the midst of the business which overwhelmed
him, abound in the letters.   Sometimes it is a ' Buck
from Whaddon Chase,' which Sir Kenelm Digby requests, in a large bold hand covering a foolscap sheet
of paper ; sometimes it is for the future of his young
niece, Doll Leake, whom he has taken to live at
Claydon, or for some poor old lady in London whose
interests he never forgets. At one time he is appealed
to for a ' civil Mounseer' by Lady Barrymore as tutor
to her sons, and Lady Sussex cannot buy ' a great
glas from Vennis ' without telling Ralph to ask his
father to go and see whether it is worth the ' forty
pond they axe.'   The letters asking assistance of all
kinds, from all sorts of men, fill whole portfolios.
Lord Middlesex writes to him to get his kinsman
Vincent Cranfield out of a scrape.   Friends of every
degree appeal to him to find husbands and wives
for their sons and daughters ; sometimes there are
thanks for the loan of a valuable ' brach ' (a dog),
or for the receipt for a cake.

With his large acquaintance at Court, in the

army, in Parliament, and the country, and always in close attendance upon the king, he was often able to speak the word in season that could advance the interests of his many applicants, yet he never misused his influence. He was at this time equally intimate with men who were about to take the most opposite sides in the impending struggle—with Lord Clarendon, then Hyde, at that time on the Parliamentary side; with the Hobarts, Lord Saye and Sele, and Lord Brooke; with Lord Pembroke, the high chamberlain, representing the Puritan interest; with Lord Warwick, soon to be admiral of the fleet under Cromwell; with Lord Carnarvon, killed on the king's side at Newbury, whose wife's picture by Vandyke hangs at Claydon; with the Dillons, both Lords Roscommon, of whom James was brother-in-law to Strafford; with Sir William Uvedale, paymaster of the king's army, and with Lord Cork and his family. The letters from men and women of such different characters and stations show a remarkable degree of respect and affection for Sir Edmund, each after his and her kind, while in the closer knowledge of those at home, among his own and his wife's relations, he was beloved in the highest degree. Mrs. Isham, his sister-in-law, once lends him a thousand pounds for a time, apparently money borrowed from him by the king, and is almost angry because he insists on paying her the interest for it. 'I hope God will take the will for the deed,' she says to Ralph, 'you will bear me witness that I have done my best.' His mother-in-law, the very cross though excellent Lady Denton, who plagues her friends all round her in spite of the kindness which she shows towards them, has always a good word for Sir Edmund. Writing of Ralph's 'little boye,' who is staying with her at Hillesden, she says, ' My sweet child Mun, and your grandson, is very wel, and I will pray that he maye prove as onest and true harted a man to his frends as you have byne to your frendss.'

After the year 1630 we learn much more of the family history of the Verneys, the details in the letters increasing greatly as Sir Edmund's ten children gradually grew up, particularly when the eldest of them, Ralph, comes to a letter-writing age. Hitherto Sir Edmund had only kept papers on business, with an occasional note from his wife, but as they were seldom apart for long, their written communications were few. After this date, however, every scrap, however indifferent, was preserved by Ralph with scrupulous care ; they were a very affectionate family, and voluminous and indefatigable correspondents, the sons when away from home complaining bitterly if a few weeks pass without their hearing from their father or Ralph, so that the accumulation soon became great, sometimes 400 to 500 letters and papers in a year.

Lady Verney, with a fresh baby almost every year, became less and less able to help her husband in the multifarious business, public and private,

which occupied him incessantly, and it more and
more devolved upon his right-hand friend and
councillor, Ralph, who, old before his time, a husband
and a father before he was out of his teens, was far
more learned in affairs and punctual in his business
habits than Sir Edmund with his different nature
and training could ever hope to be.

During the next few years Sir Edmund was still
living in Drury Lane, in constant attendance at
Court, and when his wife and children were not with
him in London, riding down to Claydon whenever
he could spare the time.   There was no other mode
of conveyance excepting the slow waggons, or the
'coch'—a private carriage, which was merely a sort
of cart without springs, with leathern curtains against
the weather, and which most unluxurious luxury
was used only by infirm persons or delicate women
who could not ride.   An enormous trunk belonging
to the Standard bearer, which only a strong waggon
could possibly convey, still exists in an outhouse at
Claydon.   The distances, which were thought nothing
of by gentlemen on horseback, appear from different
royal progresses and journeys.   In 1612 Prince
Henry, being at Richmond, goes to meet the king,
his father, at Belvoir Castle, the distance being near
ninety-six miles, and 'the weather extreme and
unusual hot, he set out at one in the morning with
his attendants [Sir Edmund was then among them],
and travelled threescore miles in nine hours.   He
came to Hinchinbroke, belonging to Sir Oliver Crom-

well K^t. master of his game, and remained the night, and the next day rode 36 miles to Belvoir.' He, however, does not seem ever to have recovered from that exertion. In 1633, when Charles went to Edinburgh to be crowned, he returned ' coming post in fower days from Barwick to Greenwich,' as noted by Laud to show the haste with which Charles hurried back to his wife.[1]   Again, in 1639, Sir Edmund is described as riding 260 miles with the king from Berwick in four days.

In 1634 Sir Edmund established himself in a large new house on the north side of Covent Garden, which was only pulled down about twenty years ago to build the Floral Hall.   The 4th Earl of Bedford had a valuable estate stretching northwards from the Strand, where his own house was situated : upon this he laid out a square and built a row of houses called the Piazza.   It was the most recent addition to the ' West End,' and probably was considered the South Kensington or Tyburnia of that generation. Sir Edmund took the two last houses, running from Russell Street, upon lease, at a rent of 160*l.*, with coachhouse and stables behind.   It is particularly noticed that though the ordinary rooms had only casements—i.e. shutters—the principal apartments were arranged with ' shuttynge wyndowes,' and that the doors had ' stock locks.'   Part of the houses,

---

[1] Henrietta Maria had refused to accompany him to Scotland and to share in his coronation there, as she had done before in the first ceremony at Westminster Abbey ; she would have nothing to do with such heretical performances.

too, were 'waynscotted.' There was no sewer as yet in the new district, and Sir Edmund stipulated that if he were so much annoyed as not to be able to live there 'with any convenyency,' he might give up his lease at a six months' notice. The state of the square, indeed, is described as very barbarous in the letters of the period. 'In Covent Garden a filthy and noisy market was held close to the dwellings of the great. Fruit women screamed, carters fought, cabbage stalks and rotten apples accumulated in heaps at the thresholds of the Countess of Berkshire and of the Bishop of Durham,' says Lord Macaulay, describing its state in the latter part of the century.

Part of the house was occupied by Sir Edmund's mother, and Sir Nathaniel Hobart, who married his niece, had a 'study,' or chambers, also there, though his home was at Highgate. Divided only by a 'fence wall' was another house where lived Sir Edward Sydenham, with whom and his wife the Verneys were extremely intimate. He was about the Court, and she and her sister, Lady Vere Gaudy, were almost like sisters to the Knight-Marshal and his wife.

Sir Edmund's attendance on the king seems to have been continual, and even when guests were staying in his house at Claydon the master was often unable to be present. In March 1636 he writes to his wife, who has her sister with her, just married to a man of large property in Leicestershire :—

'I pray remember my service to my brother &

sister Poultney & tell them I am hartily sorry that
I am not with them.   Commende mee to all my
friends.   The King goes tenn miles hence a huntinge
tomorrow morning, therefore goodnight.   Yours Ed.
V.—My Lord Carlile is dead.'

Charles had inherited his father's love of hunting
and hawking, and often visited Theobalds, which
had been bought by James I. in order to secure a
constant supply of deer and a ' chase ' in the immediate neighbourhood of London.

Sir Edmund's money matters unfortunately did
not improve as time went on.   It must have been a
considerable addition to his pecuniary troubles that
the dress of a gentleman of the privy chamber and
' Kt. Marshall of England' about the Court, of
which Henrietta Maria was the ruling spirit, was
not only extremely expensive, but was continually
changing.   Besides which, it must have demanded
constant renewal ; the ' crimson sattin dublit and
scarlett hoase laced with gould lase,' which appear
in Sir Edmund's tailor's bill for 1632, must have
suffered damage under the wear and tear of even
holiday use.   The ' black velvet cloake lyned with
plush ' would look shabby after the horseman had
splashed in muddy weather after the king, on a
progress, or in a shower of rain.   Signs of Court
festivals and masques, where the Court appeared in
splendour, can be traced by the Verney lists of
clothes, and in 1633, when Charles, attended by his
Court, went down to Scotland to hold a Parliament

and be crowned, the amount of fine garments required is tremendous, as may be seen in the following account :—

The 'purple satten suite'; the 'cloath-of-gold waiscote and cappe'; the 'willow colored satten suite, and cloake laced all over doble, cutt in small paines' (whatever that may be); and the sum paid 'to the Embroderer for setting on the lace,' equal to about 20*l.*, probably mark the particular dress worn at the great ceremony itself.

The 'shamoy leather dublett with scarlet rockett, and hoase for rideinge'; the 'Cordovan skins for a Buffe coat'; 'the cloath sute, the skirts wrought in Pickendell, with two sharps on the hoase, and rich buttons,' mysterious though the description may be, sounds more in harmony with his soldier taste. The sum total, 260*l.*, of money at its present value must have made a deep inroad into Sir Edmund's income, encumbered as it was.

He was one of the most sanguine of men, and an account of the number of schemes which he entered upon affords a pretty good list of the projects by which men attempted to obtain good interest for investments of money in the years 1625 to 1642, when the spirit of adventure had risen high in matters of commerce, and men of all conditions were trying their unaccustomed hands at trade, often with borrowed money.

Sir Edmund had very little success of any kind. He began with a share in a patent for 'garblinge tobacco [i.e. inspecting it] within the realmes of England and Ireland, the dominion of Wales, and the towne of Barwicke [which had still a separate existence] with an allowance of fower pence in the pound.' Next came his long negotiations for buying some of the confiscated lands in Ireland, which, fortunately for him, came to nothing, as during the rebellion which broke out but a few years after, his money would have been absolutely lost. The tobacco patent came to an end in 1638, when the Lord High Treasurer Juxon, appointed under the influence of Laud, 'the first Churchman who had had it since Henry VII.'s reign,' as he writes himself with pride, demanded the surrender of the monopoly (for which the king was expected to give a ' consideration '), and granted it to a new company with Lord Goring at its head, who bought up all the tobacco they could find in England on their own account, their powers proving a ' fruitful source of very shameful fraud.'

Another patent in which Sir Edmund had an interest was for hackney coaches. These, it is said, first appeared in the streets of London in 1625, when a stand of them was established at the Maypole in the Strand. Under pretence, however, that ' the King and his dearest consort the Queen, the nobility, and others of place and degree were disturbed in their passage, that the pavement was destroyed, and the streets pestered by the number of coaches for hire, the king began by limiting the power of hiring hackney coaches to persons who wanted to go three miles out of town.' He then allowed licences to fifty persons, each holding twelve horses, the Master of the Horse, Lord Hamilton, being at the head. Sir Edmund's share often got him into great trouble with the coachmen, who were rebellious subjects in more ways than one. He was also partner in a 'patent for sealing woollen yarn before it was sold or wrought into cloth.'

Another of his investments was taking shares in a lease of some of the fen lands reclaimed by the Earl of Bedford, an old acquaintance. He writes to his son : 'I have sent down 600*l.* to stoare the fenns, in hopes of a good return,' and soon after adds : 'I will provide to make good your part of the bargaine in your absence,' for even the prudent Ralph had been persuaded to join in the adventure. 'I am confident you will have a good bargaine of it, but it will cost you more than I believe you expected.'

Sir Edmund is also mentioned in a patent 'for the supply of turfe to be taken from the waste places of his Majesty's dominions for 14 years,' in conjunction with Sir Thomas Culpeper, but the deed remains unsigned, and appears not to have been carried out. Sir Thomas was a very untrustworthy man, and Sir Edmund drew back in time.

In 1640 the king borrowed 1,000*l.* from him, as from the rest of his household, and considering the uncertainty of affairs, Sir Edmund arranged that, in lieu of repayment of the principal, his heirs after his death should receive an annuity of 400*l.* for twenty years. The money was secured upon the 'Aulnage,' a tax paid for the measuring of cloth, and as he had only a life interest in his landed property, he left this annuity as a chief part of the provision for his younger children. It turned out a very bad investment eventually, and after Sir Edmund's death the family were involved in endless legal proceedings, and petitions to Parliament, and in such a mass of correspondence, that the very name of the Alnage has a terrible sound to any reader of the Verney MSS.

Finally, the outlays for land in Virginia, New England, and 'the Barbathos' which were made by Sir Edmund for the advancement of his vagabond son Tom, must have amounted to a large sum which never brought him in a penny of return, except once, when a cargo of cotton was sent by Tom to 'Amsterredam,' with grandiloquent promises of its extraordinary excellence, but which proved, as with most amateur merchants, not to be exactly what was required, and had therefore to be sold at a very low price.

Sir Edmund never seems to have realised that the making of money is a profession in itself, requiring knowledge, time, and care, none of which in his busy life was he able to afford to his many schemes. Indeed, by none of these adventures does it appear that he bettered his finances, while he enormously increased his anxieties and his burdens by the money which he borrowed to carry them out.

CHAPTER V.

SIR EDMUND'S FOUR SONS—RALPH THE HEIR.

> . . . . 'good brothers,
> . . . . I'll be your father and your brother too ;
> Let me but bear your love, I'll bear your cares.'
>
> 2 *Henry IV*. v. 2.

THE strange variety of character in members of the same family is seldom seen in a more striking degree than among Sir Edmund's four sons. Ralph the heir is a prudent, cautious man, affectionate and conscientious, who spared no pains for those who loved him, and for many who behaved very ill to him, in the difficult times which tried the spirits and temper of all men to the quick. On his shoulders his friends and relations laid their burdens without mercy, and often without thanks, and relied upon him, not in vain, in all their troubles. He had inherited his father's helpful nature, but whereas Sir Edmund's kind deeds were those of a grand seigneur, with whom no one dared to take a liberty, Ralph, on whom the cares of life had fallen early, with a great love of business and a most practical mode of doing it, was made use of and reproved in his early years by the older members of his family—always excepting his

SIR RALPH VERNEY   C. JANSEN

Ralph Verney Esqre
from a picture by Cornelius Jansen
at Claydon House

Raphe Verney

father—and sponged upon by the younger, as one who had married a rich wife, and to whose assistance in purse and influence they had a right. Somewhat precise and formal in these early days, Ralph's long, elaborate compliments, painfully worked out in foul copies which he carefully preserved, fill his letters to the exclusion of what would be really interesting ; one such is headed : ' This was never writ to anyone,' and was evidently reserved for some transcendently important occasion which never came.

After all, his style is only an exaggeration of that usual in the letters of the period, which are full of provoking excuses that ' there is here no news ' at the most important moments, or that the receiver ' will have it from better hands.' In 1631 the family were all living at Claydon—the four sons coming and going ; the girls still children ; and Dorothy Leake, fair and lively, daughter of a half-sister of Sir Edmund's, evidently a great favourite with the household, and not less so with Ralph's college friends, whom he brought with him from Oxford from time to time.

The duty of a good father in those days required that an eligible marriage should be arranged for his sons at the earliest possible opportunity. A little heiress, Mary Blacknall, had been left an orphan at about nine years old, her father, John Blacknall of Abingdon, and his wife having both died in 1625, at

' one instant time,' of the ' great plaage.' [1] He is
described as an excellent man. He had been called
to the bar, and was respected ' for his learning and
judgment in the lawes ' ; but having a good estate in
lands and rents . . . he little ' esteemed the profitt
of his practice, but was ready to give any man
(especially the poorer sort), his advice and counsell
without fees. . . . He laboured to take up contentious
causes, and to make peace between parties ; of an
humble, meek spirit, and gentle nature ; affable and
full of clemencie and curtesie.'   His kindly qualities
descended to his daughter, as well as his large estate.
This included the site of the Abbey of Abingdon,
curious papers relating to which, among the deeds of
her property at Claydon, have been published by the
Camden Society. Mary, as an unprotected orphan,
came under the jurisdiction of the Court of Wards.
In feudal times, as a woman could not perform the
services of a soldier, the theory was that the king
might marry her to one who could fulfil her duty ; but
at this time the ancient right of compelling an heiress

---

[1] There is a monument to Mr. Blacknall and his wife in St. Nicholas' Church, Abingdon :

> ' When once they lived on earth, one bed did hold
> Their bodies, which one minute turn'd to mould ;
> Being dead, one grave is trusted with that prize
> Untill the trump doth sound and all must rise ;
> Here death's stroke even, did not part this pair,
> But by his stroke they more united were ;
> And what they left behind you plainly see,
> One only daughter and their charity,' &c., &c.

There died seventy-four persons of the plague that year at Abingdon.

Verney Papers (Camden Soc.), p. 139.

to marry the king's nominee was always commuted
for money. Lord Cottington had greatly increased the
revenue from the Court of Wards, ' by which husban-
dry,' Lord Clarendon admits, ' all the rich families
of England of noblemen and gentlemen were exceedingly incensed, and even indevoted, to the Crown.'

At the Restoration, one of the first acts of the
Convention Parliament was to abolish ' all Crown
rights of wardship and marriage,' ' in lieu of which,
and of other rights, Charles II. accepted a grant of
100,000l. a year.'

In Mary Blacknall's case four of her relations
procured from the Court a lease of her lands and the
custody of her person, with the privilege, when she
should be fourteen, of bestowing her in marriage, for
which they paid down 1,000l. to the Crown, and gave
bond for the payment of another 1,000l. One of the
guardians, Libb, concocted a match between her and
his son ; ' the licence was had, the wedding apparel
bought, and the priest ready,' she being only eleven
years of age. The fourth guardian, however, her
uncle, Wiseman, appealed to the Court against this
arrangement, which was clearly a breach of trust,
and an order was made ' that the ward un-married,
unaffyed, and uncontracted ' should, under a penalty
of 5,000l., be sent to Lady Denham of Boarstall in
Bucks, mother of the poet, to be brought up with
her own daughters. Three of the guardians then
offered her to Sir Edmund Verney for his eldest son.
Sir Edmund agreed to take the child, and pay the

1,000*l.* still due to the Crown, her uncle stipulating
that she should not be forced in marriage, but should
be well-bred, ' and be allowed to make her choice at
years competent.'   Still there were difficulties, but
Sir Edmund procured a decree from the Court of
Wards in his own favour, and in May 1629, aged
thirteen, she was married to Ralph, who was not yet
sixteen.   Lady Verney writes to Mrs. Wiseman from
Claydon : ' Your neece and my sonne are now
marred.   God send them as much happiness as I
wish them, and then I am sure it will be to all our
comforts ; ' she excuses herself for the privacy of the
marriage, but hopes to see the Wisemans at Claydon,
' wher, though you will not find a wedding feast, yett
I will assure you of the heartiest wellcome I can give ;
and shall allwayes rest thanckfull to you for the
favour.   Mr. Verney is gone to Courte, but commanded mee to present his love and service.'

The girl herself writes : ' Good aunt, besides the
desire I have to heare of your health and my uncle's,
I thinck it fitt to acquaint you that now I am maried,
in which state I hope God will give mee his blessings
and make it happy to mee.'   She then says that she
was anxious the marriage should be ' privatly done,
and soe it was. . . . As I had your loving advice to
it, soe I assure myself I shall have your prayers for
the good success of it.'

Mrs. Wiseman replies : ' I pray God send them
as much joye and happines as ever anye cuppell had.
I could have wissed that Sir Edmund Verney would

have settelled his land upon them, according to his
promise, before they had bine maried. [This was
afterwards done.] I make no douth but he will dou
it . . . otherwise hir frinds will blame Mr. Wiseman
and me, whoe weare the case of the mache. . .
I humbelly thanke you for your kind invitacione :
I will hav a tim to wayt on you. Our accasion of
bilding this sommer is great, wich will be the let.'[1]
To her niece she complains that she was not more
consulted, although she and her husband 'ever
intened this mache.' She desires her always to
honour the Verneys 'as your parants, for so now
thay be, and God will give a blesinge upon you.'
She mentions that Aunt Libb, who had striven to
marry the girl to her own son, 'sayth that shee
hoppeth that I shall repent the mach as much as
anything that I ever ded, but I have a betere beleafe ; '
and thus the unseemly quarrel over the possession of
the poor child ended. She had fallen into good, kind
hands, though as it were by accident. The married
couple did not live together for two years. Mary
returned to her relations for some time, and an effort
seems to have been made even then to induce her to
repudiate the marriage. There is a mysterious letter
from Crowther, tutor to Ralph, who was spending
his vacation at Claydon in August 1631, advising
him to come back to Oxford immediately, and sending
a messenger for the answer. Ralph hurried over,
and as the next letter advises him not to give up his

[1] Collect for Fourth Sunday in Advent. 'Let and hindered,' &c.

studies for Hymen's delights, and tells him that the sweetness of a kiss will relish better after the harshness of a syllogism, with much in the same strain, it is evident that all is right again.

Ralph, aged nineteen, was now spending the college terms of each year at Oxford, studying at Magdalen Hall, where his father's friend, Lord Clarendon, and his young uncle William Denton, had been shortly before. Dr. Denton was at this time practising at Oxford, having lately been appointed physician to the king. He was the youngest but one of the large family at Hillesdon, and only seven years older than his nephew, with whom all his life he was on terms of brotherly affection. In the reign of James I. Magdalen, which was very specially the Bucks College, had been called 'a very nest of Puritans,' and the Hall retained this character when the College, under the influence of Laud and his visitors, had become a thoroughly Royalist centre.[1] The Hall at this time was not only a numerous, but a very powerful body, to which all the chief Puritan families in England sent their sons. Henry Wilkinson was the prominent tutor, under whom young Edmund Verney was afterwards placed in 1636. The proportion of matriculations at the different colleges contrasts strangely with the present day. In the earliest year for which the lists are given (1638) the numbers are : Christ Church, 27 ; Merton, 7 ;

---

[1] *Register of the Visitors of the University of Oxford.* Camden Society. 1881.

University, 10 ; Balliol, 26 ; while Exeter, 41, and Magdalen Hall, 40, stand far the highest of all. Here Ralph continued for about two years, and long letters from his tutor Crowther, in a cramped scho: lastic hand, give many details concerning the course of study at the University. The difficulty of obtaining good text-books was extremely great, a difficulty not remedied, indeed, till within the last forty or fifty years. Every man had more or less to compile his own, and Crowther sends Ralph astronomy notes which he had himself put together for his pupil, with ' a sheet containing the differences and computes of time.' Afterwards he gives him ' a generall scheme of the Arts and a genealogy of the Kings.' Again, he begs ' that he will devote to Logic and Divinity from three to four houres a day.'

' I have not initiated you into the science of geography [the Geographical Society is now trying to get the science introduced into the schools]. If you cannot have leisure to come over hither, I'll attend you for a week or soe at Claydon till I have shewed you the principall grounds,' says Crowther. He intends to ' draw forth his notes after a more stately form ' in a short time, and lends him books out of his own collection. ' If you have done with my Bilson,[1] send him.' ' At the sale of a study at the 2nd hand, I have bought two books, scarce to be had and fitt for your use, " Grymston's Estates and Principallities of the World," 20s., and "The History

---

[1] After Bishop of Winchester.

of Venice," 10s., which I will let you have or reserve
them myself at your pleasure.'

Ralph seems to have acquired a fair knowledge of
Latin, scraps of which he sometimes quotes in his
letters, and he possesses several Latin 'Historyes,'
but there is no mention of Greek either for him or
his brother.   Languages bore a smaller proportion
to the rest of the studies of the University in 1630–
40 than they do at present.   Belief in astrology and
divination of various kinds was still strong.   The
importance of ascertaining the exact moment of a
birth, in order to calculate nativities, is seen in Lord
Fermanagh's genealogical record of the Verney family,
where the instant has always been recorded with
minute accuracy for each successive generation—e.g.
'Sir Ralph Verney was born at Hillesdon on a
Tewsday, betwixt x and xi a clock at night, being
the 9th day of November in the 11th yeare of y^e
Raigne of K. James,' although the date of a marriage
is often omitted, which would now be considered a
more important question.

'A fate' was often forecast by a chance verse out
of the Bible, or a line from Virgil, who seems to
have retained something of the sanctity with which
Dante regarded him three centuries before.

Cowley, when secretary to Lord Jermyn, writes :
'The Scotch treaty, I hope, will come to pass.   The
King is persuaded of it, and, to tell you the truth,
which I take to be an argument above all the rest,
Virgil has told the same thing to that purpose.'

Charles and Lord Falkland, being in the Bodleian Library, made experiment, it is said, of their future fortunes with the ' Sortes Virgilianæ,' and met with answer sequally ominous. The king fell upon ' His men discouraged and himself expelled, his fall untimely by some hostile hand.' Lord Falkland's choice, ' Harassed by the arms and the fight of the audacious people,' was hardly more consoling.

When Charles was a prisoner at Carisbrooke Castle, in 1647–8, an astrologer was consulted as to the most propitious hour for his attempted escape. During Ralph's stay at Oxford the death of Thomas Allen, aged ninety-two, is recorded. ' He was the best astrologer of his time,' wrote old Aubrey, ' and made use of by Dudley, Earl of Leicester, for casting nativities [astrologist, mathematician, and conjuror were counted the same in those dark times] ; he had a great many instruments and glasses in his chamber, and his servitor would tell freshmen that sometimes he should meet the spirits coming up his stairs like bees.' ' Sir Kenelm Digby loved him, and bought his excellent library of him, which he gave to the University.' [1] A horoscope among the

---

[1] He goes on to tell that ' one time being staying at Horne Lacy in Hertfordshire at Mr Scudamoor's, he happened to have his watch, then a raretie in the chamber. The mayde came in to make the bed, and hearinge a thing in a case, cry " tick tick," presently concluded that it was his Devill, and took it by the string with the tongues, and threw it out of window into the mote, to drown the Devill. It so happened that the string hung on a sprig of alder that grew out of the mote, and this confirmed them that twas the Devill. So the good old gentleman got his watch again.'

Verney papers, belonging to a few years after, shows the whole array of planets and the qualities and events which they forebode. 'The seventh son of a seventh son, the man of much might,' is mentioned in one of the letters as having been consulted.

The seventeenth century must always be the period of English history most interesting to Englishmen, culminating as it did in the Civil Wars, when the battle of the Constitution was fought out, not only for the advantage of England, but one might say, for that of the whole world.

In 1631, Mary Verney came to Claydon, where she and her young husband, aged nineteen, lived with the rest of the family, Ralph still going on with his studies at Oxford, and riding over twenty miles to his home, sometimes in such a storm of rain, that his tutor Crowther laughs at him for his zeal. The marriage turned out a singularly happy one, except in the matter of health. With one of the sweetest tempers and most cheerful dispositions that ever woman was blessed with, which she seems to have inherited from her father, Mary Verney had a backbone of sense and spirit and of high principle, which made her indeed, as Crowther wrote of her to Ralph, 'your sweetest comfort.' She kept the peace with the brothers—the selfish Henry and the scapegrace Tom; Edmund, who was warmly attached to her, always calls her 'my sweetest sister.' 'Mischiefe' was one of the pet names for her in the family. Dr. Denton never mentions her without some tender epithet, and to Sir Edmund she was a favourite daughter, to whom he turned on all occasions for sympathy and affection. In those difficult relations of life entailed by having no separate home, but living always with her mother-in-law, it is to the credit of both that Lady Verney was quite as fond of her as was her husband, and at her death, in 1641, it is Mary who is condoled with and pitied for the loss of 'our mother,' far more than her own daughters, mostly children.

It gives a pleasant view of Ralph's character to see how kindly the good advice, which his tutor pours upon him somewhat lavishly, is received, and even after his Oxford days are over the little lectures are still accepted. Crowther, sending some of his notes on logic and astronomy, says, 'Had I not watcht late at night, I could hardly have despatched them. I shall desire your paines in the reading. God hath given you sufficient intellectuals, and he then requires that you be not wanting to yourself. You know what honour to his family, what a credit to himself (to let goe relligious motives), doth a gentleman purchase, who hath not only the outward gifts of fortune, but is fraught with the diviner perfection of mind. Make not your natural weaknesse [his health was not good] a fond plea for your future neglect.'

Two years after, in 1633, Ralph loses a child, and he and his wife have just recovered from the small-pox. 'Bee sure you forget not the Author of both but make a right use of your afflictions. Look abroad and see how many of as greate fortunes and hopes as yourself, of as young years and greater strength, hath it pleased God to cut off in this infectious malady, out of which he has given you an escape. Bee you more humble and thankful. Where the Lord hath in a more espetiall manner conferred mercies, there he expectes in a greater measure obedience—otherwise His past favours will but hasten on in the future severer judgements. God has obliged you in a double mercy, he hath restored unto you the delight of your eyes, which was ready to be taken from you, and after a gentle chastisement hath restored you as a comfort to her. My hopes are that your religious care hath prevented these admonitions. You have had many sad crosses, your fall,' etc. How kindly are the answers is shown by — 'Your kind acceptation of my last letter is more welcome to me than any of your favours, in that I see you soe seriously affected with what most of our gallants would take distasteful.'

Crowther goes on, 'As I truly partake in your affliction soe it affects me with noe little joy to see you soe patiently bear it. Bound you are much to God, that whereas He suffers thousands of your rank to run on in their sinful vanities, it has pleased Him through his Fatherly chastisements to bring you to a knowledge of Himself. We are all Prodigalls,' etc. 'I should blame myself for not sending before, but what else the court may alter in others, it hath not made you soe little reall as to

measure a friend by a compliment.' He ends by
' desiring a service to your sweetest comfort.'

Mr. Ralph Verney's tailor's bills for 1632-33 com-
prise such very fine clothes, that they evidently have
served at the king's coronation in Edinburgh, where
he accompanied Sir Edmund and joined in the fes-
tivities of the Court before and after, but he and his
father were almost always together, and the letters
were few at this period. Such clothes were worn by
all gentlemen of a certain condition, and were not in-
consistent with a very sober and practical manner of
life. Sir Benjamin Rudyard complains that ' hearty
protestants should be branded as Puritans,' showing
that the two ideas were quite distinct at this time.
The term Roundhead was never heard until 1641.
Servants, apprentices, and workmen of all kinds
had their heads closely cropped, and as crowds of
these men filled the approaches to the House after the
meeting of the ' Long Parliament,' the members who
were in sympathy with them were taunted as Round-
heads by their opponents ; they retorted by branding
the king's friends as ' soldiers of fortune,' or Cavaliers,
which soon became the designation of the Royalists.
Nicknames with disagreeable associations are convenient for the many in labelling their enemies of
whatever colour.

As to the dress of the ladies of the Parliament
side, Mary Verney in her portrait by Vandyck, 1636,
affects no ascetic simplicity. She wears a pale blue
satin gown, open over white, looped up with pearls,

a string of which is round her neck, a fringe of light hair curled on each side her forehead ; she is ' bigg with E. V.' (her eldest son) according to the catalogue, and is proud of her condition.

It is not a first-rate picture, and has been cleaned to the quick.   A fine bust of her, done at Rome after a miniature for the large monument at Claydon, is far more characteristic of one who was the mainstay of the family in every sense after Sir Edmund's death, until her own in 1650.   The face is not handsome, but very pleasant, full of sense and goodness combined.   Ralph remarks later, ' she never remembered her own claims,' in spite of the large property that she brought into the family.

From 1631 to 1640 she was living in the happy Claydon family party, or at ' Coven Garden during the terme,' which seems to be considered as equivalent to the season, and where she and her husband always accompanied Sir Edmund when he was required at Court.

The relation between the father and his eldest son was extremely touching, in an age when the distance between such relations was great, and the formalities of respect exacted were often extremely burdensome Sir Edmund's letters are playful and easy, with unbounded confidence in Ralph's judgment, good sense, indefatigable industry and kindness, though he permits himself a laugh at his son's want of horsemanship, his little care for field sports, his over-caution for his father in time of war, and his small formalities and particularities.

In fact, Sir Edmund was very much the younger man of the two, and continued so to the end of his life. Brave, chivalrous, buoyant in the midst of all his perplexities and all his troubles, it was not till the year 1641 that the loss of his wife, the arbitrary course taken by the king in politics, and the almost Popish proceedings of Laud in Church matters, seem to have broken his spirit or rather his heart. 'You ar so good a sone that I see your father can do nothing of bisness without you,' writes Lady Sussex to Ralph, and to Sir Edmund she writes : ' you have a son truly good ; i pray God make him happy every way for i thinke ther cannot bee a bettir yonge man.'

There is a pretty little note from Sir Edmund, to his 'good daughter Mary,' from Bath, August 1635. 'I cannott prevaile with y^r Husband to leave mee without a quarrell, therefore good heart forgive us boath, since his absence is against boath our wills, hee is every day in the bathe, I praye God it may doe him goode ; for my parte, I am suer I find none in it, but since I am come heere, I will try the uttermost of it, that I may not be reproacht att my returne for doeing things by halves ; att our first coming the towne was empty, butt now itt is full of very good company, and we pass our time awaye as merrily as paine will give us leave ' . . . ' and soe deare heart, farewell, yor lovinge father and faithfull frend.'

Ralph has been writing about his father's greyhounds, and Sir Edmund replies, ' I am glad you are soe merry with my Hounds, I am contented to reprive them, but it were Alms to hang you, for I knowe you can accuse them only by hearesaye, for you will not take the paines to informe yourself by taking a view of them.'

Sir Edmund went very thoroughly into the management of the estate and garden, the letting of farms, &c., and sent frequent and minute directions for everything connected with them to be carried out by Ralph and the steward. In one letter he says : ' The Gardner shall pleach noe Hedge this yeare . . . if you fiend him fidle about his woarke, agree with him by the great[1] for trewly I will noe longer indure his daye woarke ; it is intollerable to beare with his knavery.' His horses were many, as was required in those days when riding was the only means of going from place to place ; but the number of farm horses were eked out by ' plowing oxen.' ' I am not sorry the gray nagge is sould, though I should have been glad to have had more for him, but I will not part with the white geldenge, unless I may have £35 for him,' a large sum for a horse in those days. ' I am sorry to heare your horses thrive as ill as myne. I would send as many cart horses as I could to the fenns [where he had property], there they would gather flesh at an easy charge.'

The perpetual trouble of buying new and expensive horses to take the place of those which go lame and grow old and sick and have to be sold at a loss,

---

[1] 'To work *by great* is to work by quantity instead of by the day.' —HALLIWELL'S *Dictionary of Archaic Words.*

everyone will sympathise with who has had to do with horse flesh. ' I think it will do the colts no hurt to play abroade in the heate of the day, but I heare the pied coult got his mischance by a stroake of one of the cart horses, and that must be by carelessness of servants.' The colts come to grief, the dams miscarry, the old horses go blind, and the war-horses which have to be sent down to the army fall lame upon the road.

He is very fond of his greyhounds, and complains that ' Tho. Asham has never sent woard of them since I came from home.' Even a hedge cannot be made without his decision, between ' Roomer poole and the Ridings,' when he has let the first farm. ' I praye call upon Raphele to sell the sheep, he is mad to keepe them soe long. If Lea will deale for the cloase for twelve yeares, I will ditch and quick sett it, and mownd it well, but then hee shall be tied to mayntaine itt, soe that his cattle maye not spoyle the quick, or els hee will every yeare carry awaye my hedges and make mee bring new.'

The question of the rents for land two hundred years ago is very interesting at the present moment ; the fields at Claydon continue to bear the same names and can be identified without difficulty. ' Send to goodman Grace and if hee will give 20 shillings the acre for little Napson, or £5 in grass, let him have it ' ; and again, ' I would take 19 shillings the acre for little Napson, but I think you may gett more for it, nor under 20 shillings for great Napson I will

not take.   Bid Roades have a care for the timber of
the ould barn att the Inn and lett him laye the ould
thatch where itt may make muck or els uppon great
Napson meadow, if hee thinck itt fitt.   M$^{r.}$ Wells has
writt to mee to take Knowle Hill and Bignells mead
for one yeare att £143 rent, which I am well content
hee should have it, unless you can bee sure that
Roger Daly will for that and Mayes house give £145
and take it for some longer tyme.'

The fields in question are among the best at
Claydon, and taking the value of money in 1636 as
representing about four times, or a little more, what
the same sum does at present, the rent of the land,
far from having increased, does not bring in anything like the same sum, even before the immense
fall in its value which took place about twenty
years ago.   Little and Great Napson were then worth
about 3*l.* and 3*l.* 10*s.* an acre.   Knowle Hill farm is
more difficult to determine, but as it is bounded now,
as then, by great woods on two sides, the extent cannot be very different.   Between five and six hundred
pounds, which Sir Edmund seems to have obtained,
would be now an impossible rent to ask ; even before
the present bad times, the rent was only 450*l.*

In the same year Ralph asks his father to get him
sent with Lord Arundel, who was going as ambassador extraordinary to the Emperor Ferdinand II.
Sir Edmund writes a merry letter in answer, saying
that ' My Lord Marshall is goeing a fine journye, and
noe man would bee gladder of such an opportunity

to lett you see something abroad, then I should bee,'
and then proceeds to give his many reasons tail foremost, the real one at the end. ' In the first place,
you know I cannot settle my business without you ; '
secondly, ' that my Lord must be gone on Munday
next att the farthest. If neyther of thes will sattisfy
you, the third shall ; that is, hee will take noeboddy
with him, for hee has refused my Lord Russell, my
Lord Grandison [a nephew of the Duke of Bucking-
ham], my Lord Andrues, and in breefe all others, my
Lord Dawbingny only excepted, and hee goes with
him. Now, I thinck your journy is att an end, and
soe with my love to my daughter, I remain your
loving father.'

There is hardly any gossip in their correspondence or stories concerning the Court, which with
Henrietta Maria as its head was full of unpleasant
incidents. The only exception is a letter concerning
Elizabeth Paulet—second wife of Lord Essex—and
Sir Edmund's friend, Sir William Uvedale, paymaster of the king during the Civil War, who is described as ' a most accomplished man, handsome, and
knowing as much as learning, long travels, and great
observation could make him.' The story is a bad
one : he was found in her room during her husband's
absence by Essex's brother Sir Walter Devereux, who,
having been warned, came to the house and pounced
upon ' her maid, who had been sent down for some
beer.' He went up and attacked Lady Essex for her
conduct, Uvedale not going, but only looking out of

the window. Sir Edmund says : ' I find the citty and
the country differs in oppinion, for here my Lord and
his brother are most despised, who is undone for
taking so mean an office, unless hee had done more
to ; the ladye by most much doubted, and her discretion by all condemned, but Wm Uvedale [who
was a great friend of Sir Edmund], blamed for
nothing but not having cared inoughe to advise her
to be more circumspect.'

A duel was fought between Lord Essex and Sir
William Uvedale, to whom Sir Edmund was second.
' Sir E. V. Knight Marshall and Sir W^m. Udall
fought Robert, Earl of Essex, and the Lord——'
left blank, says the old genealogical book. Lady
Essex was soon afterwards divorced by her husband.

It was by no means always on matters of business
that the father and son wrote to each other. Scraps
of 'noos,' absurd incidents, come in between the
letting of the homestall and the close, the selling of
the sheep, and the account of his dogs and horses.
' To requite yor noos of yor fish, I will tell you as
good a tale from hence, and as trewe. A merchant
of lundon wrote to a factor of his beyoand sea, desired
him by the next shipp to send him 2 or 3 Apes ; he
forgot the r, and then it was 203 Apes. His factor
has sent him fower scoare, and sayes hee shall have
the rest by the next shipp, conceiving the merchant
had sent for tow hundred and three apes ; if yor self
or frends will buy any to breede on, you could never

have had such chance as now. In earnest this is very trew.'

Arrangements concerning marriages were almost always settled by the parents and friends, as is still the case in France, with a greater regard for the suitableness of the portions than for the inclination of the parties. Sir Edmund was often consulted, and sometimes applies to his son for information. 'I am desired to inquire after Mr. Tho. Turvill's estate, because his sonne is tendered to a frend of myne for a marrage. I praye informe yor selfe the best you can from my brother Denton and others, and let me heare what you fiend. Commend me to all my frends, but my particular blessing to yor wife. Farewell, yor loving father.'

In April 1639, when Sir Edmund was with the king in the Scotch war, Ralph wrote to him : 'I am infinitly sory to heare the Scotts continue in there stubbourness, for I feare if they come to blowes the business will not be easily ended, but we must referre all to God. I have been a little too negligent of getting my armes,' says the unwarlike Ralph, ' but now I will hasten them.' He asks his father to enquire of Captain Sydenham 'where and when I shall have my Pistolls . . . I pray send mee your opinion whither I had not best bespeake a Waggon presently and what other provisions I had best make. I should be loath to bee utterly unprovided. You that are soe near and know more, may judg better of it then I can, therefore I humbly crave your advice. I confess I say not this that I am at all fond of the jorney, or that I can say I shall leave your affairs heere in soe good order as that I may conveniently come. I hope if need bee you can furnish mee with an horse, that will be readier than any that can be brought by mee.'

This very uncheerful letter is a contrast to Sir Edmund's merry postscript to his reply, ' I pray goe to Nedd Herbert from mee [one of the Pembroke family], and tell him I will not wright to him till I can send him an inventory of the Skotts I have kild,' he still retained his buoyant spirit, little as he approved of the war in which he had to take part. 'I will inquire for a nagg for you,' he says another time, 'but charity beginns at home, and I will first provide for myself if I can.'

Fortunately for Ralph the campaign came to an end before he was able to join his father, and he went on diligently with the work for which he was so much more fitted, managing his wife's and his father's large estates, some of them much scattered, helping his mother, looking after the affairs of his nine brothers and sisters, uncles, aunts, and cousins innumerable, writing politics to Lady Barrymore, Lady Sussex, Dillon, Burgoyne, &c., doing commissions in London for his most exacting friends, and finally at the end of 1639, looking after the seat of Aylesbury for that Parliament which it was evident that Charles would so soon be obliged to summon.

Captain Thomas Verney,
from a picture at Claydon House.

Tho: Verney

CHAPTER VI.

TOM VERNEY. A 'PICTURESQUE VAGABOND.'

'Spend not on hopes, they that by pleading-clothes
  Do fortunes seek when worth and service fail,
  Would have their tale beleeved for their oathes,
  And are like empty vessels under sail.'—GEO. HERBERT.

OF all sons 'doomed their father's soul to cross' (for
worse reasons, however, than that of rhyming), Tom
Verney was certainly the most trying. He had
hardly left school when, aged nineteen, he proposed
to take to wife the 'good daughter' of a Mr. Futsin,
in whose absence he wrote to the mother of the girl,
but without the smallest pretence of asking his own
father's leave. 'The thing was commonly spread
about the house and I verily thought it came to my
father's ears,' he says jauntily, when reproached for
his conduct. Sir Edmund, much displeased, resolved
to send him out as a settler. The Puritan emigration
to America had now been going on for several years;
thousands of the best men in England—merchants,
lawyers, farmers, scholars—were flying across the
Atlantic; great landowners, like Lord Say and Lord
Broke, were preparing to follow, believing that Eng
land would no longer be a free home for them; it

was therefore quite natural that Sir Edmund should consider the opening a good one for his young son. Lady Verney undertook the arrangements with an emigration agent, who writes to her at great length setting forth what was the outfit necessary for a settler in 1634. He recommends that he do take three servants at least with him, which will cost 12*l.* for ' passage and apparel.' He had better ' bringe up with him fether bed, blanquetts, and three payre of sheets, it is but a spare [pack] horse to bring them. Although many howshowlds in Virginia are so well provided as to entertayne a stranger with all things necessary for the belly, yeat few or non are better provided for the back then will serve their on turne.' He must take some corne, ' least ther should happen a scarsity in the cuntry, which some tymes doth fall out, through the covetousness of the planters, that strive to plant much tobacco and littell corne. I have already bought the flower, the fowling peeces, the strong waters and the grosery wares. . . . if he settell a plantation for himself he shold have som seasoned men of his own.'

Lady Verney immediately packed Tom's apparel, and sent him off with an affectionate letter, saying that ' my sonne hath neither beene bread abroade, nor used to any bartering at home, but only bredd at schoole, and so I doubt wilbe to seeke in that im-ployment that he is goeing to undertake ; therefore I shall entreate that favour from you, if any one is going out whom you can trust, a littell to direct him

in his coarses ; I shall take it as a great favour.'
' If they will but acknolledg him to be the sonne of
his father you shall engage both his father and myself to acknolledg your courtesie.' She sends up a
servant to buy all necessary things. The various
' casks, and barrels, shot, and muskets, goods, provisions and servants, with the charges, doe amount to
117*l*. 13*s*. 6*d*.' A good cabin was secured for him.

In nine months, however, Master Tom was back
again, and his outfit wasted, which in the state of his
father's finances was a serious loss.

Ralph, in the emergency, was most kind to him,
and helped to make peace with Sir Edmund, who
was naturally much annoyed.

Tom was next sent as a volunteer on board a
king's ship, the ' St. Andrew,' in the ship-money fleet
now cruising in the Channel, and he writes to ' his
loving and kind brother that we are bound to the
French coast to see what they will say to us ' ; in July
1635, ' there is a fleet of Spaniards lyes off Falmouth
is the newes' ; ' there is warre proclaimed with France,
the King of Spaine is soe much the more joyfuller,
by reason that our kinge's fleet doth assist him in
it.' After which come the usual postscripts, ' that
you will speak for mee to my mother, for travellers
ever want money. Your loving brother as long as
life lasts,' writes the incorrigible, who in a few months,
having grown tired of the sea, announces that he is
setting off for Flanders, which must have been a
great annoyance to his father. ' I do not intend to

make a long stay there, only to see what fortunes a
younger brother might attain unto, and withall to
see how I shall like the country, and so to
live there, and serve the Prince Cardinall.' He
' never intends to go for Holland, because wee have
better paye from the Cardinall than from the States.
I hope you will speake to my friends for a little
money to carry mee over thither, ffor if they will
send mee non, I am resolved to goe over with that
little I have.'

A few months afterwards he is back in London,
lodging with the keeper of the Marshalsea, a servant
of his father's, and writes to Ralph that he understands Sir Edmund ' hath given express command '
that no one is to buy anything for him without his
leave, ' which much discontents me, for now I must
desire to have those things that are fitting for mee
to weare.'   To his father at the same time he writes
that, he ' doth desier when you have heard the good
report my Captaine will relate to you, out of your
noble mind you will remitt and forgive all my former
offenses, and those faults which I have formerly and
in such a base manner committed against so good a
father as you are.'   He hopes for the future ' to beare
a noble mind in all my actions, as where before I
was ignoble.'   ' Let these lines stirr you to have
pitty upon mee, that I may receive one smiling and
merry countenance from you, which I have formerly
seen angry and frowning,' signed ' your true penitent
and obedient sonn till death.'   Words were never

wanting to Tom ; his protestations of amendment, his
demands for money, his pious reflections, his crazy
scatter-brained projects for some fresh change which
is always to make his fortune, run as off a reel from
his pen, never ending, still beginning, during the
whole of his long misspent life, which lasted until
he was 92, outliving all his brothers and sisters.

The next letter shows how kind Sir Edmund
always was to the scapegrace. Tom writes to
his father that he has had a message from him
through his brother ' which did containe so much
comfort, that he could not choos but present to your
mercyful eye these lines, that you might thereby
understand that I am leading a new life, which shall
not only yield great comfort to yourself, but be a
comfort to all my friendes. Therefore deare father,
let mee again upon my bended knees crave att your
mercyfull hands pardon and forgiveness for that ill-
spent life which I have formerly lead. I doe the
rather crave pardon to you in writing, becaus I cannot by word of mouth so freely utter it.' He desires
his mother's blessing and so *da capo* begs for money
and clothes.

Shortly after he takes service in the army of
France and draws bills upon Ralph for his equip-
ment; the amounts are always to be ' faithfully paid '
after the next fight.

' I understand that my father and you doe mis-
trust that I am run away from my Colonel, which is
noe small grief to me ; becaus I have brought soe

many letters from my Collonell to his ffrinds in
London, and I hope in God to carry him as good
news back. This is the last you shall receive from
mee as long as I have being, sinc you have so ill
opinion of me. If you are troubled at this letter, I
will meete you at another hous to speak with you,
becaus I will not come where yu and my father have
a being.'

In a few days, forgetting his wrath, he says he
shall ' be with them, by the grace of God, with my
best love within a fortnight.'

' Time has been very short with me for two
months. I would willingly continue our former
love. Consider of mee as I have sinc my coming to
England this last time behaved myself, and not as I
have heretofore carried myself.'

In May 1636.—' About my imployment, since
my arrivall in France, I find it will cost me 40*l.*
more. My father is pleased to pay for thos men
whom I have for the present, he will not venter very
much until he hears it is for certain.' He then begs
for 20*l.*, but desires Ralph to keep it from his
father's ears ; ' lest it hinder me of that money.'

Paris, July.—' My Lieutenant-Collonel hath not
restored to mee my clothes, which doth very much discontent me. Having orders to march to La Chapelle,
I wanted money to buy me a hors and other necessaries fitting me.' He requests the money may be
sent quickly as he has got some one to lend it who
knows his family, ' and I know you are of too good

and loving a nature to see mee disgraced for so small a sum.'

'Within two months after our fight, I will repay you with an innumerable of thanks . . . and I shall have more caus than ever I had to pray for the hous of Verney. I have orders to march to La Chapelle, which was taken within this fortnight by the Spaniard. There we shall remaine most part of the summer. If it pleases God to send me life, after the fight is over, I shall by his grace send you a true relation of it.'

Again from Noyon comes a fresh letter demanding 'that small courtesy of the money. My honour and fortune lyes ingaged in it.'

A few months after, without any reason, he has left France, and is on his road to Sweden, and writes from Gottenburg. 'Dear father, your goodnes hath been so often expressed unto mee that I cannot omitt any occasion of presenting you with these lines,' and in an airy manner he mentions that he is on his road to 'Stockhollam,' and that letters enclosed to 'Collonell Vavasor or Collonell Fleetwood' will find him. 'Speak to my father,' he writes to Ralph, 'not to send for mee back by any means, becaus I am in a very hopeful waye of preferment, and all this winter I intend to study the language that I may bee the better able to undertake the imploymente. Make my apologie to the vertuous gentlewoman your wife [who is at other times 'sweet sister'] for not writing.'

At ' Stockhollam,' December 1637, he came across some old Scotch veterans, belonging to Gustavus Adolphus's army, who were still serving after his death, in the Thirty Years War.

' Honoured Sir,' he begins, and talks of his 'extraordinary deal of busyness.' ' Colonell ffleetwood hath had within this month, or such a matter, four of his companies cutt of by the enimy, only his officers saved, which doe lye heavy upon his hand; therefore I believe he will not be able to do me any curtesy where he is now.' He hopes to have an answer within less than two months, ' if the passage be not stopt.' ' Concerning my own occasions, I do according to your commands stay in Swedlan, partly to learne the language, and partly in great hopes of præferment, with one Collonell Lasly, neer allyed to felt Martiall Lasly, and all this cannot possibly be done without great expence. It costs mee two and twenty shillings a week for my diet, lodging, and washing, besides other expences,' &c., &c. ; and he desires money will be sent to pay his master for teaching him, &c., &c., or else to send for him home ; ' yet one thing I forgott, noble S^r, to putt you in mind of which is humbly to desier you to write a letter to Colonell Lasly, Colonell Vavasor will relate the business to you.' In the next letter he has taken up ' two and fifty pound starling, to cleare my lodging, and the rest which is left to bring mee to Collonell ffleetwood, if the enimy will permitt mee ; I must pass through three of the enemies countreys, through Denmark, through Pomerland, and through great part of Poland'; he has 'engaged an englishman, bred a souldier, which can speak the language extreamely well'; but as all this expense is incurred when Col. Fleetwood 'hath more officers than he hath souldiers,' he does not believe he will be able to give him any preferment; he hopes his father 'will not think amiss of him for taking up so much money, for if my life lay on it, I could not help it; for everything is soe extreame deare that it would greeve any one to see it, as you shall see by that little bill which I have enclosed; and besides my true, and faithfull freind Collonell Vavasor will be able to informe you . . . His busynes proceeds soe unfortunately here, that he intends to returne, when the waters are open . . . If he had received any moneys from the crowne of Swedland, I should not have had any occasion to have been obliged to any other. But he is soe short of moneys himself, that he is forced (as well as myself) to take up moneys to defraud his charges in Stockhollam . . . He is joyned with mee for the payment of the money'; ending with 'I rest your most dutifull sonn.'

He was back himself in England a month or two after this, and during the rest of the year 1638 he is either in London getting into debt and quarrels, or down at Claydon where his father sends him to keep him out of mischief. Before he starts, he has a duel on hand, and he writes to his brother Edmund, 'at

the Pehatzo Coven Garden,' for his countenance.
'I would entreat you to be with mee by 7 of the clock
in the morning, or els not at all, becaus I am to meet
a gentleman att eight of the clock about some words
which past between him and myself on Friday, and
would entreat to make noebody acquaint with it,
becaus I would not have it known. If you are not
willing, I pray send me by the porter my russett
shooes, and my greyest pair of worsted stockings
with garters and ribbins to them, and laced band and
cuffs if they bee don; if not, a plaine band, to put on
tomorrow. I have a great company of young gentlemen with mee, which goes forth in the King's fleet, or
else I had come over myself to-night.'

Next he tries to make Ralph buy some horses of
his ('as for the mare you never had a better in your
life') ; in another letter he acknowledges they are
worth nothing, and sends him a 'fox coat' in payment of ten pounds he had borrowed of him.

When he gets to Claydon he is miserable 'at living like a hermitt or a country fellow,' and 'would
goe anywhere, to the West Indies or some unknown
place in the world.' 'I should prove myself worse
than a Turke if I did not take your good counsel,'
he says, after receiving five pounds ; a further
supply being refused, he can only scold. He pro-
poses to go to the Palatinate a few weeks after under
Colonel Hunt, or to New England if his father
will give him 200l. in money and goods, which he
says he will see well laid out. He acknowledges 'that

disgrace I have formerly done you in taking such ill
wayes of life,' but declares he 'shall give much content in future.' The next letters are full of requests
of all sorts. He has 'hardly any clothes left, neither
bands, ruffs, shirts, boot-hose, boots, or anything else
but is upon my back.' His father seems to have
desired that he may be kept short, lest he should rush
off again somewhere. The tailor, however, 'charges
for a gray cloth sut for Mr. Thomas Verney,' and
again 'for a collor, and callyco to lyne and stich a
tafety doublet'—at this very time. 'Ther is a sute
of cloths come to me, but never a coat with it, it will
be very unseemlie for mee to wear my sute, and
never a coat but one sorey thing which I bought
about two months agoe, att a broker's, and some say
as it is your old coat that you gave to your man, and
I confess that it is very like yours, and as farr as I
know it was yours; therefore I pray doe but judg of
the goodness of it.' He then asks for 'three small
parcells of things' as a sort of appendix, 'and then I
will not trouble you noe more this three months—2
paire of gloves, 2 paire of linen stockings, 2 paire of
plaine boothose topps, 2 paire of woollen boothose
and three handkerchiefs. A very small matter buyes
them. I know that you are not troubled with thees
things, but howsoever your comfort is you will be the
readier to buy your owne children such small things
hereafter.'

Presently he breaks out again; there is no one at
home but children. 'Rather than lead this hellish life

[i.e. in the quiet of the house at Claydon], I will take a rope and make an end of myself, and then neither father, mother, brother, nor sister, nor any friends els shall take any more care of me.'

The servants at Claydon and his grandmother at Hillesden were warned not to lend him money, or even a horse, lest he should sell him, which he says 'is extremity itself and this is not the way to make mee lead a reformed life ' ! His debts up and down appear to be many, and he is afraid that some of his creditors may go to his father ; he declares they have good pledges, all but six and forty pounds, which he cannot account for. Sir Edmund refused to see him, and Tom continued to the end of the year at Claydon, when he became more and more violent at the dulness. 'Idleness puts many wicked thoughts in one's head. But perhaps you may object that I may read, or walk up to Mr. Aris [the Rector] sometimes and conferre with him, or to walk in att one doore and out att the other. Too much of one thing is good for nothing, but a little of each will refresh a man's witt. For to spend my time wholely in reading doth but exercise my mind and not my body!'—'it is a poore miserable and uncomfortable life,' though he acknowledges he is in duty bound to his father, 'in that you are pleased to harbour mee under your roof.'

A number of his little sisters are at Claydon with him, and a baby of Ralph's, but he never takes the trouble to notice such uninteresting personages. His profound belief in his own importance and excellence throughout the letters, and his threats to father and brother that he will never write or speak to them again if he does not get what he wants, as if such a terrible penalty were enough to bring them to any terms, are inexpressibly droll.   On one occasion he writes to Ralph, 'there is no excuse for you not doing as I ask; my father is busy, but for you, you should send every day unto the docks enquiring after a shipp for me.'

Another time he excuses himself for having accused Ralph of ingratitude (!) 'becaus I had not yet heard from you, but I knew not that you had been with my father into Scotland [where Charles had been for his coronation], but you are now returned, so,' &c.

The next notice of him is that 'he is gone to the Barbathos,' Ralph writes to his brother Henry, 'and I feare not at all amended, for about three days before hee went, hee played mee a slippery tricke, though I had many deepe protestations to the contrary.   It was not discovered till he was goan.'

Tom was sent on the recommendation of the Earl of Warwick, who had a 'plantation' in the colony. He was a friend of Lady Sussex, whom he married a few years after the death of her old husband, and was afterwards Admiral of the Fleet for the Common-wealth.   'A man in no grace at court, and looked upon as the greatest patron of the puritans, because of much the greatest estate of all who favoured them,' is the account of him by Lord Clarendon.

Tom was sent off in a good ship, with an ample supply of necessaries by his father, and there seemed fair hopes at length that he was disposed of satisfactorily, for some time at least. In a few months came a long letter to Sir Edmund containing a clever and amusing account of the country. ' I have obtained 100 acres of land, but not knowing how to dispose of it unless I can have such a supply as the invoise makes mention of, which, if I can have a supply according to my expectation, I make noe question but by the grace of God to rais my fortunes in a few years, nay, I shall be able in one yeare, to return back the principall, which is a great incouragement to you that doe disburs the money, and a greater to have mee continue here, which could never yett stay anywher.

' In regard you were pleased to lay your commands upon mee to send you a true relation of the cuntrey, I have now don it with as much brevity as I could devise.

' It is the best and healthfullest in all the westerne islands ; thanks be to God here is want of nothing nourishing, both for soul and body,' and he proceeds ' to give particulars of what good doctrine, good laws are here, and soe to proceed to the fruits, and last what doth most annoy us here. First, to begin with our teaching [the humbug] it is not soe good as I wish it were, yet in some places it is very good, but I hope if my Lord Warwick hath bought the island, we shall have better order in the

island than hitherto. Next is the law, which I thank
God is indifferent good ; and it would bee far better,
were it not for some justices that doth make laws
one court and break them the next. Until Mr. Mar-
sham comes, wee that bee under the law, must be
obedient to the law as it is, as I take it in the 8th of
the Romanes. [The devil can quote Scripture.]

'Now another thing is the fruits that this land
doth beare every month in the year, which is a great
comfort to us. Oranges, lemons, limes, plantines,
potatoes, pine-apples, guaves, and many more I will
tell you the nature of in my next letter, pepper, cin-
amon, ginger. . . . As to your potatoes, which is
very nourishing and comfortable, it is the best provision we have in the island [evidently they were not
yet common in England], both for ourselves and
servants—they will not desire after one month or
two no other provisions but potatoes boyled, and
mobby to drink with them, which is only potatoes
boyled and press'd as hard as they can, till the juce
is gon into fayre water, and after three hours this is
good drink.

'Now the last and best fruit is your pine-apple,
and there are two sorts—a Queen pine, and another,
which I cannot well call to mind, therefor I will
omit it. Now the Queen pine, when it is in your
mouth, do but imagin a tast and that relisheth of it,
soe it bee luscious. It is held such a dainty fruit,
that King Jeames swore it was the apple that Eve
cosned Adam with. I might speak more of this

pine, but the description makes mee long after it, and I beeleeve you will long till you tasted of it, which I heartily wish you had one ; but I feare it will not be till such time as I come myself, becaus they must have a great care in the carriage of it, or it will be labour in vain.   And to proceed to my last thing : the evils that doth most annoy us, and that is partly and chiefly drunkenes, your landcrabs, &c. First drunkenness.   Were it not for that great sin, this would be one of the bravest islands I ever heard of : but it doth soe much increas, that I have seen upon a Sabbath-day as I have been walk-ing to church [a little hint at his own virtue], first one, presently after another, lye in the highway, soe drunk that here be landcrabs in the land that have bitt of some of their fingers, some their toes, and hath killed some before they wakened, yett this doth not att all affright them [probably not, as they were dead].   'More I could say, but as they are beasts, soe lett mee leave them like beasts, and proceede to a word or two of your landcrabs.   Thees landcrabs are innumerable, that you shall have them certayne months in the yeare be soe thick in the highwayes, that, doe what we can, we shall have them bite through our shoes, that we are not able to undoe them till we break their clawes ; they are very like our seacrabs, but not att all soe good, becaus most of them are poysonous : ' and so on 'about cabiges, that grows on trees,' &c.   He asks that his letter may be copied out and sent to Mr. Aris, the Rector at Claydon, whom he had plagued for so many months, and he ends about his 'new lead life,' and 'that to tell soe much of the cuntrey cost mee many a weary step and watchful night, yett all that I can ever doe cannot be a sufficient ingagement to you who hath all ways been a deare and loving father to mee. I pray day and night for your happiness here and ever-lasting life in the world to come.' After which comes a postscript, saying that his 'new requests may per-haps daunt you, but 200*l.* will pay all !' and then follows an invoice of several pages in length, of every conceivable kind of commodity to be sent out to him, from 'twenty able men, wherof two to be carpenters, and a weaver who can weave diaper,—to swords, 30,000 nayles of divers sorts, pickaxes, butter, good sweet oyle, six cases of strong waters for the men to drink a dram every morning, to keepe them in health (for my part I drink non),' (! ! !), &c., &c., &c.

At the same time he writes to his mother, to try a little supplementary begging. 'There is no newes worth your acceptance or worthy my labour, but that I am resolved by the grace of God to leade a new life, which I hope you will rejoyce when you heare of it from others as well as myself,' he adds prudently. 'For my owne part, I take no glory in boasting of mine owne actions, bee they good or bad, and soe I turn upon some better thing, which doth more befitt the time and my occasions, and that is concerning housekeeping. I am now a building a sorry cottage to harbour men when I have them.'

He wants 'household stuff, plate, spoones, and the like, then pewter and brass of all sorts, and linnen of all sorts, both for mee and my servants.' He will not trouble his father, 'becaus this does not belong to him. I will leave them wholly to your own discretion, which knoweth better what to send, then I can in reason aske.'

In May 1639 he repeated his demands on his father, sending a fresh and enlarged invoice of his requisitions, and forwarding a testimonial from a Captain Futter who had authority in the island, and who certifies that Tom 'is an extraordinary good husband and careful !'

In answer, Sir Edmund, full of business as he was, with a bad attack of sciatica which had forced him to leave the King at Berwick on leave for a visit to the Bath, found time to write the following kind and wise letter. 'Tom, I am newly come out of Scottland, wheather I am instantly returning again, soe that by reason of my short stay heere I cannot for the present answer your letter so fully as I would doe, but I have left order with your brother to doe what can be done, but this ship makes such haste away that I believe hee will hardly gett any servants for you to send by this passage, nor doe I think fitt to send manny now, for I am informed for certaine that my Lord of Warwicke has bought a greate iland neare the place where you are, and that he intends to plant it presently. I conceive you maye have better conditions much then wher you now are, and I am

sure you shall ever fiend my Lord noble and favour-
able to you. My Lord intends in Feb. next to
goe for this iland in person, and I thinke it will bee
much for your advantage to transplant yourself
theather. Assoone as I return and that I know more
of the businesse, I will informe you particularly of it.
My Lord of Warwicke intends to fortify his iland
presently, and then to plant wher hee is safe from
being beaten out of it, which is a cource I like best.
Inable yourself to knowe what is fitt for plantations
and lett me alone to assist you if you proove indus-
trious and careful of my directions, soe that I may
putt a trust and confidence in you which as yet I
dare not doe, because I have found you false to your
woard, and careless of all I have sayed to you. I
doubt not but with your own helpe to make you a
fortune, but if you continue in your old cources I
will certainly forsake you. I pray God direct your
heart so that I may have cause to wright myself your
loving father.' And so for a time Master Tom was
out of the way of his much-enduring friends, who
are luckily free from his letters for the remainder of
1639.

But in 1641 the vagabond, after getting into
trouble and debt in Barbados, returned to England apparently penniless. He was given a fresh
start by his long-suffering father, and sent back to
his plantation in Jan. '42. With characteristic importunity he continued his requests for more supplies
up to the eve of his departure from Gravesend, but

whether the 'doz. payer of tan lether gloves and two payer of summer bootes and six bands and six payer of cuffs' were supplied to him is not recorded.

Nothing more was heard of him until April, when he wrote to his father and asked him if, ' with the great help of bridewell and the prisons,' he could procure him 100 men in August : those that he took out had fallen sick, and he had been ill himself and unable to look after them, so he had sold them to a ' chapman.' On his return to England in the summer he finds it convenient to conceal this fact from the people at Claydon, where he wanted to find more recruits for his plantation. He writes to Roades : ' if any of my men's friends doe enquire of you . . . how they are disposed of, I pray answer them with as much brevity as may be that they are all well and are upon another man's plantation till my return thither agayne. And if they should tell you that I have putt them of [sold] to other people, tell them it is not soe, and endeavour to the uttmost of your power to perswade them to the contrarye. . . . As for the brewer let him not be payed till my commeing doune, and then it shall be payed wth use, but not in money but in very good blows. I have not, as yett, forgott his former courtesye he did mee att my de-partuer out of this kingdome, and it shall be rewarded accordingly.' He had good reason to fear his father's displeasure at his speedy home-coming (though he did bring a cargo of cotton and tobacco to sell), but all that he says is, ' I hope my father is not offended

wth mee for my soe sudden returne from the Barba-
does. In case he be, I am extreame sorry for it and
shall indeavour to make peace.'

The cotton turned out not to be worth much, and
there was a loss on the tobacco, so he could not make
out a very good case for himself, and when at length
he was about to return to his work he writes a most
nonchalant letter to Ralph, who had ventured to chide
him for leaving the country in debt to a tailor. He
first asseverates his intention to pay the man, and is
furious with him for having appealed to Ralph and
'blazed it abroad both farr and neare.' He then proceeds : 'Now whereas you write mee word that I
will never leave borrowing of such poor creatures, let
me tell you lords and knights, and gentlemen of farr
better rank then myself are and will be still indebted unto Taylors, and therefore I count it noe
disparagement. There was a kinsman of ours (he
shall be nameless becaus he is dead) that lived after
a verey high rank, and perhapps you thought that
he would have scorned to have been credited by a
poor taylor, yet I know where he was deeply indebted
to one, but the taylor is now dead and soe is he.'

The breaking out of the civil war came oppor-
tunely for Tom, who was glad to defer his return to
Barbados, and offer his services in the king's army.

CHAPTER VII.

EDMUND THE YOUNG CAVALIER.

'It is a gallant child, one that indeed makes old hearts fresh ;
they that went on crutches ere he was born desire yet their life, to
see him a man.'—*Winter's Tale.*

THE third son of the Knihgt Marshal was the most
like his father of the whole family, spirited, brave,
affectionate, and with a very high sense of duty and
honour throughout his short career, for when a little
over thirty, he was 'put to death in cold blood' after
the taking of Drogheda in 1649, not long after the
execution of the king.

There is little change in this England, loving to
keep to the ancient ways, in a young man's education since 1630. The lad began with a school at
Gloucester,[1] and was sent at sixteen to Winchester,
where his letters to Ralph in a schoolboy hand in
1633 declare that 'his schoole master being at London, the propositors begin to affront mee, which my
companions are free from, I doe intende to intreate

---

[1] John Bellows, of Gloucester, has been good enough to make
enquiries, and writes that, 'it would be safe to conclude that the
King's School (otherwise known as the College School), at Gloucester,
would be the most likely one for a Royalist to send his sons to,' but
the School Register does not begin till about 1680.

him to suffer mee to enjoy the same libertyes that
they doe,' if not he thinks that his uncle Denton's
writing would prevail.   After a kind answer from
his brother, he takes heart and finds out that ' the
propositors words are more than their deeds, and
your fraternal letter has made me careless, not fearing
what they can doe unto me.'   Later he says, ' I hope
to see you at Crismas, if my mother goeth not to
London, as I believe she will not.   If you please, do
your best endeavours that I come.   I shall acknowledge myself much beholden.'   ' The Commoners
custom and the childrens are not alike, the Children
cannot goe home without the consent of the Warden,
the others need only that their parents should desire
their coming ; our stay is but three weeks, the
earnestness of my sute makes my father, I feare,
mistruste that I neglect my time, but it is not
soe.'

Letters from school at the present day are meagre
enough, but at least the boys tell us of their cricket
and football ; there is something painfully ludicrous
in the laboured letters to his father about nothing at
all, which such a bright, charming boy as we know
Edmund to have been, writes from Winchester.   He
has been reproached for his silence, and this is how
he makes amends :

Winton Coll : Feb. 10 1635. . . . . ' Not daring
to present any unpolished lines to such a judicious
reader, but finding how farr greater a crime it is to
neglect duty than to lay my defects to a wel wishing

father, I have adventured to write to you, humbly
beseeching you to pardon what I have written, by
which meanes you will encourage me to make a
second adventure. With my humble duty remembred
unto you, I remain your most obedient sonn

EDMUND VERNEY.'

In April 1635, something had gone wrong, and he
wrote to Sir Edmund, 'I feare you have been informed against mee more than is true, though I
cannot denye that I have sometimes by company
been drawne to doe what did not befit mee.'

After two years at Winchester, he wrote to his
brother, ' I think I have behaved myself soe fairly
since Whitsuntide, that Dr. Stanley can inform my
ffather of nothing that I have committed that I neede
be ashamed of, therefore I would intreate you to urge
him to forget my former misdeeds.' He was now
going to Oxford, to Magdalen Hall, where Ralph had
been before ; he adds in a postscript, ' I think it best
to send my bed by the foot post, which goeth from
Winchester to Oxford.' It would be curious to know
how long it took by this primitive conveyance.

Soon after his arrival he inquires ' whether my
father will pay for the carryage of my trunk and bed
and my chambers rent for Michaelmas quarter, which
amount to the sum of 19s. 10d.'

Sir Edmund had written to the indefatigable
Ralph, ' I praye send yor Brother to Oxford assoone
as you can ; I will allow him forty pound a yeare

[equal to about £200 in the present day], & hee shall have a cloath sute made him against easter or sooner if neede require. advise him to Husband it well ; for I knowe it may maintaine him well if hee will ; & more I will not allow him.' A little time after he wrote, ' Now for Mun, I did ever intend to paye for his gowne over & above his allowance, but what the other charges will come to I know not. If he will provide his gowne himself, I will allow him for that & his entrance fee £10 besides. You shall herewith receive a letter to his tutor.'

The lad was well pleased with his start at College, and wrote to his brother, ' Oxford & my tutour I lyke very well. The Vice Chancellor spoke to me very courteously when I came to be matriculated, he could not find fault with my Haire, because I had cut itt before I went to him. I must not forget to give you many thankes for the loade of woode y^u gave me. Had I time I would be more large, but now I must crave pardon for my brevity. I pray command in whatsoever I am able.'

In the next letter, dated Magdalen Hall, Oxford, he writes to Ralph about the fee to his tutor, ' the fiery Henry Wilkinson ' who is described as preaching before Cromwell and Fairfax in 1649. He was brother to Dr. Wilkinson, formerly Principal of Magdalen Hall, and then President of the College.

' According to your desire I asked Mr. Sessions what it were fit for mee to give my Tutour. He told me Mr. Jones gives him £1 5s. the quarter, and that he would advise me to give him the lyke. I must needes make me a sute of clothes presently, but as I will doe nothing without your advice, so I will entreate you to name the stufs and to speake to your man to give order to Miller [his father's tailor, where a ' sober grey sute for Mun ' followed by ' a red one ' appears] for the making of it. I pray retaine so much of my quarteridge as you think will discharge this. Let me beseech you that my own ignorance may be appologie for my boldnes with you.'

Fast days were still kept rigorously at Oxford ; ' all the newes is that Mrs. Gabriel is lyke to dress noe more meate on fasting nights. It was my fortune to be there on Friday at supper, with a Master of Arts and two Batchelors of our house, when Dr. Browne of Christchurch came in and tooke us, commanding mee to come to his chamber next morning. I made use of Doctor Wall, who obtained a promise of remission, but that he would speake to mee, but would not tel Dr. Wall what it was aboute ; when I came to him he spoke very courteously unto me, and asked me how my father did, and desired me to remember his service to him in respect he stood obliged to him for many courtesies, and to let him know that he would doe mee any favour for his sake ; ' so the lad got off easily for that time.

In August of the same year the king visited Oxford, and it is curious to find his arrival given as the reason for enforcing shortness of hair, which is commonly supposed to have been the badge of Puritanism. 'There is a Proctor for every house during the king's continuance in Oxford, and the cheifest thing that they will endeavour to amend is the wearinge of long haire. The Principal protested that after this day he would turn out his house whomesoever he found with haire longer than the tips of his eares. I believe this severity wil last but a weeke, therefore I pray, if you can conveniently, send for mee towards Satterday'—hoping to save his hair. 'Beggars must be whipt, I pray execute this law upon Sessions, who is resolved to beg a peece of Venison of you. I think my Tutour wil be there, who wil better deserve it than that Miser who in my conscience if not boyle it,' evidently a crime of the first water, 'yet wil put it forth, he finding venison, and the other finding crust.'

A few months after, matters are going very wrong with the lad, and Dr. Wilkinson writes to Ralph, 'I must needes confess, for tis extorted from me, that your brother Edmund doth not carry himself so ingeniously as he ought in every respect. He hath in a strange manner (for what reason I know not) absented himself from my lectures, and likewise from prayer in the Hall. I would say more, but I desire to speake with you y^r selfe. I will meete you any day at Sr Fleetwood Dormer's, that you appoint in this week.' The list of Oxford misdemeanours does not apparently vary greatly from century to century.

In April 1637, matters were growing worse, and again Ralph was appealed to, who went im-

mediately over to Oxford to see if he could help,
but apparently in vain, for Edmund writes that
' I know I am infinitly condemned for making you
partly lose your labour ; the love of my credit was
the sole cause of it. I am confident that to yield
to your demand would have made me the laughing
stock of the whole university.' Ralph had offered to
lend him money to pay his debts, but he demanded
some condition which, although acknowledging his
' respect and thankfulness for your greate love,' Edmund still refused. He says ' his misery is unsupport-
able,' and in another letter that he is ' utterly undone.'
He had borrowed money from those who could little
afford it. His unpaid tavern scores, and many worse
misdemeanours, greatly distress his father. There
is a touching letter from Sir Edmund, who evidently cannot bear to find that his favourite son
has fallen into bad ways, and is stern in proportion to his love : ' Sonne, And now I have said that,
my griefes grow high upon mee, for you were a sonne
in whom I tooke delight, that I had a p'ticular
affection for, above some others, and above most of
my children. But God has in you punisht mee for
that partiality. For your former offenses, though they
were great and of a base nature, yet when I had your
many faithful promises for a reformation, my love
to you was such that I was not only content but
desirous to remitt them . . . that indulgence has
wrought no other effects than to encourage you to bee
more wicked ; you are now grown so lewd and false

that I blush to think you mine. You have not only beene content to forfeit your owne credit, but you have, as much as in you lyes, suffered mee and my reputation to fall in the opinion of friendes. I find by your mother's importunity that if I would now pay those debts, you have promist a greate amendment, and I find you have foold her, as heertofore you did me, into a belief of it. . . . As you have been so unnaturally base as to follow your drunken, lyinge, false humor, and as you have left yourself and mee for your meane company '—his father will not pay a penny more, and if he does not change he ' will take no further care ' of him, ' but that by beinge my unworthy sonne I am made your unhappy father.'

Edmund meantime writes to his unfailing brother to help him out ' of the ill cources I have hitherto taken,' saying humbly that he finds unless he ' leaves Oxford he cannot leave them. I can impute it to noe other cases than my own ambition in perpetuall desiring of greate company, for had I associated myself with low quality, I should have found it noe hard matter to have shaken them off. . . . I know noe better way than to fly to you to make a motion of this to my father. It is not any hate I beare to learning, but my own facile nature, soe apt to be drawne the worst way,' that leads him astray.

In these circumstances Ralph appealed to Mr. Crowther, who had lately married and settled in the living of Newton Blossomville which Sir Edmund had procured for him, and the old tutor willingly under-

took to do what he could for the poor lad. Sir Edmund thanks him for his 'curteous offer of receiving
my ill-disposed sonne ; truly I was never in more
paine for anything than how I might dispose of him
where I might have hope to reclaime him, and now
your goodness hath relieved me, to my infinite comfort. I shall not despair but that I may againe love
him. Sir, I commit him wholly to you. I pray bee
careful what acquaintance hee makes with any of
those greate families about you, for there is dainger
for him that is soe apt to these vices.'

Ralph also appeals 'for the prodigall committed
to your care, which I know shall not be wanting.'

Mr. Crowther sets zealously to work upon his
new pupil, whom he 'finds by his owne confession
hath wholy lost all his time at Oxford, and understands not the very first grounds of logicke. or other
university learning, and hath no bookes to initiate
him in it.' He therefore asks Ralph to send him
'those notes which I collected for you, to go on with
for the present.'

In another month, however, the poor tutor is
'taken extreame ill, and I fear,' says Edmund,
'past recovery, though Dr Bates [a great university
physician] put him in greate comfort, saying there
was no danger, and his lyfe for his own.' There was
no will, for his wife had been afraid that making it
would hasten his death, but Edmund had written
down what the dying man intended : 'he endited so
fast that my fast writing made me forget, and in

Latin, as he entreated me, because his wife should not
understand ; and he hath made you the overseer of his
will.' It is not signed and he is insensible. If the lad
was able to write the will in Latin he could not have
been so entirely ignorant as the zealous Crowther
intimated. The poor widow was in much trouble, and
Edmund proved himself extremely kind and thought-
ful for her necessities. He remained until after the
funeral, when he was taken in at Hillesden by his
grandmother and his uncle, Sir Alexander Denton, as
Sir Edmund and his mother were still in London.
And, unlike Tom, he took kindly to the quiet country
life, which brought him back to his better self.

He continued at Hillesden for the rest of the
year, and the beginning of the next, and wrote
affectionate letters to Ralph, trying all through the
summer to do little acts of kindness and consideration
to everybody who came in his way.

Lord Warwick was at this time engaged in a
great scheme of colonisation, and Edmund writes in
August 1638 : ' When my father was here he made a
proposition to me by my uncle $D^{r.}$ and $M^{r.}$ Aris, of
my going my L^{d} of Warwick's voyage ; he prayed
them to propose it, and to learne whither I were
really addicted to such an undertaking, and would
not motion it himself first, least I should accept it
however. Truely, $S^{r.}$ in my opinion it was a most
noble and free way of propounding it. Who can
sufficiently honour such a father ? I have undertaken
it, and writt him my answer since. My brother

Thomas goeth the same voyage. I can tell you nothing of it yet.'

The plan, however, for some reason came to nothing. A month after he 'presents his reallest love and service' to Ralph, trying to put in a good word for Tom, who was staying at Claydon in disgrace. 'He carryeth himself without all exception. . . . He is not so ill as his own indiscrete discourse argues him. It is really thought that it is his facile nature that hath ever wronged him. As you have done many good offices for him, soe truly he doth often acknowledge them by protesting that he thinks there's not a more kind and loving brother in the world.'

But a few weeks after he can only say : 'I know I am noe judge to pass my censure on him ; I must rather admire your continual love towards him, for truely it doth exceede the possibility of my commendation. I believe my brother Tom will continue well so long as he is heare, but rather feare how 'twill be when he goes hence.'

Next comes a letter concerning a 'poore woman,' wife of a servant of Ralph's, who has sent her no money, and 'she is neere her time. The towne [i.e. village] say they only tooke her on your account, and ask for some present relief from the husband, lest she and her child perish.'

In the next week he is appealing in favour of his sister Susan, who had got into trouble with her father and mother—' shame and a kind of amazed fear hath deterred her from pleading an opening.'

The difficulties of transport made it impossible to take the six girls each time to London, where Sir Edmund was obliged more and more to live, and Lady Verney, torn in pieces between the claims of her husband and his children, was often obliged to leave several of them to her eldest daughter, Susan, now about seventeen or eighteen, a high-spirited girl, not always 'amenable' to advice, while she herself, with the last of the babies, made her difficult way up to town. 'My aunt Isham went to Claydon,' Edmund goes on, 'to look on my sister's crookedness, and I wayted on her there.' There is a tremendous bill from 'the poticary' for pills and potions, boluses, plaisters, 'snail waters,' &c., 'for Mistresse Penelope' enough to kill the girl. The physic of the day was of a murderous description; bleedings, caustics, setons, cuppings, abound in all possible states of health. The third daughter Margaret was much away from home, having been adopted by her aunt and godmother, Mrs. Poulteny.

Finally Ralph's eldest boy Edmund, aged two, was at Hillesden for his health, and his uncle is constant in his attentions to him, unlike Tom, who despises the children. 'The baby is froward with his teeth'; 'hee is very like his mother.' 'He imparts his affection to me, which I am not a little ambitious of. Were I as skillful as Œdipus I should be puzzled to say whether I love him or his father best. His gummes are so sore that he will suffer none to look into his mouth, but he presented this morning his duty to you as well as hee could doe it.'

At last, in February 1639, while on a visit to his family in Covent Garden, the wished-for opening comes. His father gets him sent as a volunteer with the army marching to Scotland, where he is himself going with the king.

Edmund writes to Ralph : ' Sweete Brother, I came away in that unexpected sodaynes [suddenness] that I had scarce time to give a farewell to those freindes that were then within, and beleeve me I was much greev'd that you were not of that number, allthough I know it would have brought me to a farr more sad departure, because then I must have bidden the adue to one whom I may truly terme dearest to me. For my part I think the journey will prove but an ordinary progresse, and then I shall have the happinesse of seeing you again in winter. But if it should come to blowes, yet why should not I think of escaping as well as any other, although I'll speak it and yet forget vaine glory, that I'll endeavour to attempt as much as any in a brave way.'

After he has joined the force he writes to his brother—' We marched from Selby [the rendezvous] when I had divers shrewd fits of an ague. But I thank God it left me, and I am as well as ever I was in my life. We are at Ryton, within 5 miles of Newcastle. . . . Till the foote come up to us I beleeve will be at least this fortnight, for we left them at Selby, and not half of them gathered together.'

Shortly after his father observes with much satisfaction that ' Mun carryeth himself very well.'

The army was disbanded after the pacification of
Berwick in June. Edmund returned from the North,
and soon after started to join the army of the States
in Flanders.

He stopped at Hillesden on the way to · see his
friends, and took the opportunity of going over to
the Oxford 'Act' ['for the creating of Doctors '].
He sought out the creditors who had been hitherto
left unpaid, and settled everything but 17*s*. or 20*s*.
which he was indebted ' to the tapster at the Grey-
hound, most of it mony out of this poore man's
purse.' The tapster was not to be found, but Edmund
wrote to Ralph to beg that as soon as enough of his
' quarteridge ' was due, he would try and see that the
man was satisfied, as he heard he was still in Oxford.
' I think I shall be free with all the world when this
man is discharged, and so I shall endeavour to keep
myself while I breathe '—a promise to which he ever
strove to hold.   He was now ensign in the company of Colonel Sir Thomas Culpepper, who received
him kindly, on account of old obligations to Sir
Edmund.

' My Brother Harry was the bearer of my last
letter to you by Bredaes post, and was in such hast
himselfe that he made me end allmost before I had
begunn. I shall deferr begging of a furr coate till next
yeare, because the army is now upon goeing out of
the feild, and I am in a free garrison, wher I shall

never be put to any watches, but if you find my
ffather willing to part with any of his sutes of
cloathes, I pray further him in it, for I shall ever
desire to goe as handsomely cladd as I cann possible.
I am in a pretty good stock of cloathes allready, soe
that now and then a sute from my ffather will maintaine it at the same height ever, and then I shall
think to live as handsomely as any Gentleman in
Holland, and I hope my ffather will still grant me
this, because he hath hitherto dealt so with my
brother. My Colonel and I are as great as two
beggers; he is often repeating his deepe obligations
to my ffather, and sure he would never doe it to me
unlesse he meant some great requital.' Another
letter is written from the army by 'Hulst in flaun-
ders.' 'There is a hollands post that goeth weekly,
by whom all letters come very safe. My brother
Harry is goeing over to England. For my part I
dare not soe much as dream of such a happiness yet,
though it be never soe pleasing to me. I have set
up a resolution to banish all thoughts of it, till I
have either got a fortune [i.e. a captaincy], or am
past all hopes of it. My Collonel useth me with very
great courtesy. I am confident that I shall have at
least the second fortune that falls, but I must walke
step by step without any leaping.' In the next
letter he is beginning to find out the worth of Sir
Thomas Culpepper's promises. 'I would desire that
my ffather would take the course with my Collonell
that Sir Harry Vane doth. He tells him that what

courtesyes and favours he showeth to his sonn he
will studdy to requite, but will acknowledge none
but what shall appear reall, and hath possessed my
collonel with such a feare of him, that he hath confess'd to me that he [Sir Harry Vane] is not a man
to be incensed.   If my ffather keepe him at a kind of
distance it may work something on him . . .   I can
get noe answer to three letters which I writt to him
at the Hague . . . his sordid and base dissembling
makes me more admire the faithfull and reall affection which you have expressed to me . . .   My
Collonell told me at my first coming, that it might
ly in his power to putt me into a partizan or a company within a twellmonth.   I know him so well by
his dealings with other men that I vow to God I
cannot credit his fairest and greatest protestations,
for I am sure his great god, Gold Allmighty, is able
to make him deceive the best freind he hath in the
world.'

Edmund was next sent with his troop to
Utrecht, where they went into winter quarters, he
took advantage of the university town to make up
for former idleness and studied seven or eight hours
a day for many months together to acquire a better
knowledge of Latin and French.   He hopes his letters
to Ralph arrive safely.   ' I may truely say I take the
time from my studdy of french and latine, but most
of latine hitherto, for I have not had the opportunitie
till this last week of beginning my french, but my
frenchman, which is the same that was Sir Humphrey

Sidenham's, tells me he will warrant I shall speak it perfectly before we draw into the field, and truely I am confident I shall. I repent me of noething so much as the bringing over soe fewe bookes. You have many good latine historyes which I most proeferred, and divers other excellent bookes in your studdy, which I believe you seldom make use of. If you would be pleased when you heare of any gentleman's coming over, to put some in his truncke, you would exceedingly oblige me. Think not I pray that I intend to begge them for I knowe they are not thinges to be so easily parted with, all that I desire is that you would be pleased to lend me some.'

In January of the next year he describes the utter indifference of the army as to the events going on in England, and as to politics, except as regards the chances of war.

' I wonder none of your letters mention news. We are as full here as ever we can hold ; for it is credibly reported that there are thirty thousand men raysing in England, that my lord of Northumberland is generall of the field, my lord Connoway of the horse, Sir John Connyers his leiuetenant generall ; and that Collonell Goring shall command a third part of the Army ; and that these forces shall goe God knowes whither, for the truth is wee heare noe certainty of that. This is the newes that sounds merrily in our eares. We know that you are to have a parlyament, but we care not to aske whither the payment of shipp money shall continue, or whither monopolyes shall downe, or what

lords either spirituall or temporall are lyke to be
questioned.   None of these last trouble our thoughts ;
but truely wee would gladly be informed of the
former ; therefore I pray Sir when you write will you
please to signify what trueth you know of these forces,
or of what continuance they are lyke to be of, and
when they set forth.   My cousen Tyrvile continues
very ill and full of payne, and doe but thinke what
aggravation the newes of these present stirres are
to one of his spirit [Edmund has been nursing his
cousin for several weeks at the Hague, to his own
great inconvenience, but without a complaint], for
I dare sweare he longs to be an actor in this come-
tragedy or tragicomedy, or whatever it proove.   His
sickness is soe greivous that there is a greate doubt
whither he may escape with lyfe or noe.'   A postscript is added to say that Edmund has just heard
to his sorrow that the troops being raised are intended against the Scotch.

He is very earnest to get the place of a certain
Lieutenant Flood who is about to be cashiered.   ' It
is really worth £100 if my father can get it for that.
I pray take heede that my Collonel over reach you
not in it, *latet anguis in herbâ*. I desire your good word
because I esteem so much of your affection that I will
not propose the least thing to my Father, but I will
endeavour to work it first by your means.   Sweet
brother, tis worthy my most deliberate thought to
consider how noble my Father hath ever been to me.
He hath written most affectionately to me thrice, and

now it has pleased God of his infinite mercy to give
me a clearer insight into my former rebelliousnes
against him, and the leudenes and vanity of it is now
even odious to me.   God is wiser than man, and
knowes when we have neede of His greater mercy,
even when we live in the strongest temptations, for I
could never say till now that I livd good for goodnes
sake.   Now I thank God I proeferre a good conscience
before all the world, which is the sweetest comfort
any man can conceive.   I have now writ to my
Father for a Furre coate, I pray doe mee the favour
to plead for mee in it.   I pray be pleasd to send mee
a pocket prayer-book, for here are none to be got.'

Without dragging his religion in by the ears in
the fashion of Tom, Edmund, after speaking of the
books which he wishes his brother to lend him, says :
' There is one thing I would begge of you to make
a guift to mee of, which is Mr. Bolton's workes.
Most of them I can name to you, being these : his
walking with God, his Instructions for the comforting of a right afflicted conscyence, and his four best
things.   These I begge of you, because I would make
myself obliged to you for whatsoever good I shall
ever be capable of, for dear brother I esteeme of you
more then I can express, and though I think I shall
not in any little time come into England to give you
thankes in person, yet know and be assured that my
heart is with you allwaies.'

The tender feeling which the young soldier preserves for his home is a great contrast to Henry's

indifference to everything but his promotion and position, his pay, his horses, and his outfits—topics which fill his letters exclusively *ad nauseam.*

There was some uncertainty as to whether he was to serve on foot or in the cavalry. The cost of fitting him out for a cornet of horse sounds high. ' I shall goe neare to get it, for the Queene [of Bohemia] will engage the Rhinegrave who is the Colonel of that regiment. But if he doe, and my ffather approove of the keeping it, I shall then write to him for £150, for so much it will cost me to mount me and furnish me with saddles and a carre, with other provisions necessary for that place.' Ralph had sent him just before some of the books which he requested : ' An Historicall Collection of the most memorable accidents, and tragicall mattarres of France under the reigns of Henry II, ffrancis II, Charles IX, Henry III, Henry IV ; the Historie of Scanderbeg ; Plutarch's lives in French—these 3 Bookes I sent my Bro' Edmund.'

In March '40 Edmund, still at the Hague, wrote to Ralph, considering whether it would be for his advantage to join the army which the king was once more gathering against the Scots. ' Your advise was ever good at home, if you can give me any now I am abroade I pray let me have it, for I vow to you I am in such a streight that I know not well what to doe, or to what regiment to betake my selfe. I doe thinke I may doe much better in England, for a Captaine's pay being fifteene shillings a day, besides the allowance of 4 deade [men's] payes and his own mens, I am confident a company will be worth £400 a year honestly, and I am noe such ill husband now but that I could pick something out of it, besides the saving my father his allowance ; and yet I doe thinke I could ass soone get a fortune in this country, ass I shall if I stay here all the time, and then I shall have the more pretence to a greater place here, which truely I ayme at, for I confesse my ambition of rising is not small.'

There is an interesting letter dated April 9, in which the young soldier shows his wish to keep to a higher standard than was the fashion among the officers of the unscrupulous armies then fighting in the Low Countries. ' I desire to live in a perpetuall obedience to my father's pleasure, even while I live ; I am confident he wisheth that which is best for my proeferrement, and truely I am much affrayde that my continuance here can never advance it ; for ass the case stands I may very well stand 2, 3 or 4 yeare without a colours or a leiuetenant's place. And when I have got a leivetenants place, it is not soe good to me by £20 a yeare, ass it is to my Brother harry, or to any other that cares not to make a false muster, for noe Captaine will give any thing extraordinary to a man that will not help him that way, nay a captaine will strive all he can to avoyde the having such an officer, for it may very well be £100 yearely out of his way ; but what inconvenyence should not a man runne, before he should proesume to commit a sinn which his own conscience convinceth him of, and truely I take a false muster to be noe other. And this I confesse is one greate reason of my desire to come over.'

In May Edmund came to England with Sir Thomas Culpepper, and in July was sent with the troops against the Scotch. There was great disaffection in the army, but, young as he was, he seems to have managed his men with considerable tact and success. The expedition was mismanaged from first to last, and on September 10 he writes from York, after they had been defeated at Newburn : ' It is now very long since I writt to you, and yet truely none of my fault, for on the march we have noe time at all, and when we came to New-Castle we were soe buisy both by day and night, that I dare say we had scarce 3 houres rest in a 24 all the time we stayde there, and since we have been noe lesse hastily employ'd in running away. . . . Boyse and I have lost all we have, and soe have many more ; it hath undone me if the warr breake of, otherwise I shall esteeme it a gaine. My father is dayly expected here, otherwise I would have written to him now ; I pray wish us better successe and anything but peace, and then you will continue your obligations to your most loving Brother,' &c. On the same piece of paper he continues on 21st : ' By the date of this letter you will find it hath beene written 11 dayes since, but I could not send it with any security till now, for I heare that most of the letters that come by the post

are opened. . . . When you write next I pray let me
heare what became of the Cart-horse [which he had
lost on the road]. This postscript was written in
the feild, and this is my day of having the guard in
towne, and the houre of marching thither now drawes
neare, and I have only time to tell you that I am soe
much that I cannot be more your loving brother,' &c.
' 25 Sept. Judge you whether this dolefull newes
of disbanding is not enough to kill a poore man that
is allready undone by the losse of all that ever he
had at Newcastle ; assoone ass ever I come home
expect me singing good your worship cast your eye
on a poore souldyer's misery, and then your liberality
will be very wellcome to your most beggerly Brother
Edmund Verney.'

However, in another fortnight the aspect of things
had changed ; there seemed to be no prospect of peace,
and he wrote : ' I pray tell my younger Brother,
leivetenant Verney, that now I begin to looke up
againe, for certainely tis God's will that our warr
should continue, for the trueth is here is little signe
of the contrary. . . . I am confident I cannot put
my selfe in the same equipage againe for £70, for I
lost all I had save one sute of cloathes which was my
buffe coate and cloath hose, one band, one paire of
Cuffes, one paire of bootehose, one shirt, one halfe
shirt, a cap and a handkercher, which were all of the
very worst I had ; my father hath beene very noble
in his proffer to me, but I will make use of it ass little
ass I can.' Apparently Henry was not very sympa-

thetic about his brother's losses, for in the next letter
the latter wrote : 'for my Brother Harry, let me tell
you that he is but merry at what I should be very
serious in if I were in his place, for unlesse the Scotts
had shreived me to the skinn, 'tis impossible they
should have left me poorer. . . . Well may I say
with Byas, omnia mea mecum porto. . . . Farewell
and beleeve the proverbe of me, though poore yet
honest and your truely loving Brother,' &c. In a
postscript he gives ' the bignes of his necke and
wrists,' that he may have some new shirts made of
stuff at 8s. the ell.

Edmund had some friendly intercourse with the
Scotch leaders, and apparently the lost luggage, or
some of it, was restored to him, for on December 10
he writes : 'I have lately been at New-castle where
Lasly us'd me but indifferent kindly, for he bid me
twice or thrice get me about my buisnes, but that
was because I did not stile him his exellency, but
indeede I found infinite civillity from the Earle of
Ancram's sonn the Earle of Lodyan [Lothian],
who assured me he had sent one truncke up safe to
my father.'

Jan. 15, 1641.—' This is an age for newes, and
an intelligence from you would have beene more wellcome to me then from another, because I know
through your judgement and insight into the trueth
of things, you are able to give a more just information ; the trueth is one maine buisnes I desire to
know is in what estate wee stand, or how long it is

lyke to be before wee shall be casheir'd, or whither you are lyke to employ us any other way. This I will say for you of the parlyament [Ralph was at this time M.P. for Aylesbury], you are the worst paymasters I know.'

Jan. 24.—' Your blaming me for not writing came very unexpectedly to me, for I have written soe often, that I rather thought to have heard that your parlyament affayres would not have suffered you to have reade halfe my letters.'

CHAPTER VIII.

HENRY THE RACING MAN.

'A' plays at quoits well . . . and rides the wild mare . . . and such other gambol faculties a' has, that show a weak mind and an able body.'—*Henry IV*.

HENRY, having been intended by his father for a soldier, was early sent to Paris to learn French, by which his English was certainly not improved, and his spelling and diction all through his life are a strange jumble. His thoughts wander from his French grammar to the horses and dogs at home. 'pleade for me,' writes the boy of seventeen to his elder brother, 'in my behalfe to my ffather if I have not write in french so well as he expects, but howsoever I presume a line to testifie some little knowledge in the same, and hope in time to expresse myselfe more radier, as the old proverbe is—il fault du temps pour apprendre—. . . . please to send the doggs by a frenchman that is lately gone over for doggs for my lord. . . . . I hope my father will not fail to send them for my lord expects them, with theare names, theare ages, and coulers and markes.' He took part in the war of the Palatinate with the son of his father's friend, Sir E. Sydenham, his cousins the Turvilles, and a number of other friends and connexions. Horse-racing is his particular delight. He writes, in 1637, to his brother, saying, as to his profession : ' I tell you truly I doe not like of it. I wod have you think it is not the firing of the boullots that fears mee at all, but the true reson is that I have alwayes givin myselfe so fer to the sports and plesurs of the wourld that I cannot give my mind to this course of life— but to give my father content and the rest of my frinds, I will tarry this sommer in the contry, for to learne the use of my armes and to knowe the duty of a soger, that when I come of it, shall bee for my credit and honnor. it shall not be mee that will be judg of it, but my Captaine. If hee say noe, belevet I will not come of. for I had rather louse my life then to come of to bee laught at, or bee slighted by my frindes which I doe think dous love mee. If my father is angry, I knowe hee will spake with you of it, let me intreate you to passify him as well as you can.'

He next desires his letters to be sent ' unto Buekelay his Captain's garison. it's a great frontier and wee have hard duty for to doe in the winter. we must wach much and the nights will be very could. I will ask for a fur couth which will doe me great pleasure.' He takes his horse-racing seriously, and talks contemptuously of ' your spruce courters, and shuch as think uppon nothing but goeing to playes and in making of visits. I can right you noe nuse but of a horsmache, as is to be run yearely at

the Hagge for a cupe of 50 pounds, as every offecer
gives yearly 20 shillings toewards the bying of it.
I hope to winit afore I die myselfe. I have rod but
to maches cince I saw you, and have won them both,
I hope likewise to win the cup for the third.' In
another letter to poor Ralph, whom he seems to have
considered fair game, whenever he wanted anything
that his father could not supply, he asks first for a
pad, then for a bit, then for the horse furniture fitting to it, then for a saddle, and, lastly, adds (as in
the gradual accretions of the stone-broth) the extra,
that 'a horse willbe very wilcom, for sommer drawes
on apace, and if I am unmounted I know but wan
way I must trust to, which is to march afout. and
I am an ill foutman. I would have sent you money
to have bought one, had I any to have spared, but
seeing I have non, I refer myself holy to your kind
nature, and make no dout my desire will be accomplished, eyther uppon credit or gift.'

In another letter he says : ' if I have a horse, twill
be to ease my weary limes not try his speede for the
cup,' which he thinks may further his request.

' I doe not at all wonder,' wrote Edmund at this
time, ' at brother Henry lyking a souldier's life, senc
he can follow that and horse maches too.'

In October 1637 Henry was present at the re-
taking of Breda by the Prince of Orange, one of the
most gallant deeds of the fearful Thirty Years War.
The Spaniards had reduced the place by famine after
a siege of eleven months, wherein the sufferings of

the inhabitants were terrible. There is a magnificent picture bristling with lances, by Velasquez, at Madrid, called ' Las Lansas,' painted to commemorate the surrender of Breda, showing how proud the Spaniards were of the exploit. They were now themselves besieged in the town. Henry writes : ' In our a proches there has bine nothing done cence the taking in of the hornworke, but in count William's a proches, wee lost some to hundred men of the choitches, and divers offesers besides, in faling in of the hornworke. After, as thay had sprung there mine and where in the worke thay where beate out of it for want of there seconds comming up which were the Ducthes. This was all the servise that was seene afore the towne that is wourth speking of, but wee lost great store of men that where shot in our a proches by misfourtune. The towne is now ours and it was given up the six of October, nue style, and the 10 of the same mounth they [the Spaniards] marcht out of it with wan and fifty flying coulers, and there was not at all gest [guessed] to be a bove sixteene hundred men, straglers and all. This is all the nues that I can wright you word of.'

After the taking of Breda Henry remained in garrison there. He declares that he is ' not yett so absolute a soldiur though I love my profession to dispise and contemne those sports so farr forth as they tende to pleasure and recreation, but to settle my whole intencions that way as formerly I have absolutely left.' Nevertheless he explains : ' I rod a

mach of six mile with a Dutchman for 50 pounds
and won it, but it was not for myself but for a
friend.' He had been begging again for a horse,
'not such a one,' he says ungratefully, 'as my
kind aunt Pountne sent me'; and observes afterwards, 'if you had sent me a courser, it would not
at all have made me more in love with rasing.' In a
postscript he begs for a speedy reply respecting the
horse, as 'if not I must make use of a Dutch Dogg.'

That Ralph was no preaching prig, unable to
enter into the amusements of his brothers, appears
from a good-natured letter to Henry at the Hague in
1639. Henry seems to have been at home for a short
time and is anxious about the matches at Brackley.
'My Lord Carlile's white nagg,' says Ralph, 'hath
beaten Dandy, and Sprat woone the cup, and Cricket
the plate ; and which you will most woonder at the
Weavor hath beaten the Sheepheard shamfully, and
offerrs to run the same number of miles for £500
with the Sheepheard, and bee tied to hopp the last
12 score y$^{ds.}$ My Lord of Salisburies horse Cricket
was matched with Banister's bauld horse for £1000
a horse and £200 forfeiture—they are to run the
four miles at Newmarket—they would never run for
so much money unless they certaynly know Banister's
horse to be sound.' He then asks kindly how Henry
likes the Low Countries, and tells him to let his
friends know who uses him with most courtesy ' that
they may find some way to thank them for it. I
pray brother practise your hand and write often to

my father. The dun horse is well of his heeles and
is now one of the bravest that ever I beheld. My
father intends it for your Coronell. Captain Sydenham hath writ much in your commendation, and for
a greater allowance for you.'

In the autumn of 1639 Sir Edmund bought a
lieutenancy for him, and he becomes friendly with
his captain, a Vere, and his other officers. He is
tolerably satisfied and only desires his friends to send
him '6 yards of coarse cloth, and 4 yards of baize,'
to make him a winter suit 'to lie upon the gards.'
A recruiting agent had been sent over from his regiment, and he was anxious that a horse should be sent
by such an opportunity, and explains how 'the nag's
meate by the waye is to be provided for.' 'If you
can help him to a man or to,' he adds, 'I pray doe.
Bridwell is seldome so empty but they may spare
some, and, for his honesty, I'le promise you not to
enquier after it, for let him be neer so bigg a rouge
the beter. I can no wayes requite you with newse,
but I am now in the Hauge and if you have any sute
to the Queene of Bohemia you need not doubt to
prevayle in it, if you please to command her greatest
favourite.'

The Queen of Bohemia, Elizabeth, daughter of
James I., had taken refuge with her family in Holland, after having lost both shadow and substance of
sovereignty. The ambition to become a queen had
made her urge her incompetent husband to accept
the crown of Bohemia offered by the States ; in con-

sequence of which they had been driven from his
hereditary dominions in the Palatinate, and the
remainder of their lives was spent in fruitless endeavours to recover them.   James employed all
the resources of his beloved kingcraft with every
means in his power, excepting those that cost money,
to help her, but in vain.   Her two sons, Rupert and
Maurice, were among the most active of Charles's
commanders in the Civil War.

The ' Queen of Hearts,' as she was called by her
many admirers, seems to have been very kind to both
the young Verneys when stationed at the Hague.

Later on, after her husband's death, she privately
married Lord Craven, concerning whom there is
a curious letter from Sir Nathaniel Hobart, who
married a half-niece of Sir Edmund's, a sister of
Doll Leeke.

He begins by saying that the Spaniard is ' very
angry with his Matie,' who is expected to assist his
nephew, but that the king replied that he would
only do as the King of Spain did for the emperor.
' In this action the Hollanders and my lord Craven
joine.   Though I dare not ranke him with kings and
princes, yet, trust mee, his bounty may challenge a
prime place amongst them.   I dare say there are
some Itallian princes would shrinke at soe great an
undertaking, nay, and they should pawne their titles,
and spoyle their subjects, they would not bee able to
furnish such a summ.   Yet what is all this but a
small part of those vast treasures left him by his

father ?   And what was hee ?   *Filius populi.*   What
stock had hee to begin withall ?   A groate ;—an ex-
celent pedigree !   What saies the court of this man ?
they laugh at him, and desire things may be reduced
to their first principle.   Would you have my opinion
of him ?   Truly, his wealth is his greatest enemy,
and yet his only frend.   It begetts, in his inferiours,
a disguisde friendship ; in his equalls, envy.   His
vanity makes him accessible to the one ; the meaness
of his birth, person, parts, contemptible to the
other ; and though in those great ons envy bee the
true motive, yet his many follies rendring him ob-
noxious to a just censure, that passes away unscene.
Had fortune conspirde with nature and ranked him
according to his degree, he might have crept away
among the rout, his levities unknowne, or if discovered, they might have procurde him as gay though
not soe rich a coate as now he weares.   Are you
not weary ?   Truly, I am.   The candle bidds mee
goe to bed ; therefore, good night.' . . . Dated ' from
my cell in Coven Garden '—Sir Edmund Verney's
house.

Henry Verney remained in the service of the
States, though not very well satisfied with his position.   He writes from the Hague in February 1642,
begging Ralph to get his father to buy him a company : it could be had for £700 ; ' it is not deare
considdering the profett of it.'   He envies his brother
Edmund, who he hears ' is gon Captain for Ireland,
and doe hope a will kill a 100 tyrannical rebels for

his part.' The queen had gone over to Holland,
carrying the crown jewels with her, which she sold
to buy munitions of war. Her coming to the Hague,
says Henry, ' is expensive to all,' and also lessened
his chances of getting a captaincy ; for ' here are
divers gentlemen of great qualities wch are come
over with our queene that stands for the first company that falles of our Platton . . . and all they
can pretend to is hopping to imbrace a fortune by
the queene's favour more than for their good service.'
Sir Edmund must have been sorely put to it to pay
such a large sum for his exacting son, but he promised to do so, and Henry writes very gratefully to
Ralph for having ' moved his sute.' He hopes for
the good offices of the Prince of Orange in the matter,
as he writes :

' When I went to take my leave of his Highness
a incouraged mee much [Henry, life Falstaff, uses *a*
for *he*] in promesing mee to doe for mee : wth all
a has given mee an act under his owne hand volun-
tariley of himselfe to remaine in the Armey this
sumer ; it is a favour, and a great one I can assuer
you ; I dare sware it is the first a hath given to
any of a strange nation in his life. I hope if any
fortune fall sence a hath don this a will thinke of
mee ; in earnest it is a good signe, though a greate
charge to mee and my ffather. I have sent to him
for a nagg, I hope a will be plesed to send mee wan
. . . for I am so lame of my leggs that I cannot
march.' A few weeks later he writes to his father

full of vexation, having failed of promotion, though three places had fallen vacant : the queen had recommended one man and Lord Goring the two others. He attributes his ill-success to the conduct of Sir Edmund and Ralph in Parliament. ' Now sence this I have bine with Sir Thomas Stafford and . . . intreated him to move the queene to recommend mee to the Prince ; a reply'd a durst not, for a sed a was sertaine her Majestie would not be plesed to spake for mee. Wth all like a noble freind as hee conseved a tould mee the reson of it : thinke but of Wickcom and Alsberie and you may both easley find the sence of it ; the truth is, I beelive, a has tryed her and was deneyd . . . truley I find by him that I am far more unlikeley of getting a companey then I was the first day a come here : my lord Goring hath bin the occasion of this and non else ; had I deserved the lest unkindness from him it would not have troubled mee ; his being my enemie I am confident will cast mee out of my coronells good opinion, and then to get higher it is impossible. . . . This weeke I goe to my gareson and there shall stay this summer.'

Lord Goring writes to Sir Edmund to justify his action in the matter, and begins by saying, ' we have knowne and loved long, and I shall desire you first to reade what I shall heere lay before you, and afterwards iudge of me as upon dew examination you shall finde cause.' He goes on to say that he had been pledged for many years to the man whom he had recommended, and for the other place, though he

had been applied to by men 'of great experience and
long service in these countryes,' he had refused to
engage himself : also that Henry had not applied to
him 'till many days after ye prince had bin moved
for him and all ye Towne full of it.'   In a later letter
Henry refers again to his father and brother's action
as affecting his promotion : ' for Wickham and Alis-
bery stepping in my way, I believe that is noe hin-
drance, though, indeed, I have bin tould by more
than one or teu it has.   The opinion, I see, of the
great ones most att the Court is that my father and
you are all for the Parleyment and not for the King,
wch here I find they take not kindly.   My father's
lett^r will let you see more playneley how little I
regard shuch falce jelosies, and truely as times goe
now, and considdering the diffeculty of getting mee
a company, a need not much regard it ; for, let mee
travill where I will, soe I go not to hell, a more baser
place to make a fortune and less beelive I cannot
finde ; and were it not more to obay my father's will
and my friends' desier then any love I bare to my
masters the States, the divill their godfather should
serve them, and not I.   Had I gon, Captaine, for the
North att first, as I desired, when divers other offecers
here did, wch had bet^r command then myselfe, and
now for Eirland, I had had more then five hundred pound in my purss, when now I have not a
grao^t to speeke of, or else I must have spent my
time ill.'

In a later letter, when Ralph had apparently been

suggesting that he should join the army of the Parliament, he wrote : ' I confess the imployment wth you I hold to bee much better, where [were] the continuance of it soe certaine as thes here, and the cause soe just as that of Ireland ; as earnest as I am in pressing to ataine to a bet^{er} fortune, yett my prayers are daley for peace in that kingdome. To speake the truth, I must needes say of late I have bine much crost in my advancement, and when I am alone and thinke of the maliciousness of that man wch did prevent mee of it makes mee madd, and in a maner weary of my profession, for if a possess my coronell once against mee, as long as a lives I shall not gett a company.'

It is evident that Henry had no principle to guide him in the course that he should take in the Civil War except his own interest. Ralph, who had no illusions with regard to him, writes candidly in another letter about the possibility of his engaging himself on either side in case these troubles should increase. ' I presume the army will not entertain him, what they will do I know not but I believe they value him not, nor do I think unless he hath great hopes of a speedy settlement. . . . he will easily engage for he is naturally idle enough.'

Eventually, by the advice of his father, he offered to attend the queen on her return to England, where he obtained a post in the King's Army.

He writes to Ralph from the Hague in November 1642 :—' In my last letter I sent you word of my misfortune in missing of the company I wrote you word of, now I must let you know that I have by favour of my friends, procured leave of his Highness to hold up my place for 4 mounths, soe that I shall assuredly attend of our queene over. I goe from hence wthin this hour to my garison to fetch my things there, but make noe stay att all, for Her Majestie as I doe here is fully resoveld to depart from hence wthin this 12 dayes, if the King be so neare London as I have reported, where I hope to have the happiness to see you suddenly. I cannot now send you any directions how you may write to me, for I know not where I shall be myselfe, but as long as I live be confident I shall continue,

' Your most affectionate loving brother and humble servant, H. VERNEY.

' My brother is gon about his business but where I know not ; a tould me when I tooke my leave of him, a would see you suddenly. My choyest affection to my sweete sister your wife, and to the rest of my sisters and freinds. Once more farewell.'

The queen returned to England in Feb. 1643, after a most stormy voyage, and in the same month Henry writes : ' Sir Ed. Siddenham hath got mee to bee Maior of hors to Sr. Ralphe Dutton, his garsson is Sisseter.' He hopes his colonel will help him to raise his company. ' The King's hand I have kist ; a lookt earnestly uppon mee, but spake not to mee ; in time if the warr goe one I hope to be better knowne to him, if not I shall hardly get my sute granted.'

Surely a cold reception for Charles to give to the son of his faithful servant, slain in his service at Edgehill, not four months before ; and himself a soldier, who only asked to be allowed to serve him.

CHAPTER IX.

THE COUNTESS OF BARRYMORE——SIR NATHANIEL HOBART ——SIR JOHN LEEKE——AND SOME IRISH FRIENDS.

' . . . troops of friends.'—*Macbeth.*

SIR Edmund's connection with his many Irish friends was of old date. In July 1626 there is a letter from the ' great Earl of Cork,' commonly so called as if it were part of his title, thanking Sir Edmund for his ' noble carriadge' to his daughter Alice and her husband Lord Barrymore and little son, ' of which I will as I have good cause, reteign a moste thankfull remembrance.' He entreats him to present ' a leash of falcons [3] to his Majestie. They ar the ayry of Smerwick, bred in the veary fort which the Spaniards held . . . till putt to the sword by Lord Arthure Grey, then Lord Deputy of Ireland [1580]. The King's late father of blessed memory vouchsafed yearly to write unto me for these hawkes and did esteem yt a great blessing to have birds of pleasure bred in that rocky fort in which his late sister of famous memory had an army of Spanish enemeyes which came to bereave her of this kingdome lodged. That affection of his late majesty gives me the bowldnes to offer soe poor a present which I praie maie be humbly tentred to his highnes.' He goes on to beg Sir Edmund to try and get certain moneys repaid, advanced by him to make tenable both the famous forts of Cork and Waterford. 'The works given over for want of money laste year, I, to prevent the further rejoicings of the ill-affected papists (who wrote poorly thereof into forreign kingdomes), have weekly imprested them with my own monies and doe every Saturday pay them fifty pounds upon account not doubting but in due time these monies and 500*l*. which I lent to supply th'extream necessities of the soldiers his Majesty's fleet landed here shall be repaid me. From Lismoor the xvii[th] of July 1626, your affectionate frend and servant R. Corke.'

His daughter Alice and her husband, Lord Barrymore, lived on their estates and did their duty by their surroundings ; they were earnest Protestants of the type of Sir Edmund and Sir Ralph, and had sermons for the few Irish Protestants about them at Castle Lyon on Sundays and Wednesdays.

He is called a good and brave man, and was for some time President of Munster. Lady Barrymore seems to have been an Irish woman of the best kind, the most charming type in the world, very energetic and capable, very amusing and very lovable. In each of her yearly visits to the 'Bath' and to London, sometimes with her father, sometimes with her husband, Sir Edmund appears as

ANNE LEAKE
LADY HOBART

Anne, Lady Hobart,
dau: of Sir John Leeke,
from a picture by Cornelius Jansen:
at Claydon House.

Ann Hobart

one of the foremost friends on whom she relies for help.

Sir John Leeke, who married Sir Edmund's half-sister, was a retired officer, connected with the Barry-mores, from whom he hired a house and took to farming the park at Castle Lyon. He had several daughters ; Mary married a Beresford ; Anne married Sir Nathaniel Hobart ; Bridget, a Captain Hals ; Doll, who lived so much at Claydon, died unmarried ; they were all extremely Irish and voluminous correspon-dents. None of them lose anything for want of asking their English relation at Court, who was re-quired to use his influence for every variety of favour, such as getting a would-be son-in-law made a knight, &c., &c.

Sir Nathaniel Hobart—'sweet Nat,' as he is continually called—was as a brother to Ralph, and he and his wife ' Nan ' were much attached to Sir Edmund. In 1630–40 he was a young lawyer, working hard at his profession, living with his family at Highgate in a house which he apparently inherited from his father, Sir Henry Hobart, Chief Justice of Common Pleas, who is spoken of as ' of Highgate.'

In 1635 Sir Nathaniel seems to have got into money troubles in the scheme for draining the fens, where he invested his money in a share with Sir Edmund, probably not very wisely. The 'great level' round the isle of Ely, covered by the overflow of the Ouse, was a dreary swamp in summer and a waste of water in winter. Vermuyden, a great Dutch engineer, had been employed first to rescue the immense waste of land inundated by the Humber; he next undertook the draining of the Bedford swamps in 1634, under a company with the Earl of Bedford at the head, who were to receive 43,000 acres divided into twenty shares. In three years, however, Bedford had spent £100,000, but the work was still incomplete; waters poured over the reclaimed land, there were great complaints, and Commissioners were sent down to examine into the state of things. They imposed a tax to carry out the works; Sir Nathaniel became liable for his share which he could not pay, and for some time the young lawyer was in hiding, sometimes in his study under Sir Edmund's roof, where probably the protection of the Knight Marshal was of use to him. Sir John Leeke, his father-in-law, writes to Sir Edmund that he was 'loath to be in durance . . . the fenns have nere drowned him : give yor ayd, yor cowncell to that Honest sweet man that he may looke uppon poore Nann and his pretty Babes. you have bine a father to all mine. be so still.'

After a time the king, without waiting for the settlement which the Commissioners had been specially sent down to make, announced that he intended to take the works into his own hands, as he considered them imperfect. He was to receive 57,000 acres in return. In point of fact Bedford and his associates were not injured, as they received a large part of the reclaimed land promised them, without the obligation of finishing the works, but the look of the thing was against Charles, who was apparently benefiting himself and injuring a popular and useful man like Bedford. Moreover the king, amidst his own money troubles, was quite unable to spend anything on the fens. Vermuyden's plans were not altogether satisfactory, hardly anything was done after the undertaking came into his hands, and, as far as Charles was concerned, the whole matter continued in abeyance.

Sir John Leeke, writing to Sir Edmund of poor 'Nat's' share in the loss, says : 'I am relieved [? grieved] above all earthly things that have befallen me, my loss of my deare boy excepted, that honest Natt hath not only sould his brave lordship, but that most of the money about the ffens is wasted, and hath and must pay much more for the bewittinge bill and that his liberty is taken from him. He is so loth for to be caught, but it will be hard for him to escape the fowlers that lay lime for him. I know your help and the parliament help may advantage him much but the ende will be most dangerous. I would have him to see us here in Irland as soone as the parliament shall be ended up till some fair composition may be had. I know poor Nan will be loth to have him from her armes but it would break her heart to have him in restraint and I am sure would go near him. Let him adventure a welcome hither, if it be not as harty as he can expect, let us be blotted out of his remembrance. You know Nan brought him five hundred pounds without a johnture or provision. God hath blessed them with many sweet children. I wish they were cared for in some measure. I need not invite your care, I know your wisdome considers for necessity.'

Sir Nathaniel was eventually relieved from his difficulties ; he was appointed a Master in Chancery in 1652, and was knighted after the Restoration, Charles II. having reappointed him to his post.

Besides Sir John Leeke's daughters and their husbands, Magdalen Faulkner comes into the story ; a niece of old Lady Denton's and a poor cousin of Ralph's, she became a lady-companion to Lady Barrymore, and her letters from Castle Lyon during the Irish rebellion are very valuable. She afterwards married Mr. Bruce, a clergyman in the neighbourhood of Youghal, connected with ' Mr. Moray of the bedchamber,' who, coming from France, was taken prisoner at Gravesend and closely confined in the Tower for bringing letters from the queen to Charles. In May 1631 Lady Barrymore, who had been at Bath with Sir Edmund and his son, writes to him as 'noble governour' from Dublin, saying she had received a letter from him assuring her of what she had never doubted, 'for I knew it was impossible that so ill a thing as forgetfullnese should harbour where so many vertues are.' The remainder of the letter is compliment, ending by presenting 'her love and servis to all the good company at Charing

Cross and to my noble sarvant Ralph—your assured friend and charge to command.' It is addressed ' to my moch honored frend Sir Edmon Verney Knight. Knight Marshall of England att London.'

Sir J. Leeke writes to Sir Edmund in 1635 : ' Now that the Deputie hath browght into the King's power 3 Counties and they have submitted themselves to the King's mercy, it is conceyved the Kinge will take the fowerth of each countie. My Lord Clanricard hath most of his lands fallen into the King's mercy. A great plantation wilbe and exelent lande. My lord Clanricard or his sonn or my lord Willmote cann best instruct you. Be quicke for many gape after this plantation. Thes lands are in the prvince of Conaught whereof my Lo. Willmote was governer many yeares. If you may w^{th}out hurte to y^{r}selfe speake a good worde for me, I shall bless god and you for itt. I have littell hope of the sowre Deputie. I have given 200*l*. for a lease for Capt. Hals. We have 36 years to come. The lands is my Lord Barrymore's. I must give him 100*l*. to renue the lease to 51 yeares, out of wch my Lord Dungarvan will have 50*l*. for you. [Sir Edmund managed for his half-sister Lady Leeke.] But this money must not be had until the capt. come home, who I expect every day. He hopes to bee with us on Michalmas day. God sende him safe, for he hath suffered much in his goinge, a moneth and five dayes storme, lost 12 men, and were not in that time able to sett on a kettell, and hadd much of the Beverage staved in, so much that he came to a pint and a haulfe of water a day. I hope his goods will prosper that is gotten wth so much hassard and difficultie.'

Captain Hals married ' Bidde,' Sir John's fifth daughter, and though after his death she consoled herself with two husbands in succession, it would seem that her first choice was a happy one, judging by her father's letters. ' God all powefull hath effected this match, and I dowght not but that arme will still and ever cover and bless them, for never man I beleve cann more truly love then he.'

Letters seem always to have been sent by hand. Sir John has written to Sir Edmund by a merchant, or by Lord Cork's ' too younger sonns ' who are to be at Eton. ' This I sende by a most deare frende of mine, Mr John Barry. Had not my lord Barrymore issue male, this gentellman must Inheritt his Honor and Landes. I am confident of noe man's faythfull love to me In this Kingdome but of this man's, yett I must say I have many wellwishers as any poore man hath, but I may truly call this man my frende. He is a man of seaven hundred pounds by yeare and may live happily att home, but his desyeres are to be abroad and in the warres, whether his Intentions now are. If uppon good conditions he may, I am resolved to send Jack Leeke wth him, who will use him as a Brother and will allow him a good meanes. Hee will carry over 1,500 men. My sonn doth begine to be toe sturdie for my government and this must be his way. I hartily desyer you will take

Mr. Barry into your love and good opinion, he will deserve itt, a more valiant, honest younge man liveth not. nether is ther a man, I beleeve, that for exercises of the body cann out doe him abought the court. He is a papist, but we have hopes he will be other.' In a later letter he writes : ' For my deare Mustris [Lady Barrymore] you send me most joyfull newes of her comminge for Irland. Itt will make us rich here and your barbarus England poore by her depar-ture, for if you once fall to killinge and beatinge Captains and Leiftennants you will next fall to injuringe Ladys . . . You will sorrow enough when you goe by the Savoy and find the juells re-moved and nothing left but beggars and bedds. I desyer, though you be somewhat Lame, you will not take a lodginge ther in your sorrowes.'

Sir John Leeke writes again when the Barry-mores are gone on another English visit :—' My deere Mustris hath bestirred hirselfe to perfect this lease for me from her father. She is the trewest frende and most constant Lady that ever wore the mark of the Moone. Well may she prosper and inioy what hir brave hart desyres. Sinn were itt she should ever be crossed so much as in hir thought or wishes. See hir, good S^r, and say or doe somethinge that may expresse my thankfullness by you, for shee hath a great oppinion of yor noble respects to hir. You shall likwise find wth her a sister Katherin, my deere cossen, a more brayve wench or a Braver spiritt you have not often mett wth all. She hath a memory

that will hear a sermon and goe home and penn itt
after dinner verbatim.   I know not how she will appeare in England, but she is most accounted of att
Dublin.   I am much obliged to hir, and lastly you
shall incounter wth a younge peere that stands in
feare of you already.   She howlds downe hir head a
littell and my Mustris tells hir that when you see hir
you will not spare to chide hir.   I know not how itt
goeth, but ther hath bine an overture [of marriage]
made for the new Earle of Thomond sonn who you
know.   I pray doe some good office in itt, if itt come
in yor way.   She is a sweet disposed Lady . .

   ' You shall have all thes winter att the Savoy, in
Sr Tho. Staffords howse, the greatest familie that
willbe in London (I praye god the ould man [Lord
Cork] houlds out) . .   I often heare of you by my
good frendes att Stalbridge [where Lord Cork's
youngest son Robert Boyle the philosopher lived].
My Mustris sent me worde that she had receved a
letter from you from Barwick, and that you had
promised to see Stalbridge. . . .   The Lo : Deputies frownes lie very heavily uppon me and con-
sequently not favorable to my daughter in hir
busines.'

   Capt. Hals had died and Sir John was negotia-
ting the re-marriage of his widow with a Mr. Badnage,
who, he says, came purposely over to Lord Cork to
gain his approbation, ' wthout which shee had promised his Lo^{pp} not to marry and he would take itt ill
if she showld . .   You shall find him a rationall

man . . Shee is now worth 2,000 markes, hir debts payd, and hir child well provided for ; so as you may conceyve that she is a mach for a right goodman, and if you were acquainted wth the woman as you are wth the rest you wowld say that she deserves a good husband for she is right good and worthy. . We have almost persuaded the Mann to be mayd a k^t for o^r women and good frends here so wish itt for as she was my dawghter beinge the eldest k^t in Irland now knowne and as she was Capt. Hals his wife who hadd a companie att the Ile of Ree of foote she had a good place, and now by marrieng Mr. Badnege she comes in the reere of all wch will goe neere to breake all and hee understands itt well himselfe. If itt may be browght to pass in England wee all showld be gladd for it will hardly be in Irland if itt concearne any of mine, the great mann's hate to me is so much.' In another letter : ' Truly I finde Bidde's affection well enowgh to the mann were itt nott that hir place must be in the [?] ouse of all the country and I beleeve if any thinge hinder itt that wilbe the rubbe, for wee stand heere more uppon place then in England heere are mayny startupps that wealth doth advance from baseness to prferrment.' The question of precedence seems to have been waived in the end, however, for Bidde shortly after married Mr. Badnage, and he remained unknighted. In another letter to Sir Edmund, Sir John Leeke writes :

' Noble brother, you have now obliged me my poor fortune, wife and children and my ould carcase for sending against yoar will my deare Mustris, the worthiest of woemen. Believe it ould Corke could not begett nothing foolish. I am with all my hart glad we have her, and by this time you find the misse of her for had you had her conversation any wit longer she wowld have much advantagd you to have bine a Counsellor a Deputie or anything. You say shee is very discreet and of great understanding. By my soule I dare swear itt, for I hadd rather have her judgment in businesse than the greatest concelor amongst us and if I had a desier to be merry, better company is not. If she hath either got Doll or her own more pretious sister Kate, to whom Doll comes short, surely if you shall ever see her you will say that you have seene the unparaleld cossens, but my pretious Katherine is somewhat decayed from the sweetest face I ever saw (and surely I have seene good ones). She is keapte and longe hath bine by the foulest Churle in the world; he hath only one vertu that he seldom cometh sober to bedd, a true imitation of Sir Robt Wroth.

'For my daughter Hals, considering how pro-testant husbands goe here and this mann's thrift the mach is not enough, she will live happie for he loves her. I cowld wish with all my hart that Doll had such another.' She was still living at Claydon.

Another letter :

'I am tomorrow going to kiss my Mustris faire hands, once in twenty days I must see her. Mustris is the best chronicle of the court and town of any

living that spent no longer time ther than she did.
She dashes me over the face with some stories of my
youth, but I pass them bye as not remembrᵍ them.
She hath half complained to me and so hath Doll
Freake, that they had heard that you were a ready and
complete man for the pleasure of ladies, and expected
at opportune times to be put to it, but that you had the
sciatica and such ill savours about you that Doll yet
makes a face at the remembrance. You have deserved ill of them, they speak not a good word of
you. At the first coming over you were their discourse especially in my presence, but time has cooled
that fancy. Now they talk of Robin Welsh and
such gallants, let it not trouble you, it is the way of
all flesh, but Mistris will ever in three days vouch-
safe to drink to me, as it goes down the meaning I'll
not enquire. . . . Your ould Tom is with Mustris
and fools every meal with drinking a glass of sack to
your health and when he doth pray itt is for you
only.'

Sir Edmund, at Sir John Leeke's desire, thanks
Lord Cork for signing some leases of ' divers plowing land,' and for adding twenty-one years without
raising one penny rent. Sir John writes : ' I have
itt as itt was lett 20 years since wᶜʰ was 31 pound.'
He is underletting it for a hundred. ' I acknowledg
this a frendly guift. . . . I am especyally bound to
Dungarvan and Mustris, who never left the ould
Lord untill he had granted signed and sealed my
lease . . . and truly the Noble Earle's willingnes

incountered wth ther intercession for he is not psuaded
to doe thinges beyond his Judgment. God reward
them all for they are really my trew frends.'

He tries to persuade Sir Edmund to adventure in
some of the confiscated lands so much recommended
in a former letter, and which were being allotted by
Lord Strafford. 'I have sent you divers letters
concerninge the plantations that are like to be in
Conaght in the Earl of Clanrikards Cuntry and did
wish you to advise wth him how you may be planted
in some convenient place, for I am assured they are
good lands as any in the kingdome.'

In October 1635 he says : 'My Lord of Incyquin
is a fortnight married to my Lord President's [1] delicate dawghter, and to this marriadge this sommer
came over the tow dawghters of Sr John Ogle, daintie
fingers and most exquisite musitians. They are here
untill the springe.' To which wedding also came
James Dillon, Ralph's great friend. The bridegroom was the first Earl of Inchiquin, and is said
to have been 'distinguished for military skill and
many soldierlike exploits during the Irish Rebellion.'

In 1639 Lady Barrymore writes from Castle
Lyon to Ralph to ask if Sir Edmund will find a
tutor for her little son. 'Noble Sarvant,' she begins,
and says she has had a 'distillation out of my head,
which is fallen into my jaws and teeth,' and has put
her to so much pain that she could not write before
'to aske the favour to find a good tutor for my young

---

[1] Sir William St. Leger, President of Munster.

master. I would have him a mounseer, one that might teach him to right and a good garb, and that might still be with him when I send him to school. I would not have him too old nor too young, but one of a very temperate carrage. For his wages I refer it holey to him for what he agrees to I will God willing see paid. I like him so well for a governer for myself that I humbly desire he may choose one for my mad boy; and that he may come over with as much speed as may be, for he be spoild for want of one. Good sarvant let me desier you to rite at large about this bisnis what you think fit, and in so doing it shall add to the innumerable numbar of your other favors and bind me ever your mistress to command.'

Sir John Leeke, at the same time, says that 'Lady Barrymore hopes you will favour her so much as to send her a cyvill monsiere to breed her son. Mistress ffaulkner and my lady do well fadge [agree] and I believe she doth not repent her coming over for my lady doth much respect her and keepeth all her promises most justly and not without many gifts and expressions. Mistress ffaulkner is very sickly and melancholly, we merrily tell her it is for some love she left behind her.'

Lady Barrymore writes that 'Lady Denton has sent her niece ffaulkner a cheese. She says you shall not keep it but shall have haulfe. At the beginning of April, God willing, my dear Elin and Faulkner with Garrot Meagh shall for England for help for her lameness which grows much upon her. Pray tell my lady so much that I may have her advice fust.'

She next writes to Sir Edmund in favour of a relation of Lord Barrymore's, who wishes to appear at Court : ' I have sent unto your protection a kinsman of my lord's who I desier you will please to afford the favour that in the court where his desiers are Sir Edmon Verney's acquaintance and conversation may give to a stranger. I dare promise he shall endeavour to deserve your favor in all his ways. And soe will ever your charge to command.' She sends a message to ' swete Mrs. Hubbard ' that she is her humble servant. ' Faulkner holds down her head and keeps on her gloves worse than I did and that is for your credit.'

Later on, when Ralph has taken side against the Court, Lady Barrymore writes to him : ' Noble Enemy, it is not one of the leaste of your vertues that you are pleased to caste your eyes from the gallantry of the courte, and the bravery of the citey upon a cuntry lady living in Ireland and convercing with none but masons and carpendors, for I am now finishing a house, so that if my governour [Sir Edmund] please to build a new house, that may be well seated and have a good prospect, I will give him my best advice gratis, for all the quarrell I have to him in letting me be so neare the happinese of your conversation almost a twelvemonth, and never bringin me to that honor. The maney favors you conferd upon me daley at the Bath makes me the

more resent of my misfortune, and be confident
nothing can make my pease with you and him butt
your promised journey heather, by which meanes I
shall obledge the whole kingdome to me, by bining it
so greate an honor; and it will make me if it bee possible more your sarvant than now, in which degree
you have not a more powerful command over any,
than over Your Enemey and friende to surve you.'

In July 1641 Magdalen Faulkner writes : 'You
writ to me about strawberry treese [evidently the
arbutus] which were green all the yeare, but a think
you are mistaken in the name of the tree. I believe
you mein the cane apel tree, but it tis past the time
of the yeare, thay must be set at the beginning of
fbbry, there is none of them nere ous but one at my
lord of Corke's. I make no doubtt but to get some
of the slips and send when the time of year sarves.'
. . . ' Sir John Leeke begins to repente his dawghter's marrag and wishes he had loste his hande when
he joynd thare's, but kipe this to yourself. Now I
knoe you are knited [she is writing to Ralph] I will
give you your rite titel but you should a put me out
of that dout, and a dun as a knit of our contre did to
his frindes in the concluding of his letars, and gave
himself the titel of Sir Wilam Manerd, if you would
have dun me this favor I should not a robed you of
your titel so long.'

The difficulty of finding an investment for a
small sum of money, particularly for a woman, seems
to have been immense. Magdalen had been left a

hundred pounds by her aunt, Lady Denton, and she had a little money of her own, which seems to have been lent at interest to farmers at Hillesden. [An old French governess of ours had a certain number of hundred francs lent in this way to peasant proprietors ever since the time of her grandfather. She had had no interest for several bad years, and, like Magdalen, had been much put to it.] In prospect of her marriage Magdalen was very anxious to get together three hundred pounds, 'as my portion,' and writes to Ralph, in 1642, about getting in the various little sums : 'If you have called that money into your own hand pray let it remaine till you heare from me ; except the business goes on fairly betwixte the King and Parliament about the rebels' land which you will kno better than I can. If there bee a fair proceeding, I shall desier you to return it to me by my Lord of Dungarvan or my lord of Corke. But I leave it to you own judgment to advise me which you think best for me. For I am resolved to tak the way that you advise me.'

When Strafford's rule in Ireland had come to an end, Sir John Leeke wrote to Sir Edmund in December 1640 : 'I writ this purposely to give you to understand of the petition and remonstrances our Lower House of Parliament submitted to the new Deputie [Wandesford], and that they might be suffered to go into England a selected committee to make good the grievances for we groan insufferably under them.

' P.S.—I received lately a most kind and courteous letter from my late mistress, the Lady Mary Wrothe. . . . She wrote me word that by my Lord of Pembroke's great mediation the King hath given her son a brave living in Irland. . . . We hear from good mouths that our Lord President must be removed, for which I am sorry heartily, for he is and always hath been my good and noble friend, yet if it please his Majesty to think him fitt for other employment, I then wish with all my hart I had as good a friend in his place. It is worth £1000 per annum from the King, a troop of 50 horse and a company of foot, with some other duties and perquisites it may be worth £2,500 per annum. I could wish you had it, if you could be content to part from the eyes of your master, or think this a better place than the marshal's ; it is a thriving place, for our noble president doth thrive exceeding much. But if you shall not hold this a place for your content, then put to all your friends and power for honest Barrymore. Oh it were a blessing and a fortune inexpressible for that same noble lord and his, then might he soone pay his debts and make Castlelyon flourish. Receive this from my deare mistress. Lastly from myself I have so much ambition that I do desire you were the Deputy. Examples have been that in Queen Elisabeth's time some of your rank and some of meaner condition as Sydney, Fitzwilliam, Parrott, Chichester, after a lord, and this Wandesford lately dead. Let Sir Ed. Verney have some ambition to be our governour or our kingdom's governour. I pray take this close to you as things not impossible.

The misery and destruction of the rebellion of 1641 must have fallen like a thunderbolt on the happy and useful household of the Barrymores. The particulars will be given in a later chapter. Within a year the country was sacked and ravaged, and the owner and his people alike ruined.

CHAPTER X.

SIR RALPH'S FRIEND—JAMES DILLON.

'Friendship is healthful and sovereign for the understanding as
for the affections . . . In a word, a man had better relate himself
to a statue or picture than suffer his thoughts to pass in smother.'
BACON.

THE most intimate of Ralph's Oxford friends was
James Dillon, eldest son of the second Lord Roscommon, who, having been converted from the Catholic
faith by Archbishop Usher, sent his son to Oxford
for education. Usher recommended him as ' a jewel
of price' to the Master of Exeter, who, finding him
' a young man of pregnant parts,' placed him ' under
the tuition of the nephew of the great Sir Thomas
Bodley,' founder of the Bodleian Library. He became
' a person of several accomplishments, and was afterwards third Earl in his own country,' says Anthony
Wood. His mother was a sister of Lord Barrymore's, so that the friendship of the two young men
was hereditary. They went to Oxford about the
same time and left the University together.

James Dillon was continually at Claydon during
the years 1631 to 1636, and the side lights in
his letters give a pleasant picture of the family life

there, the household including the very youthful couple, Ralph and his wife, besides a large detachment of the younger children, and their cousin Dorothy Leeke. The young Irishman evidently admired her very cordially, and there was more romping and kissing when they met than would be permitted at the present day. In all his letters to Ralph little words of recollection and allusions to 'brother Doll' appear, and little presents, a thimble, a comb, &c., are sent from time to time.

His first letter is written from Cloncullan, and shows the difficulty of travel from England to Ireland in 1631. He had ridden post from London to 'Chester water,' there to pick up some little sailing vessel, which might be a week or more on the passage to Dublin if the winds were contrary. He begins his letter by calling Ralph 'dear servant,' the word meaning only friend. Dillon signs himself 'your affectionate mistress,' and always mentions Sir Edmund as his 'grandfather.' These fancy relationships were much the fashion at the time. Sir Edmund directs a letter to his wife as 'my much loving sister Lady Verney at Claydon.' Mrs. Eure addresses her nephew Ralph as 'cousan,' while Ralph and his wife are always addressed as 'brother' and 'sistar' outside and inside their letters by Anne Lee, and they return the compliment in the same terms. Dillon's letter goes on : ' You will expect an account of my journay, and truely whilest it lyeth in me to answere your expectation, I will never deceave you—

take one brifely then.   Within two or three dayes
after comming to the water-side from London, I with
many more was entized a shipboarde by a flattering
winde, where we were noe sooner in a readinesse, and
even uppon the weighing of anchor, then there arose
a terrible tempest, the winds blew beyonde measure
high, and the rayne fell downe so violently and soe
fast as one might have thought the floodgates of
Heaven had beene sett wide open.   We landed presently and truely 'twas well, for had we stayed
aboarde our lives had beene all endangered though
within harbor.   How soe, doe you demande ? I
will tell you sir.   Our barke was beaten upp to a
fulle sea-marke, where she had her bottome strucken
out and was unseamed. . . . You see, servant, what
a deliverance this was, and how I have been preserved once more (and that peradventure ere you are
aware of me) to embrace you really and in your
proper person as now I doe in my thoughts, and
those ideas of you which doe still accompany your
most affectionate and obliged mistress James Dillon.'
The letter is addressed ' to my noble freinde Raph
Verney Esquire, at Mr. Hubberds house in Channell
Rowe, right over agaynst Sir Henry Fines his
stayres, deliver these. London.'

   In June 1633 James Dillon had failed in coming
to Claydon, where he was expected, and Ralph writes
to reproach him.   He defends himself by saying,
' though you will not invite me any more to Claydon
I dare goe thither without any more invitation, and

that you shall by the end of the weeke following or beginning of next, see by God's leave.   Present my service to my noble Lady Verney, my service to Mrs. Verney, my brother Doll, and the rest.'

After his visit Dillon writes from London to Ralph but more than half his letter is really addressed ' to the tow sweet soules,' as he generally calls them, i.e. Doll Leeke, and Mary the wife of Ralph, for whom he had evidently a sincere affection, as for her husband.   Mary, although the mother of a baby born in 1632, to whom Dillon was godfather, was still only a girl of seventeen, and she and her cousin enclosed in one of Ralph's letters to his friend a folded sheet addressed to him with ' Open not this letter till you all meet,' and ' doe us the favor nott to censur our lines,' in Mary's writing.   The paper was blank inside.   Dillon replies, ' I have here enclosed the letter from the tow soules that give life to the company wherein they are.   Reade it and see what it was they were haching when you writt your last to me, but for the world betray not any secret in it.   Upon Wednesday next with God's leave you shall have me there, till then farewell.   I should write to y^r goodly creatures but that Mrs. Hubbard [Doll's sister] is come.   Meats now at the table, I must end and to it without more words than that I am yours.   tell the tow faire ones from me that I am ashamed to see a letter from them tow wherein there is not one modest word.'   He is paying them out for sending him the empty sheet !

In July, Dillon sends ' five little combes ' to
Claydon, ' whereof there are three intended for my
Lady Mother [who seems to have joined in all her
children's quips and cranks and merriment], tow for
my daughter Verney [i.e. Mary], and my niece
Leeke. For these tow there are tow thimbles that the
one should not hurt a fine finger by the making of
my handkerchiefs, nor the other receive a prick in
working of my Lady's buttons. . . . Meate we cannot soe soon at Oxon as I thoughte, for I may not be
there this Act [i.e. commemoration], for some unexpected occasions defer my going. My humble
thankes to my Ladie for all her noble favours. unto
the tow sweet soules that are with her the services
of theirs and yours,' &c., &c.

Both Ralph and his father had some intention of
buying lands in the confiscated counties in Connaught
and elsewhere, which were much recommended by
their Irish friends. Lord Dillon was anxious to
forward any business which would help friends of his
son's. ' I am emboldened,' says Ralph, ' to desier you
to inquire how my Lord of Carlile's plantation in
Ireland goeth forward. His worship hath not the
whole Sheire to himselfe, for one of your welewishers
hath a verball graunte of a little share in it. . . .
I am easily persuaded that the Deputy (as well for
his owne benefit as the King's) would gladly have
the plantation in Connaught goe forwards.'

Dillon replies that ' my Lord of Corke ' had opposed Lord Carlisle and the Chancellor Loftus ; ' thus

of all hands they tugged when I came awaye. Since, all theire addresses were made to the King, who has referred all to the Deputy. This I learned within this quarter of an houre from my Lord Wilmot. . . . More cannot be absolutely said ere the Deputy comes to declare himself.' Lord Strafford had only lately arrived.

In another letter James Dillon says : 'I have lost the faythfullest shee-freinde, as by letters from my Lord of Corke I am too well assured, that ever I had or ever looke to meet with. My lady Digby is deade whom neither the teares of her father ; nor the sighs of her husband ; nor the prayers of the poore ; nor the moane of her friends nor (in a worde) the petitions and desires of all that ever knewe or hearde of her could withhold from the jawes of death.' Dillon's 'shee-freinde' was Venetia Stanley, wife of Sir Kenelm Digby, who was so proud of that somewhat frail beauty, that he devised all sorts of strange cosmetics, vipers' broth, &c., to preserve it, and set up a gilt bust on her tomb to commemorate her perfections. There is a picture of her painted after her death ; another, which was at Claydon with a crimson feather, probably given to Sir Edmund by her husband, who knew him at Court, has unfortunately been lost.

'My trouble for the loss of my Lady Digby has been great,' Dillon repeats in another letter.

Ralph soon after inquires for some 'noats,' which Dillon had made of Archbishop Usher's lectures. These appear in due time with proper depreciation on the part of the writer ; 'how to praise them more then to call them Dillon's and Usher's, I cannot imagin,' replied Ralph courteously.

His sister Betty was born on September 12, 1633, and Dillon sends congratulations and his service to 'the Ladie Verney the Elder, the yonger, the Lady Mairasse of Abingdon [Mary's father had been Mayor there], and to the prettie plumpe rogue, my brother,' signing himself 'Gilian Boyland,' the joke of which is lost.

'Out of Ireland I heare that the Deputy . . . hath . . . warned the countrie, that if men come not to him to compound for defective titles, they must looke for plantations [i.e. English colonies], which men say are very likely to go forward in Connaught and elsewhere. This I heare, but not from my father ; yet I advertise it, that if any use be to be made thereof it may be donne in tyme. Your father went yesterday to Theobalds [a hunting seat which had been bought by James I.] ; he was pretty well, but not perfectly soe after his fall.' Sir Edmund's horse had fallen with him on the road to Scotland with the king, and he had been reported as dead.

The question of titles to estates in Ireland was an exceedingly thorny one ; Charles, by an act known as 'the Graces,' had consented to accept the possession of land for 60 years as a bar to all claims of the Crown. It was one of Strafford's most high-handed proceedings, that he broke faith with men who failed to show titles by no fault of their own ; he wanted money to carry on the king's government, and the proceeds were very large of the compounding which Dillon here mentions ; he also honestly believed it to be for the advantage of the country that the turbulent lords should hold their lands of the king, instead of as heads of their septs, that tribal ownership which has been the source of so much evil in Ireland.

Ralph writes to Dillon : ' I chanced to cast my eie upon Sir Walter Raleigh's instructions that there is nothinge more becominge a wise man then to make choise of freinds, for by them a man shall bee judged what hee is. . . . Your brother Doll feares you will never leave your wild uncivill tricks, shee complaineth to mee every time I kisse her how you galled her lipps. I am sure I have had the greatest Losse, for where I have one Busse of her lipps,' &c., &c.

Dillon writes : ' I have the greatest desire that may be to followe the wise instruction of Sir Walter Raleigh ; but if . . . I looke for vertue in my friends as well as wisdome, ware being discarded ; look that you be not cast of in the firste place. . . . Present my service to my brother Doll unto whom I have sent a dozen of gloves enclosed in paper that is directed unto you, ten of them were I confesse long since due unto her, the other tow I pray you tell that I meane to make her deserve when I meet her next. farewell Sir. He ends who without end will be yours, J. Dillon.'

Soon after this Dillon was attached to the service

of the Lord Deputy, and constantly attended him
wherever he went, whether in Ireland, Scotland, or
England. He was staying with Lord Strafford in
London, February 1634, when Ralph wrote to inquire concerning the frightful sentence just pronounced by the Star Chamber on Prynne.

'Wee country clowns heare various reports of
Mr Prinn's censure. Some say hee is to loose his
hand and eares, others his hand only ; a third sort
there are that say neither hand nor eares, but hee
must pay £6,000, and endure ppetuall imprisonment.
I know none can relate the truth of this better than
yourselfe, for you love not pleasing amatory dreames
in a morninge slumber, nor lazie streachings on a
downie bed ; noe, your spirit scornes such soft con-
tentments. I dare say you rise early every Starr
Chamber day to heare the sage censures of the grave
councellours ; to you therfore I fly for information,
which I am confident you will not denie to your
friende and servant.'

Dillon replies (February 26) that Prynne was ' to
be degraded in the Universitie, disbarred at the Innes
of Court, he was fined, . . . I believe it was in
£4000 that most of the Lords did agree. He was withall condemned to the losse of his eares, whereof he is
to parte with one at Westminster, with the other at
Cheapside, where, whilest an officer doeth execution
on himself, the hangman is to doe it on his booke
and burne it before his face. He is to suffer perpetuall imprisonment . . . There were of the Lords

that counted this not enough ; they would have his
nose slitt, his arme cutt of, and penn and inke for
ever withheld from him, but these were but few . . .
he was pronounced an offender against the King, the
Queene, the Commonwealth, the Church, nay Christ
himself (said some), to whom he envied the honnour
due to his name. His booke was, you may remember, against playes, whereupon the Archbishop of
Canterbury tooke occasion to saye, that though he
was noe enemie to the lawfull use of them, yet he
was never at any in his life, howbeit others of his
coate could gett under the dropps of waxed candle
at a play, to be observed there, therefore counted noe
Puritans. This I observed spoken upon the bye,
and therefore I take notice of it to you, because I am
persuaded that you understand whom it is that this
concernes. There were other observable things, but
these . . . suffice to exceed the just measure of a
letter, which (if Seneca be to be credited), should be
perspicuous and short.'

Prynne's book, the 'Histriomastix,' was a silly
attack upon players as the ministers of Satan, with a
heterogeneous list of other sins—hunting, maypoles,
cards, music, false hair, and the decking of houses
with evergreens at Christmas. 'No man was ever
sent to prison before or after for such a mass of non-
sense,' says Mr. Green. For a libel written while
still in prison, Prynne, in June 1637, again stood in
the pillory, lost the remainder of his ears, and was
deprived of pen, ink, and paper. The absence of

sympathy for him in the nation at the first con-
demnation was curious, but as he passed to the place
where the sentence was to be executed three years
after, the street was strewed with flowers and the
people cheered loudly the words he uttered from the
pillory.   Laud, writing to Wentworth, complained
bitterly of his having been allowed to speak, and when
the remains of his ears were again cut, 'there was
such a roaring in the crowd as if each had lost a ear.'

Almost the first act of the Long Parliament was
to restore him and his fellow-sufferers to liberty.

The absence of all comment in the letters at this
time on the news given is remarkable ; facts only are
thought worthy of the dignity of letter-writing ;
opinions are irrelevant.

Ralph replies : ' I shall now begine to have a
better oppinion of my owne judgment then hitherto
I have had for makeinge choyce of a man not only
able but willinge to informe mee of Mr. Prin's censure : some men are able and not willing ; these I
canot love ; others are willinge and not able, those I
pittye ; you are able and willinge, and therin lieth
the happinesse of your freinde R. V.'

' My wife is now at Tunbrig above 60 miles from
mee drinkinge of the waters for her health ; poor
Nan Uvedall I left sick when I cam from London,
present my humble duty to my Lord your father ;
you may think there is little left but you may be
mistaken, all my servants [i.e. friends] are my fathers,
and I believe it is so with you.'

VOL. I.

On March 19 Dillon writes : ' The towne heardly did ever more abound with newes then now it doeth. It sayes that Wallesteine, by command from the Emperor, is murdered in Germany ; that the great Turke sends forth his edicts through the worlde to call the Jewes backe to theire Palestine, and the building of theire new Jerusalem ; that the French fleet and the Duch are both uppon the coast of England ; that the King of France is by the Duch and French proclaymed King of the narrowe Seas . . . and here is the King looked for tomorrowe. This I thinke is enough for me to write in one letter, and ennough for you to beleeve at one tyme. . . .'

In April, hearing that Ralph has had a bad fall, Dillon sends a messenger on purpose from London to inquire after his welfare : ' if he lives in whoes blessings or sufferings I share, you are the man.' On July 8 he writes : ' Dear S^r I am in hast ; in ex-treame hast, and readie to take horse ; yet before I goe, I must lett you knowe that I am infinitly thine. . . . Present my service to every one in Clay-don the boyes porter the kitchen boyes and the rest. Farewell, my heart, soe soone as I come backe I will see you.' On August 20 he is about to leave England and writes : ' I receaved some letters out of Ireland which expresse in my father vehement de-sires of seeing me suddenly there. To satisfie him my journey is resolved on ; and with all the speed that conveniently I may, away I goe. But ere I part, see you I must.'

Ralph, in November, says that 'nothing can be done in the Irish business at present.' He had promised his picture to Dillon ; 'it is not yet begun ; but within three weeks I shall come to London to stay for the greatest part of the winter and then it shall be my first work. There is noe newes of anything that concernes us, but that our old friend, my Lord Russell [son of the fourth Earl of Bedford], is newly come out of France, and in my judgment much betterd by his travels.'

In February 1635 Ralph says : 'I have now sat three times for my picture [copy of one by Cornelius Jansen now at Claydon], as soon as it is finished I would willingly send it to you, but I must first be informed by what way, for such a rare jewell deserves to be carried with much care ; my hart, farewell.'

There was an exchange of portraits, James sending his own, also by Jansen, to Ralph (which is now, alas ! missing). Dillon in the next letter is doubtful whether he shall be able to pay a promised visit to Claydon ; Ralph replies, ' The expectation of a misery before it falls makes a man miserable, put me out of my paine quickly, let me know what I must trust to. I had rather be knockt down with a bullet than languish in a consumption.'

In May 1635 Dillon writes from Dublin that he has had a letter 'from you sent by your kinswoman [Magdalen Faulkner] at my Lord of Barrimores. I hope to see her shortly and shall as much and as really desire to serve her as any freinde she has. I

have also a letter from your father which tould me of
a little gentleman [the picture of Ralph] whom I extreamely desire to see. He is like you I presume and
therefore I would not have him adventured over
hither, before you heare againe.' He then says that
in the north of Ireland, about 100 miles from
Dublin, his father tells him there is property to be
sold, very good land, to the value of £1,200 a year,
for £10,000. ' By taking upp moneyes, at use there
[i.e. London] ; and laying them out on purchases
here, you might with advantage discharge interest,
and after 20 years clearely gaine the lands purchased.
. . . My father says other hazards in regarde of payments from tenants, there is not in purchasing there,
rather than in other parts of the kingdom ; but in
troublous tymes, whither they be occasioned by intes-
tine rebellion or forreyne invasion, this parte of the
kingdome lyes farther from being sheltered by the
wings of the State then peradventure some others
doe.' ' I have written largely to your father and my
grandfather ' (as he calls Sir Edmund) ; he adds that
the Earl of Sussex, with whose wife the Verneys were
intimate, ' is the prime man of the Radcliffes, and one
unto whom our Sir George here is a kinsman [the
secretary and right hand of Lord Strafford, and therefore an important man to influence]. You are an
understanding man and therefore of this I shall need
to saye noe more.'

  ' For my Lord of Sussex,' replies Ralph. ' I must
tell you he is old, and his estate soe low, that few of

his kindred can gaine anything by his death, and
therefore I conceive he cannot do much with Sir
George ; besides all this, hee is under a cloud at
Court, that I may use your own language, " you are
an understanding man and therefore I shall need to
say no more." '

In June 1635 Dillon writes, much troubled, that of
' the sixe letters with advantage ' which he had written,
some on business that he ' desired to communicate to
none but yourself,' not above two or three have been
received ; one contained a bill of exchange for the
return of £20 borrowed from Ralph in London. The
difficulties of getting and sending money seem to
have been great indeed, and Ralph and his father
were always lending money to impecunious friends
who take a long time to return it, if at all.

Dillon repeats the details of the Irish scheme. ' It is
cleere that very great advantage may be had by taking
upp moneyes, and securing the use of them for 20
yeares, and laying them out on purchases here. Here
is now to be sould £1200 a yeare—my father is my
authour, who speakes knowingly—for less than
£10,000 . . . The use [interest] of all will amount
to £800 annually for 20 yeares. Will it not be a
mightie benefitt to gaine this £400 a yeare during the
20 yeares, and after the expiration of them the whole
£1,200 a yeare cleerly and for nothing ? . . . And
yet it is not more then you may have, and that of one
there—I meane the Earl of Annandale. Within these
tow yeares he would have taken £9,000, what he

will doe now I knowe not. For the rents thereabouts, my father who very well knowes it, because of his management of my Lorde Folliott's estate [brother-in-law of Dillon's stepmother], sayes that they are noe more uncertayne there than in other parts of the kingdom. Onely this I must tell you, that this estate lyes sixe score miles or neere it from this towne ; and is all planted with Scotts ; truly me-thinks these are noe considerable exceptions. The plantation of Connaught goes on. I have written to your father and my Grandfather largely of it, I will only add that my father knowes me a much obliged man to my grandfather there and thee. If he will ingage my father to serve him let him do what he thinks fitt. I assure you I thinke of the Marshall's sending to my father, not out of any fond humor, because of his nereness to me ; but,' and then comes a pretty tribute from the son to the father, ' merely and solely and totally because (I will conceale noe thought of mine from thee), I beleeve he cannot have in the kingdom a fitter instrument to further his business. He has a hande in the ordering of it him-self, he is one in the good opinion of Sir George Radcliffe and the Deputie : he goes the progress with him . . . he is one in a worde, faythful in what he undertakes and true to all trusts reposed in him. And if your father commaunds him I dare undertake for what lyes in his power . . . I shall goe the pro-gress here.'

In answer Sir Edmund writes : ' My deare Grand-

child, I cannot expresse the obligation I have to you
for your continuall care of mee and I shall presently
follow your advise . . . the businesse of the plantation has seemed here to goe slowly on ; but I feare it
hath appeared soe to keepe off Sutors : I shall now
put it home ; and then I shall trouble you with what
I have donne ; your commands to your freends heere
I shall obay ; but as yet I have seen none of them.
I hope your kindnesse to Mistress Uvedall [who was
just married] may recover her ; but I left her sick at
London and shall not see her till tomorrow. I am
in such huntinge hast that I will trouble you with
nothinge of newes, nor is there any heare worth your
knowledge.' He encloses a letter to Lord Dillon,
thanking him for ' his noble Curtisies ' and saying
that he will soon ' take the Bouldnesse to begg ' his
assistance.

The next year there were rumours of Dillon's
marriage, and Ralph writes to inquire about it.
Dillon replies: ' I was towards noe marriadge nor
crossed in any, nor by any bodie that came out
of England. My Lorde Deputie goes shortly into
England & it may be then a good tyme for my
grandfather then to order things concerning his
business. I presume I shall over with him, & give
you an account of all that may be looked for from
hence. I am very full of many things.'

In Ralph's reply there is some trace of anger at
the idea of Dillon's marriage. He was very fond of
his cousin Doll, and perhaps felt that Dillon had been

playing with her. ' I am glad to heare that those
reports concerninge your marrage are untrue. I hope
the first inventors of them will suffer by the ill
tongues of others, as you did by thers. If my Lord
Deputies cominge into England may bee a cause to
draw you hither, the sooner hee comes the welcomer
hee shall bee to mee, though I confesse I know but
few that are fond of his presence. Nues here is non,
but that your sister Nan Uvedall that married Mr.
Henslow is the mother of a brave Boy. I am now
goinge to meete some of my neighbours a Duck
Huntinge, I am told they have exelent Doggs. therfore excuse my hast.'

The allusion to Strafford's unpopularity came at
an awkward moment, for Dillon was on the point of
engaging himself to the Lord Lieutenant's sister,
Elizabeth, whom he married soon after. In the next
letter he confesses that there is a lady in question,
and says that he is coming to Claydon ' with the
leave of God on Tuesday ; ' he cannot come before
because the Lord Deputy ' goes on Saturday to Court
and I must attend him thither, because he takes his
leave there uppon Sunday & sees the court noe more
until the King comes to Rufforde. I shall tell you
stories when we meet ; you shall then heare that I
am indeed towards a mistress, & you shall ever finde
that I am wholy & faythfully yours. My blessing
& service to Mrs. Anna Maria,' his little god-
daughter.

He writes again from Windsor to Ralph, who had

proposed what seems to have been an annual visit of the two friends to Mr. Pulteney and Sir William Uvedale. ' The Deputy goes into Yorkshire and sayes I must kill a buck with him there this summer. Yet must I vehemently desire to see you.' Although Ralph will not be at home he will make a journey to Claydon and will come again later to see him. ' But I leave (under the rose be it spoken) a great pledg of my returne into these partes—my mistress not farr from London ; & if I cannot wayte uppon you before I goe into the north, within some moneth after I shall come back, perhaps of a good errand [his marriage] & in my way take you—my duty to my noble grandfather, my service to my Ladie Denton ; my Ladie Verney ; my Gossip ; my sweete brother ; Mistress Anna Maria.' Ten days after he says, ' My dear Heart, I went not to Claydon. I stayed uppon another design here. To avoyde this northern journey I have don it.' ' Say therefore by the next returne of the carrier when you will be home & thither I goe. I goe post Stonie Stratforde way, I shall be with my mistress at Hacney.' Aug. 3.—' My Lord Deputy is now going away, this night I attend *him* & the next week *you*. I sett no day because I will break none, for tow days you shall do what you will with me.'

Ralph writes : ' I wish your occasions would give you leave to go to Sir W. Uvedales with me, we would come back before the King comes to Woodstock. But I recant this wish, for I know there is one at

Hackney that would wish me hanged if I should prevaile. I will not run the hazard to lose her favour,
who though unknown to me, yet as she is yours, I
must serve.'

Lord Strafford in London writes to his wife at
Dublin : ' It is likely to be a match between Mr.
Dillon and my sister, so now I send to my Lord
Justice to perfect that which is to be done in Dublin
[about some land of Lord Dillon's], and that returned
I shall give them leave to proceed as shall please God
and themselves.'

In September Dillon is staying with Lady Elizabeth Wentworth at Hackney, and writes : ' What
might concerne in Ireland yᵉ affaire that here I attend
[probably Lord Strafford's decision about his father's
land] is allreadie dispatched. There remaynes now
nothing but to consummate it, which my mistress &
I doe intend on Tuesday come three weeks at Lowton Hall, in Essex. We shall both be gladd of the
honner of your presence at that tyme. If this ap-
poyntment hould not you shall heare from me with
God's leave before that tyme. I am not now to tell
you how much I vallew you, or what my desires are
to serve you.' There was one more visit to Claydon,
which must have been rather uncomfortable for all
parties, and for which Ralph thanks him rather stiffly
when it is over.

There is a great deal of human nature in the
world of these old letters, and it would be strange
if the brilliant young Irishman did not leave a sore

heart behind him in the breast of the girl whom he
had toyed with so affectionately (to say the lea..
of it) for three or four years. Nothing further appears in the letters, but some years later 'the prettie
plumpe rogue,' as he calls her, sends her 'humbell
service to her unkell Edmund,' and says, 'he may
rather style me his lean cozen than his fatt.' Her
father, Sir John Leeke, lost home and fortune in the
Irish Rebellion. Sir Edmund was in great money
difficulties, and Doll became a sort of lady com-
panion, treated however as one of the family, to
Lady Sydenham, who was about the Court with her
husband. They all three accompanied the king to
York before the raising of the standard at Notting-
ham, and the letters she wrote are very interesting.

In 1636 the letter carriers had been prevented
from going to London by the plague which was
raging there as early as June. 'There died this week
of the plague four score, being four more than died
the week before,' wrote Strafford to his wife, and
Ralph gives the failure of the carriers as an excuse
for not having written. He accepts the invitation to
the marriage. 'Since you are pleasd to make mee
a witnesse of your happinesse, I shall most willingly attend you at the time & place appointed,
but if the sicknesse or any other ill accident cause
any alteration in your Resolution, let mee know it,
for I shall alwaies claime the libertie you gave me,
not only to bee a partner in your Joyes, but sufferings.' Again, 'I am now at Highgate where I desier

to bee informd how you doe, how you are. Tomorrow I intend to visite my friends the Vere Gaw-
dys, & if you resolve to make Tuesday next your
happy day I'll wait on you at Lowton Hall on
Saturday or Monday, & if you please to send me
word where you shall bee this weeke I will attend
you sooner though it be but for an hower, for twill
bee very hard for mee, to bee five or six dayes soe
neere you & not to see you.'

'Dear Sir,' wrote James from Hackney, 'my day
holds. Tomorrow I must to Croydon to wayte on
my Lorde Deputie ; he is there. I am assured of it
by Sir George Radcliffe who brought along with him
yesterday the letter from my Lord Deputie, which
you may remember was wished for. Perhaps we may
meet with both on Tuesday' (at the wedding). The
letter probably concerned Strafford's action with regard to some land of Lord Dillon's. In Ralph's
report of the debate on Strafford's misdeeds (February 24, 1641), one article of the impeachment is :
' He caused the case of tenures to bee made, & caused
judges to subscribe it, & caused my lord Dillons
land to bee taken away by that case, without legall
triall.' Some arrangement had evidently been made
in view of the marriage.

There are no more particulars concerning the
wedding, at which Lord Strafford himself was present, but a month or so after, Dillon writes to Ralph
from London, hoping to see him there. There is,
however, a chill in the tone ; the Strafford connexion

naturally began to estrange him from his old friends.

' I thanke you for the honor you did me at Loughton Hall. My wife and I are now in Coven-garden ; where we finde the want of you and y^r familie. We hope to see you here as soone as the holydayes are over, for we presume you apt to doe the towne an honor and us a favor. If you can helpe the berrer to a Doe out of Whaddon Chase doe it ; its the sute of your most affectionate servant J. D. Poste. My wife will have her service remem-bered to you ; there is else noe Peace to be hoped for with her. She's angry because your wife has not had the first tender of her respects ; she sayes that shee would well have me for to knowe that Ladies should have homages donne to them ere men were thought of.' There is still one more sending of affectionate messages to ' my noble grandfather, y^r Ladie and my Gossip ; my brother and the rest.' There was still this half remembrance of poor Doll.

James writes once again before he starts for Ireland, hoping that Ralph is coming up to Covent Garden. ' The tearme [of parliament] they saye holds ; we have nothing new amongst us, nor ould that I desire to trouble you with, but the humble service of your most affectionate servant,' &c., &c. ' My wife will be your servant in despight of my teeth she sayes. Faythful Fortescue will serve you too if you will command him hee sweares.'

The plague, however, at this moment was raging

in London, and the Court had been driven away by
the fear of it ; the alarm was great in the country,
and Ralph replies from Claydon, where his son
Edmund had just been born : ' The unconstancie of
this wandringe sicknesse hath filled us with soe
much distraction that though I heare it decreased a
little this weeke, yet wee cannot absolutely resolve to
doe what wee most desier. I dare say there are few
in this family that thinke it lesse then a second plague
to bee kept from waitinge uppon your vertuous Lady,
whose goodnesse I hope will alwaies honour mee with
the title of her most humble servant.'

And so ends the correspondence. Dillon and his
wife returned of course to Ireland, where he was in
constant attendance on Lord Strafford, who often
alludes to his sister's presence with him in his letters
to his own wife. Dillon was cut off from the Verneys by all his new political and social interests, and
nothing more appears of him for some years.

His father was apparently much trusted by Lord
Strafford, for the latter, when writing to his wife
after his impeachment, says : ' Sweet Heart, I never
pitied you so much as I do now, for in the death of
that great person, the Deputy, you have lost the
principall friend you had there.' He still does not
believe in more than the death of his office. ' Yet
I trust Lord Dillon will supply unto you in part that
great loss, till it please God to bring us together
again '—that ' again,' which never was to come to
pass for husband and wife in this world.

In February 1642 Edmund writes to Ralph from
Dublin : 'here is your old freind Sr James Dyllam,
who often remembers you, and now his service to
you.' In 1642 James's father died, still young, and
he became Earl of Roscommon. When in the spring
of 1647 Lord Ormond found it necessary to give up
Dublin, &c., to the Parliament, Dr. Denton wrote :
' Hostages, wherof Rosse Common is one, are already
att Chester, and as I heare desire to stay there.'
James afterwards came to London, and saw Ralph's
wife there once or twice.

In 1647 Ralph was in France, and apparently
did not meet Dillon again ; but in 1650, about a
year after the execution of the king—a time of much
sorrow, public and private, to Ralph, whose wife was
dying at Blois—Lord Roscommon was staying in
Paris, which, Evelyn observes, was ' full of political
exiles,' and Sir Richard Hastings, the friend of both
and a kinsman of Ralph's, writes : ' Sir Richard
Browne [the Ambassador] and his lady are yours
and your lady's servants, and soe are all, I presume,
that knows you, for your civillyties will oblige an
ennemy (if you have any) to admire you. Sir, if you
have not hard itt, the Earle of Roscommon is dead,
whoe visitinge some of his frends in a compliment avoyded the light of a candell, ran hastily to
the chamber doore, and fell downe a greate paire of
staires, which caused his death.' The outer door of a
suite of rooms, in an old French town-house, usually
opens on to the slippery oak stairs, with a very narrow

landing ; hence probably the accident at once so commonplace and so tragic, which closed the career of this gifted and fascinating Irishman.

Ralph replies from Blois : 'I am infinitely sorry for the sad misfortune that befell my Ld Roscommon, hee was very unhappy in this world, but I am confident his afflictions heere are now recompensed with the joyes of Heaven, wch is a greate comfort to all that knew him, but espetially to myselfe, for non loved him better than your,' &c.

He left a little son of twelve years old to succeed him, afterwards the poet Wentworth Lord Roscommon, praised both by Dryden and Pope.

It is painful to trace the drifting apart of two friends who for seven years had been on terms of such affectionate intimacy. In a beautiful poem of Clough's, such separations are compared to ships at sea, lying side by side, 'When fell the night, up-sprung the breeze,' and at morn they can scarcely be descried long leagues apart.

> To veer, how vain ! On, onward strain,
>   Brave barks ! In light, in darkness, too,
> Through winds and tides one compass guides—
>   To that, and your own selves, be true.
>
> But, O blithe breeze ! and, O great seas,
>   Though ne'er, that earliest parting past,
> On your wide plain they join again,
>   Together lead them home at last.
>
> One port, methought, alike they sought,
>   One purpose hold where'er they fare, —
> O bounding breeze, O rushing seas !
>   At last, at last, unite them there !

Sir Harry Lee, Bart: of Ditchley.
from a picture by Cornelius Jansen at Claydon House.

241

CHAPTER XI.

THE LEES OF DITCHLEY AND LADY SUSSEX, ' OLD
MEN'S WIFE.'

' When are you married madam? Why every day, to-morrow—'
Much Ado about Nothing.

THE Lees of Ditchley in Oxfordshire, a place not
above 25 miles from Claydon, were hereditary friends
of the Verneys. Each successive Sir Harry during
five generations, for they were a shortlived race,
depended upon Sir Edmund and Sir Ralph to be
trustees, guardians, godfathers, executors, friends
and advisers in general, to themselves, and their
widows and orphans ; the amount of business for
this one family thus entailed upon Ralph throughout his long life was enormous.

The name of Sir Harry Lee is well known to the
readers of ' Woodstock.' It is idle to expect correct
historical details in a novel, but Sir Walter Scott has
made a curious medley between the later Lees, young
men of somewhat puritanic and parliamentary principles really living at the time of the Restoration,
with the 'loyal Lee' of strict monarchical and Church
views, Champion to Queen Elizabeth, who died forty
years before. There is a picture of him in his

eightieth year, with his hand on the head of a great dog,[1] and the motto 'more faithful than favoured,' now at Ditchley, painted by Cornelius Jansen, to which Sir Walter was evidently alluding in the last scene of his story.

He was succeeded by his cousin, another Sir Harry Lee, the first baronet, who married Elenor Wortley out of Yorkshire, and Sir Edmund Verney was warmly attached to both husband and wife, to each of whom he was trustee. There is a fine picture at Claydon, by Cornelius Jansen, of Sir Harry, with a wonderfully painted, deep lace collar, and a very intelligent, handsome countenance with bushy hair. Elenor's many marriages—with Sir Harry Lee and with three Earls in succession, Sussex, Warwick and Manchester—gained for her in Sir Ralph's cipher correspondence, the title of 'Old Men's Wife.' Sir Harry died in 1631, and the widow married two years after 'the prime man of the Radcliffes,' as Dillon calls him, sixth Earl of Sussex, a somewhat infirm old man.

---

[1] This 'faithful mastiff' guarded the house and yard, but his master had never taken much notice of him. He was kept for use only. One night, as Sir Harry was retiring to his chamber, attended by his favourite valet, an Italian, the dog followed them upstairs, which he had never done before. He was turned out of the room, but continued scratching at the door and howling for admission till absolutely driven away, when again he returned, and finally Sir Harry, being surprised at his importunity, allowed him to come in, and he at once crawled under the bed. In the dead of night a man entered the room ; the dog sprang forth and pinned him to the floor, and he was found to be the valet. He subsequently confessed that he had intended to murder his master and rob the house.

Sir Edmund was again trustee for her marriage
settlements, and had to look after her very miscel-
laneous possessions, ' the picture case sett with dyamonds, the gold watch sett with Turkies, the pair of
bell pendants with dyamonds, the silver warming
panne, and chafing dish, the posnett, porringers, two
cannes, the bason and ewer, and Spanish pott all of
silver, the household stuffe, black wrought bedd, and
sixteene horses and mares for draught etc.' ' My
lorde's plat,' she says ungratefully, ' not much, in his
own inventory but 179*l.*'

Lady Sussex was an energetic, active woman,
with strong puritanic and parliamentary tendencies,
and no love either for Charles or his queen. She was
very much younger than her husband, and though
' the sade retired life' which she led with him at
Gorhambury was not much to her taste, she did her
duty to ' my old Lorde,' for whom Sir. Ralph sends
down ' chise' at different times, ' which is so very
good that I am very sori i can ate non of it,' says his
wife.

She was a most voluminous correspondent, and
consulted Sir Ralph and his father upon everything.
She trusted to them to make the arrangements concerning her will, to give orders for carpets and curtains, and even gowns ; to find a husband for ' Nan,'
and to Ralph to send her parliamentary and Court
news, whenever his father was too busy ; ' as i thinke
you the best of men, so the best frinde I have next
your good father and mother.' She was godmother

to Ralph's eldest child, Edmund, and on the birth of his daughter, Margaret, she wrote : ' Non was more glader than myselfe to hear of your wife's safe delivery and that you have so brave a swite baby, which i pray god may live longe to bee a comfort to you both ; my prayes for my swite god-sone is that he may make as discrite and good a man as his father, and then i am suer he will give joy enofe to his frindes. i must ever chalenge an intrist in him, for belive me i love and wish as much good to you and yours as any can doo, ... i was telling your father how happy he was in you, and he sade he was so indede for no man hade a better childe, and many more good wordes he sade of you, which plesed mee very much to know you was uppon so dear and kainde termes.' She sends her dear affectionate love to his mother who had been ill. ' i harde of hur sicke-nes and recovery togathar or else i hade sufferde in-finetly ; she, your father and selfe are the frindes i must ever love and valy most ; i have sent my sarvant for i desier much to be asshurede how my lady and your good swite wife and baby doth ; you must remember me affecynat to your wife whom i love as much as your selfe ; when you are both wery of london i becech you com to this doll plac ; for you made me so happy in your companeyes the littill time i hade you hear, that i must bege of you to lett me have it this somer for a longer time.' On another occasion after a visit at Claydon she writes to Sir Edmund : ' I can not pay thinkes enofe

to you for this favour and your care of me ; the cold-
nesse of the day was more troublesome then hurtful ;
i cam home late but very will.'

Sir Harry Lee, Lady Sussex's only son by her
first marriage, was not on good terms with his
mother, and they saw but little of each other. He
had been annoyed at her second marriage, perhaps
at the large jointure of 3,000*l.* which she carried out
of the family, and Lady Sussex writes of her daughter-in-law's relations, the St. Johns, with great
bitterness. In June 1639 Sir Harry Lee had joined
the king's army at York, and Lady Sussex writes
sadly that she had not seen him before he went ; ' he
promisede to come this way as he went north, he has
falede me,' she says, and sends her letters to him
through Sir Edmund.

He returned from the army in July, ill, to his
house at Chelsea, and soon after his mother writes
that she is ' expecting much compiny, my Lady May
and Mrs. Garmen [Jermyn, whose husband was
afterwards engaged in the Army Plot], and my
sister Crofts, and my stable i doubt will bee more
then full with ther horses ; I belive the will stay a
wike with me. My sone,' she goes on, ' fill ill of the
smale poxe the day after he cam home, and is very
full of them. The begine to drye and the fisysions
sath he is, thinkes bee to god, past all danger. He
was extremly ill before the cam forth. I thinke you
swite Mr. Varney for your affecynat inquirie of him,
and for your fisit,' &c.

A day or two after comes a hurried scrawl : ' I cannot say much, my hart being fuller of sory then i can expres to you for my dear childe : The sent me worde he was past all danger, and now the tell me he is dede. I besech you sende this lettir to your father as sone as you can, and if your ocasyon cannot let you com to me now. i shall right very shorly to you agane.' . . . ' I pray god send your father safe and sone home '; he was still with the king in Scotland. Sir Ralph had meantime been writing to Lady Lee to enquire after her husband; he would not allow his wife to come to him for fear of infection. ' Sweet Maddame though I heard a rumour of your husband's sicknesse yet till Saterday night last that my lady Sussex was pleased to informe me I had no certainty of it, and though the same letter told me the physitions were confident hee was past dainger, yet I shall not bee satisfied untill I have it confirmed by yourselfe, for when my freinds are ill I confesse my feares overcome my hopes of their recovery, and hee is on that I soe much affect that I cannot but suffer with him.'

The loss of her son affected Lady Sussex a good deal, and she must have been pained at his will, which laid open to the world the breach that existed between them.

' This day,' writes Ralph to his father, in July 1639, ' I was sent for to Chelsey to the openinge of poor Harry Lee's will, and the deed of trust ' ; and he goes on to give the details to Sir Edmund, who was a trustee. First, certain lands are to be ' sould' for payment of debts. All his other lands in ' Bucks and Oxfordsheires' are leased to his trustees to pay his annuities, legacies, &c. ' My Lady Lee is his sole executrix, and she is to have the wardship of the heir, but if she die or marry [he remembered his mother's example], what is left to her is to be for the ward and the 'marrage' must be purchased to the ward's own use : ' hee is to be allowed £60 a year till hee is 14 and then £80 till hee is 21 and so is the daughter: and the younger son is to have £50 till hee is 14, and then £60, till hee is 21: then a farm which is about £120 per. ann. and £300 annuity for his life. The daughter to have £5,000 portion £2,000 whereof must be paid the day of her marrage or full age. . . . My Lady Sussex is not so much as named . . . which I am hartily sorry for as I know it will trouble her extreamly. Sir Harry Lee's debts are about £4 or 5,000. I pray bee advised how you accept of the trust,' says the prudent Ralph, ' for hee hath given away more then I beeleeve can bee raised out of the estate, and you are trusted already for my lady Sussex, and the writings may be soe drawne that your acceptinge this trust may bee a prejudice to her ; therfore I pray thinke well of it.' Sir Edmund seems not to have accepted the trust.

Sir Harry's widow, daughter and heiress of Sir John St. John of Lydyard, married Lord Wilmot in 1644, ' much concerned in the escape of Prince

Charles from England'; he was afterwards created Earl of Rochester, and his son, who succeeded him, was celebrated for his wit, his profligacy, and his poetry. There is a curious and interesting account of the wit's conversion to Christianity in the later months of his life, by Bishop Burnet. Sir Harry Lee's two sons succeeded each other; the eldest married Anne Danvers of Cornbury, another heiress, and he and his wife died within four months of each other in 1659, leaving two orphan daughters, wards of Sir Ralph's; one, Eleanor, married to Lord Abingdon, and the other to Thomas, Lord Wharton. There is a discussion when they wind up the affairs of the wardship whether they shall present Sir Ralph with £500 in plate or their pictures. He chooses the pictures, and two very bad Lelys are the consequence.

Another Sir Harry Lee succeeded his brother in 1659; he married Lady Elizabeth Pope, daughter and heir of Lord Downe, an Irish peer. She was a woman of a most overbearing temper, and insisted on being heir general to the North estates. The chief of them, Wroxton, went to her sister, Lady Frances Guildford, and although the trustees agreed that Lady Elizabeth had no title at all, yet they, 'being wonderfully scrupulous, advised a composition, her ladyshipp furiously protesting she would have half.'

Evelyn, travelling in a coach-and-six in 1664, tells how he came 'to Ditchley, an ancient seate of the Lees, now Sir Hen. Lee's; it is a low ancient timber house with a pretty bowling greene. My

Lady gave us an extraordinary dinner. This gentleman's mother, the Countesse of Rochester, was there.
There were some pictures of their ancestors, not ill-
painted,' says Evelyn, majestically, of the Vandykes,
Cornelius Jansen, &c.

Lady Elizabeth afterwards became the third wife
of Robert Earl of Lindsey, grandson of the Earl of
Lindsey, hereditary Lord Great Chamberlain, and
Lord High Admiral of England, in command of a
division of the army at Edgehill, where he was killed
with Sir Edmund Verney. Sir Ralph was very intimate with Lady Lindsey, who used to write him
long letters from Whitehall on all sorts of subjects,
almost as involved and exacting as those of the grandmother of the race, Lady Sussex. There is an oval
picture of her in the saloon at Claydon.

Her son, Sir Edward Lee, was created Earl of
Lichfield in 1674, and married, at the age of sixteen,
to Charlotte Fitzroy (King Charles's daughter by the
Duchess of Cleveland), aged fourteen. It was a very
happy marriage, little as this could be expected, and
Sir Ralph was called in as godfather of more than one
of their twelve children: ' 1690 Countesse of Lichfield
delivered of a son—Gossips Duke of Southampton
[one of Charles's illegitimate children], Sir Ralph
Verney and ye Lady St John,' the great aunt.

The king himself was godfather to the preceding
child. In spite, however, of this close proximity to
a daughter of Charles, Sir Ralph seems to have kept
quite apart, and never to have been to Court or had

the smallest intercourse with the king, of whose character and policy he so thoroughly disapproved.

But to return to Lady Sussex, the most important of the Lees to the Verneys. She had an unmarried daughter Anne, who was very intimate with both Ralph and his wife, whom she always styles ' Brother and Sistar.' She writes on fine paper, tied up with blue floss silk, a number of extremely *missish* letters, quizzing the young gentlemen staying at her mother's apparently, or riding down there. Each has his nickname. ' Boutared Eggs ' is one of them, ' who catches it ' from her according to the fashion not unknown to the young ladies of the present age. Another time she writes about a paste for making the hands white, the receipt for which is to be kept a dead secret. After expressing many regrets to Lady Verney, who had been staying at Gorhambury, for ' the loss of her sweet companie,' she writes : ' I spend my time most in excesing my fingers on the getar. When we parted we promised to right no comply-mentes, wich I am very glad of for I am very dall and can write no golden wordes. I am very sory that your finger is ill : the fines thing that can be my cosen baron sayth is poset curd with red rose lefes boyled in the milke and torned with ale.'

When Sir Ralph and his wife are driven away to France, ' Mistress ' Anne loses her ' playfellows,' as she calls them, and does her utmost to persuade her mother to take a trip to Blois, but in vain. She writes to Ralph : ' Sweet brother a shure yourself

that thare is no time that geves so much plesuer to
mee as when my thoughts ar on you and my deere
sistar : and I wish it ware in my power to testifi the
truth by any sarves that I might done you in this
place.   The continuance of these sade times ads much
to my unhapynes in that they will keepe mee so long
from seeing you, and to dele freely with you I think
my lady is resolved not to store.   You know hur old
umor, wich I presume she will contineu constant to—
y^t I belev nothing could prevale more with hur to
com In to those partes then your good compiny.   I
shall not be faling in what I can dow to parswade to
itt.   I will give you no forther trobell at this time
but done this right to beleeve that I am, Swet
Brother your afectnat sister and sarvant.'

Both Sir Ralph and his father were appealed to
by Lady Sussex again and again about ' maches ' for
Nan.   One of these was to the son of Sir Thomas
Middleton ; ' on of the best maches in inglande that
is to be hade,' [writes Lady Sussex] ; but the portion
demanded is too great for them she fears.   ' The
estate lies on the edge of Wales, the grandfather was
a merchant, and the grandmother a Dutchwoman ;
they . bred the young man up at home, his mother
being very tinder of him ; his father seems to be a
good solede man, very harty for the Parliament.
The sone is littell, hath wite enofe, I belife, a littell
refining woulde make him very pasable.'   The negotiation, however, comes to nothing ; Nan continued
unmarried for several years, and appears later as

the wife of Mr. Berkeley, afterwards Lord Fitz-Hardinge.

The danger from small-pox is terrible, Sir Henry had died of it two years before, and Nan is taken ill of it in 1641.   Lady Sussex writes to Ralph in much concern : 'Nan i hope is past the worst, and the till me the think, she will not have much disfiger, i pray God, keep us all from it, for it tis a grivous disise and oncomfortable.'   It had broken out at Latimer, where Lady Sussex had been visiting her mother, who married the first Earl of Devonshire as his second wife, and which still belongs to the Cavendishes.   Ralph writes : ' I am extreamly sorry to heare of the ill accident that happened at my Lady Devonshire's, but much more troubled to think how far you have hazarded yourselfe, in venturing so soon to Latimer, yet I hope the dainger is not so great, as tis reported ' ; he ends with ' the infinite Respects and favours you obleege me in, I cannot rekon them, much less express them,' and he blushes at such poor payment.

In September 1639 comes a bit of gossip from Ralph : ' Newes there is none, yet I cannot but tell you that Mrs Cary was this morning made Mrs Herbert.   I wish her as much comfort as I shall receive by our coming to Gorambery next weeke.' [1]

---

[1] Margaret, daughter of Sir T. Smith, Master of the Requests, an old friend of Sir Edmund's, first married Thomas Cary, second son of the Earl of Monmouth, one of King Charles's Gentlemen of the Bedchamber (who was afterwards said to have died of grief at the king's death) ; secondly, Sir Edward Herbert, the Attorney-General.

Lady Sussex replies : 'i am glade he hath made a good chose : it hath beene longe spoken of, but she woulde not acknowledge it to me. he is rich and full and she is a fine lady, and well knowes how to manage a good fortine. this is all i have to say now.'

Lady Sussex was apparently not of an easy temper. After her mother's death at Latimer she and her brother quarrelled fiercely about the will. She writes to Ralph in '42 : 'My brother ned is a woful man to have to do with, so furious, and everything must be as he list.' Again : 'i must not goo into the hose [Latimer] for my brother in his pasyon swore i shoulde not com within the dores, but i woulde fane know what the lawere sath was my right in all thinges ; i woulde not have them thinke me cuch a fole but that i woulde know my right in every thinge, though i take nothinge but what the will give me.' In another letter she says : 'My brother and i have hade many disputes since you was hear of thos littell poore thinges my lady gave me : let me intret the favour of you to axe some lawer whether the givinge me all in hur boxes and cabbe-nets only money exceptede whether i am not to have the golde. So for hur boxes, ther is in on boxe very fine sheets, i hear att lattimers, some roght about and with a border of golde and lasede, and cortens and cossin cloths rought all over, whether these must passe by the name of hur linen, for she gives all her linen to to of hur grandchildren not naminge hur householde linen, but in generly hur linen. let me intret this favour to your most affecyonat frinde.' Later on she says her brother and she are now 'frindes in show.'

She and her old husband had hired Lord Bacon's house, Gorhambury, in Hertfordshire, near St. Albans, from Sir Thomas Meautis, the husband of Anne Bacon, daughter of the great chancellor's half-brother, Sir Nathaniel, who with her brother inherited Lord Bacon's estate.[1]

Lady Sussex was often uneasy about her tenure of the house, the trouble of which fell as a matter of course upon Sir Ralph. Sir Thomas Meautis threatened to come and live there, and she writes to Ralph that her landlord and his wife are come to stay with her. 'I belife they will stay this fortnight. pore man he lokes miserably; he hath a belife that this are will recover him, so i could but in sifility desier ther stay as longe as the plesede.' Sir Thomas, however, died before the old Earl, and Lady Sussex continued to live there till her third marriage, to Lord Warwick. Lady Meautis afterwards married Sir Harbottle Grimston, one of the most prominent of the parliamentary leaders, yet speaker of the first parliament of the Restoration, and lived at Gorhambury, where Sir Ralph used to visit them in later years on almost as friendly terms as with its former inhabitants.

Lady Sussex continually troubled Sir Ralph with all sorts of petty commissions, even her coals cannot

---

[1] Mr. Bacon lived at Shrubland Hall, Suffolk.

be had without his help ! She writes : ' The felo was
hear this day with a lode a coles ; i thinking your
sarvant had agreed with Falcon sent thether for a
chaldron and a halfe and he sent them, but my
sarvant till mee the are very bad coles ; i becech you
let your sarvant pay him for them ; i thought he was
a knave and would not employ him any more. . . .
it will be a month i fear, for this man can buy but a
chaldron and a halfe at a time, so he can bringe but
4 chaldron and a halfe a wike. . . . i am glade
your man hath agreed in another plas for twenty
shillinges. . . . most of these feloes that carry coles
lives nine or ten myles off at Bushey.' Sir Ralph is
commissioned to get all sorts of things for her, as the
following extracts from her letters show :—' To peses
i have sent for of the golde color [damask], not that
i have any present use for it, but truly it tis so very
good and chepe i will by it for use hereafter.' . . .
' My thinkes to you for my sattine ; it cam very will ;
some of it i employ for the backes of chers ; the rest
i entende for cortines ; when the chinse stofes come
in, if you see any prity ons remember me i pray you
for to or three peses.' . . . ' I am very sory i dide not
consider of the figerde sattine when i was at chelsey
for truly though the prise be unresonable i hade
rather give it then by any of the figerde sattines that
are to be hade hear ; thorty shillinge the yarde the
axe, and the color lokes lyke dort to that i have.' . . .
' The carpet truly is a good on. . . . if i can have that
and the other for forty ponde or a littell more i would

by them ; the woulde bee very fine for a bede, but
onlie if one may have a very good peniworth ; but in
these times [1640] money is the best commodity.' . . .
' For the carpets if the gronde bee very doll and the
flowers or workes in them not of very plesent colors
i doubt the will bee to dole for to suet with my
haninges and chers.' . . . Concerning the choice of a
small carpet : ' If it will not sarve for a windo it will
sarve for a fote carpet i want for that use.' . . . He
sends her ' so many good pens and such good paper
and so chepe ' she hopes to write ' a better hande ' ;
but her scrawled letters do not show that she had any
success. She would be glad to have some ' calico
spotede with golde cuch as mrs barbordes bede is
lynede with.' . . . ' I must truble you to get me a
hansom mofe bought . . . a fasyonable mofe for one
as tale as your wife' (probably a present for Lady
Verney). For the trimming of a ' swite bage' she
sends most minute directions : ' If you woulde ples
to imploye somebody to chuse me out a lase that hath
but very littell silver in itt and not above a spangell
or to in a peke i thinke woulde do will ; i woulde not
have it to hevy a lase ; about the breth of a threpeny
ribinge very littill broder will bee enofe ; and desier
Mrs Varney i pray you to chuse me out some
ribinge to make stringes ; six yardes will be enofe ;
some shadoede sattine ribbinge will be the best of
forpeny breth and i woulde fane have some very
littill eginge lase as slite as may bee to ege the
stringes and but littill silver in it ; ten yardes will

be enofe.' . . . 'Do me the favour to chuse me sixe
wine glasses ; i have cuch littill ons and none as
my lorde uses to drinke in.' She also buys a dozen
'white plats,' and another commission is the mending
of her sable gloves.

In November 1639 Sir Edmund asked her to sit
to Vandyke for her picture, and there ensues a long
and difficult negotiation concerning it, as she is hard
to please, and cared about her personal appearance,
to judge by the following note to Lady Verney, sent
with some myrrh water : ' I have longe usede it and
finde it very safe. tis good for the hede and to make
on lok younge longe ; i only wete a fine cloth and
wipe my face over at night with it.' On the other
hand she writes to Sir Ralph : ' Your father sendes
me worde Sr Vandyke will do my pictuer now—
i am loth to deny him, but truly it is money ill
bestowde.'

Later on she writes to Sir Ralph : ' Put Sr Vandyke in remembrance to do my pictuer wel. I have
sene [seen] sables with the clasp of them set with
dimons—if thos that i am pictuerde in wher don so i
think it would look very wel in the pictuer. If S^r
Vandyke thinke it would do well i pray desier him to
do all the clawes so—i do not mene the ende of the
tales but only the end of the other peses they call them
clase I thinke.' Later on : 'i am glade you have
prefalede with Sr Vandike to make my pictuer lener,
for truly it was to fat, if he made it farer, it will bee
for my credit—i see you will make him trimme it

for my advantige every way.' Again : 'I am glade
you have made Sr Vandike minde my dres. when it
is don i becech you pay him for it and get a hansom
frame made to put it in and then present it to my
lady and your father from me but the frame I will
pay for to.' . . . 'I pray God the good cobbler may do
as well by your father as he hope for.' Sir Edmund
had been consulting a quack doctor. Then come
some curious details concerning the prices paid for the
picture itself, and to the man who copied it : 'I am
glade you have got hom my pictuer, but i doubt he
hath nether made it lener nor farer, but to rich in
ihuels [jewels] i am suer, but it tis no great mater for
another age to thinke me richer then i was. i see you
have imployede on to coppe it, which if you have, i
must have that your father hade before, which i wish
coulde be mendede in the fase, for it tis very ugly. i
becech you see whether that man that copes out Van-
dicks coulde not mende the fase of that—if he can any
way do it, i pray get him and i will pay him for it.
it cannot bee worse then it tis—and sende me worde
what the man must have for copinge the pictuer,
if he do it will, you shall get him to doo another for
me. let me know i becech you how much i am
your debtor, and whether Vandicke was contente with
the fifty ponde.' The price of the copy was to be
' eyght ponde.' Even supposing the value of money
to be about four and a half times what the same sum
represents at present, 'fifty ponde' is little enough
for a 'full length picture,' as it is described in

the old lists, 'in a blew gowne with pearle buttons.' The difficulties of conveying the portrait to Lady Sussex at Gorhambury were extreme, and various means were proposed. Ralph has bought her for 40*l.* a looking-glass 'from fines [Venice],' on which she had set her heart, and she writes : ' the cole wagen will be in London this weke but I doubt he cannot carry the pictuer with the glase. if he cannot, I think that may bee sent safe by the wagen of sentarbornes [St. Albans].' Again : ' I am very glade if a coppell of porters would undertake to bring it done carfully and for any resonable matter, suer that it is the saffest way. But if the will not I will sende a hors for it with paniers. what yóu adfise me i will do.'

At last the picture is received at Gorhambury, and the original writes : ' Swite Mr. Verney, the pictuer cam very will, many harty thinkes to you for it. the fram is a littell hurt, the gilt being robbede off. the pictuer is very ill favourede, makes me quite out of love with myselfe, the face is so bige and so fate that it pleses me not att all. It lokes lyke on of the windes poffinge—but truly I thinke it tis lyke the originale. If ever i com to London befor Sr Vandicke goo, i will get him to mende my pictuer, for thow I bee ill favourede i think that makes me wors than I am.' There is here good proof that Vandyke did not flatter his sitters, as he has been often accused of doing. Lady Sussex was a woman of influence whom it might have been a temptation to propitiate at the cost of half an inch of cheek, if the higher interest of truth in art had not been uppermost in the mind of the painter. The picture appears again in the correspondence in 1646. Lady Sussex announces her approaching marriage to Lord Warwick, and she is anxious that Sir Ralph should allow her to purchase from him the Vandyke painted for Sir Edmund.

She writes : ' Sr i shoulde say somethinge to you but you must not misintrept me for it ; it is conserninge a pictuer ; and i know you are so much my frinde that you woulde not willinly part with any of myne ; but consideringe you can make no present use of them and i thinke you haveinge three, give me this confidence to saye this my desiers to you ; which is my lorde much desieringe a good pictuer of mee att lenth and i haveinge non ; and i confes not willinge to bringe any hether onles itt were a good noble pictuer which i cannot till how to compase without your favour and helpe ; for i never hade any pictuer drane that was considerable but that you have which Fandicke drue for mee ; that if you woulde part with ; i shoulde take itt for a great cortesy ; and so much as itt coste you woulde bestowe uppon any thinge else that woulde keepe mee in your memory the copy of the pictuer you haveinge allredy ; now i have sade all this i leve itt to your good plesuer if you can part with the pictuer ; i will not saye from whence i hade it ; never do you misintrept me for i protes i shoulde not have desierde itt from you but for this ocasyon i till you.' Ralph, however, has no mind to part with the Vandyke, and sends the following polite reply : ' Maddam It beeing impossible I should deny you anything I must beeseech you not to require your Pictur from mee ; you know to whome t'was given, how hee valued it, and that nothing but death could make him part therwith, and I hope you doe not thinke that I esteeme it on jott lesse than him that left it mee. I confesse my selfe guilty of many follies and reduced to many greate and sad extreamities, but I doe not know wherein I have soe farr forfeited my selfe (by failing in my duty and respects to you) as to be esteemed unworthy to bee the owner of that Jewell ; neither will I yet beeleeve you thinke me soe, but rather that you doe this only to try the truth of my professions even in the hardest point you could possibly imagen or invent, wherby you might judg whether I am (as I have ever express'd myselfe) with-all my hart and soule, Madame, Your most faith full and perpetuall servant.' This Vandyke has unfortunately disappeared, probably when Lord Verney's ruin dispersed many beautiful things ; the pictures, it is true, were heirlooms at Claydon, but he seems to have carried several to his house in Curzon Street, where they were at the mercy of his creditors.

As soon as the Short Parliament opened in April 1640, Lady Sussex was anxious that Lord Warwick should undertake the proxy of her old husband, who was too unwell to attend the House of Lords. She writes to Ralph : ' Swite Mr Varney i must thinke

you for your complyment to my lorde Warwicke,
which i am suer was above what we could have riton.
Your father sent me worde you cariede the proxy.
You have now the serious afares of parliment in con-
sidearasyon, won should not bee so unsivell to troble
you with littell matters . . . but i will adventer it.
my desier is to by mee as much sattin of which of
thes couler you lyke best, as will make a cote for a
child, about fore year olde but do not send it doun
yet. . . . To your good wife i am so much indettede
remember most afecyonatly with many thinkes for
ringes, which i will keep all.' In a P.S. : ' I hear from
your father that you dide not deliver the proxsy
which is due for i am suer you was willinge to have
done my lorde that cortisy.'   Lady Verney had been
ordering 'ringes with posies ' on the death of Lady
Sussex's mother, the old Countess Dowager of Devonshire. The ' sattin ' was for little Edmund, Lady
Sussex's godson, so that the gift was delicately devised. In 1642 she reverts again to her desire to make
her godson the present of a coat, and writes to Ralph
thus : ' Now i have a requist to you that you must
not denye me ; for truly i cannot sende it to anybody
that will do it to my likeinge i am suer ; but you
must not speke of it nether ; it tis to by my prity
godson a very hansom sattin cote and get it made . . .
and then sende me the bill of all ; i must give it him
holy . . i hope is ague will not do him hort if it
continue but save fue fits ; i pray god bles him with
longe life and that he may bee as good a man as his

father and then i am suer he will bee a childe of much
comfort to you.'

In August 1640, when the king was just starting
for York, on his road to Scotland, Sir Edmund,
suffering from his sciatica, 'took another turn at the
Bathe,' and Lady Sussex writes to Ralph : 'I longe
much to hear what your good father is lyke to finde
by the bath—for your selfe, i presume will, by getting
an acquantince with many fare ladyes, and much
jholity will be amonst you, but i pray be suer your
father siffility do him no hort now, but doo you
undertake all thinges of compiny, but have a care of
your health to, for i have harde the bath is a very
aguies ill are [air] therfor i pray bee not out of your
loginge to late a nights. I confes i cannot desier you
from your father whilst hee stayes att the bath, but
when you retorne i hope i shall have your compiny,
and Mrs. Varney without danger to hur. Belive me
you are both as near to me, in my affecyon as my
one, and must ever bee so. it were not sivell to
keepe you longer from your good compiny therefore
i will only assure you that you have not any frinde
that wishes you happines more truly then your very
affecyonat frinde . . . the nues of the kainge gooinge
to yorke trubles me extremly. pray god his stay
may be so littel that your father nede not folo.'

Lady Sussex was very politically inclined, and
followed every step of the great contest as furnished
by Sir Ralph with deep interest. In the spring of
1641, when he writes to her of the marriage contem-

plated between Princess Mary and the Prince of
Orange, she says, ' i thinke you for your nues ; i
see the will adventur to mary, for all the fear of the
times.'

In April of the same year Ralph negotiates again
about her husband's proxy, and she writes to him :
' i am glade you sade that to my lorde of northum-
barlende for my lordes proxsy ; you are so considerate, discret and good that it tis beyonde all that
can be sade ; i confes i will not give my consent that
my lorde robortes shall have my lorde proxsy, but
wee shall have time enofe to thinke of that.'

Another piece of business in which Ralph gives her
valuable assistance is concerning certain fishery rights
of hers which have been infringed.   Innumerable
letters pass between her and Ralph on the subject as
to how the poachers are to be stopped.   He delivers
a petition for her to Parliament in April '42, signed
by several lords, and she writes : ' Suer this com-
mande from the parlyment when it tis puplishede will
friton the fishermen from cominge uppon our watter.
. . . i woulde fane see a coppy of the order that the
parlyment gave for us. . . . you are more profident
of my pors i am suer then anybody else woulde
bee ' : for she anticipated that the petition would
cost a great ' dell of mony.'

When Sir Edmund joined the king's army in
July '42 she is much concerned for him, especially as
his health was a good deal shaken.   He pays her a
farewell visit just before he starts, and she writes to

Ralph : 'i am hartily sory to find you have so sade a hart; the wisest i know are most considerate; trublede thoughts cannot helpe anythinge . . . i becech you have a care of yourselfe.'

In the unsettled state of the country after the war had begun her friends pressed her to move to a safer place than Gorhambury, but she would not desert her old husband, who could not well be moved : 'i hope in the lorde pese will com . . . ; if ther bee not i shall bee in a most misirable condisyon, for i will not stor from my good olde lorde what some ever bee coms of me.'

She desired to arm her servants, and wrote to Ralph : 'I must becech you to get some body to boy six caribens for me and some twenty ponde of poder i hope that will be enofe to defende us hear if it bee not poder enofe, as much as you thinke fitt, for i woulde fane have you and your lady as safe hear as at london, which truly i belive you will.' Ralph and his wife paid her a visit in August '42. Apparently he thought that Gorhambury was a safe place, for Lady Sussex writes to him in September : ' To [two] lode of your stofe is com, which i have set up in the safest plas of my hose ; i hope it will bee so and all myne hear ; ' though, as she says in another letter, 'wee bee thretonede because we gave nothing to the parlyment.' Her house was never attacked, but there was much reason for alarm, and she was glad to secure through Sir Ralph a ' Protection ' signed by Essex. She writes to Ralph in September

'42 : ' I thinke wee shall all bee ransakede therefor i
becech you get cuch paper for mee as you have for
the safty of Cladon.'

She was much affected at Sir Edmund's death at
Edgehill, and wrote most sympathising letters to
Ralph. Through all her own troubles she was often
careful for his comfort, and sent special dainties ; on
one occasion 'pots of gely of pipens . . . it tis holl-
som for you . . . and the perly cakes is very good,
nothinge in them but oringe watter perle '; and
another time ' podinges.' She complains of feeling
' out of tune,' but the ' fissicke ' she takes to cure
herself does not seem to improve her : ' My fissicke
made me so out of tune in my hede that truly i
dorst not right.' Again : 'i toke some fissicke
hopinge it woulde have made my sperets somethinge
cherfuller, but truly i finde myselfe still so doll and
sade that i take littill ioy in any thinge in this worlde ;
i pray God give me a cherfuller hart.'

In April '43, when soldiers were quartered at St.
Albans, Lady Sussex fears they will come to Gorhambury to search for arms, and hears that it was
said she was a ' casicoleke '; . . . 'but the gentillman
the spoke it to assure them i was noe papes nor malig-
nant . . . i am confident the parlyment will not give
them any warents . . . but i will sende to sr tomis
chike to speke to my lorde manchester, that in the
hopper hose he will have a littill care of us ; and in
the lower hose i know you both will if you hear anythinge intendede that way.' Again : ' my protexsyon

hath don me some good : . . . the take very many horses up hear ; . . . one of the men goinge to chesome the lade hold uppon his horse so i had fane to sende the protexsyon and when the saw that the let my man have my hors agane.' Ralph's 'stofe' is now sent back to him in London, and Lady Sussex sends also to his care ' twenty dises, a foyder and to dosen of plats.' The dishes she bids him 'put of [i.e. sell] : i hope you may get fore and a leven penes hapeny an once for them.' . . . ' I am most glade your stofe cam all safe to you ; it plesede mee when i hade somethinge of yours under my care ; it gave no truble ill assure you ; nor never can anythinge bee so to me . . . but a plesuer when i may have pouer to sarve you in anythinge, for as you are you must ever be the frind i shall most valy.'

She was evidently a very determined woman, and though she desired to deal fairly with every one, she was not at all inclined to be weakly indulgent. In '43 she writes, in view of still worse times coming, ' i have a very good mynde to pay my debts whilst i have where withall to pay itt for it would bee a very great affliction to mee to have any cuffer lose [suffer loss] by mee ' ; and in another letter concerning an abatement to her tenants : ' I shoulde bee very willinge to yelde to anythinge that is resonable ; but if the make use of my fortune for ther one paments, and let mee bee without my rent, then i must loke to myselfe.' The estate of her grandchild is so lessened in value that they beg she

will abate according to her proportion and be at half
the loss that may happen to the tenants by pillaging.
In July '43 her husband died ; and she writes to
Ralph : ' Now i must till you that which may bee
you will harly belive, that I hartily cuffer for my
good olde lorde how truly grows so very weke that i
fear he will not holde out very longe.' One arm and
leg is paralysed, though they feel warm ; ' he eats his
meat as well as he used to do and slipes well ' ; a few
days later ' he is grown so infinit weke, not able to
put on anythinge but lapede in a shete and a blanket
and so lade uppon his palet . . . he hath exprest so
much love and respecte to me all the time i have
hade him, that truly i cannot but bee very hartily
sensable of his lose : i woulde not neglect anythinge
for his beriall that may expres my love and valy of
him ; it will cost me a great dell of mony, but i must
not be falinge in my last sarvis to him.' The funeral
cost her little less than 400l. He is buried at ' borom '
parish church to ' nue hale,' where a chapel, adjoining
the chancel, was built by his ancestors for their
tombs. Ralph lends her a black bed. ' Blakes '
must be provided for the relations : and a ' fale ' for
herself. She begs for a pass for all her ' compiny '—
two coaches with six horses and six that drew the
hearse, and six or eight-and-twenty men on horseback besides footmen. She is resolved not to spend
all that the herald suggested, but would be content
to have ' a greate flage, and a crone, helmett and sorde
and spors.' After the funeral she writes : ' Good

man i am confident he is happy, and i am glade he is lade amonst his one blode.' She was hoping for a visit from Ralph and his wife, ' which will bee very cordiall to mee ; truly i am so sade i know not what to do with myselfe ; and the dispersinge of my family [i.e. household] will truble me much ; but ther is no remedy i cannot holde on in the way i am in ; . . . this wike i will prepare to receve on Sonday, that will make me the better fittide to order all my affars i hope.'

In November Ralph departed for France and writes to her in the lowest spirits just before he sailed. Lady Sussex writes sad letters to him after his departure, and laments the state of the country and her own misfortunes : ' i live the saddist uncomfortable life that ever any dide ; for you know how littill i have to ples mee from any of my one blode, but i mene to trye whether i can get a rome or to att my lady gorges that i may goo some times thether ; though i belive i shall finde but littill to ples me ther, yet some littill change will bee bettir then all to gather in this doll plas.' Again in '44 : ' I am a very beger, and itt trubles me the more becase i cannot make good my promis of what you know of ; but if itt ples god wee live ever to see better times agane all shall bee made up.'

The next year, '45, matters have not improved for Lady Sussex, although she is on the parliament side and they are now in the ascendant : ' I confes i have not a frinde left mee hear whom i can anyway relye uppon : . . . i pray god give me comfort in the best thinge, for in this world i can expect none ; . . . may be you harde i was towards matrymony, but i may till you truly ther is no cuch mattir, for i thinke i shall never finde a man to my hart. . . . My sone's wife last marede the lorde [Rochester] may bee a warning to me, she haveing but nuely got hur lande of the sequestrasyon but above to thosonge ponde debts was lade uppon hur estate. . . . the time here are cuch that i dare not stor nor remove anythinge. . . . i have bene out of tune all this wintir and in a longe cours of fissicke, but now i thinke god resonable will in health and shoulde bee most glade if i had pouer to sarve you any way hear.' . . . 'It tis not to be tolde you the fexsasyons i have hade in my [fishery] suts ; picering [Pickering] hath plade the part of a most arant knave with me agane.' Ralph applies to her for a loan of money, being pressed by one of his sisters to make up her dowry : he sends her a present at the same time : ' I beeseech you bee pleased to receive halfe a dozen combs and a little combe box I bought at Paris, wch is soe very a trifle that I durst not send it had I not remembered twould sute well with your glasse trimed with silver. Maddame, though this is but a toye, yet being in fashion here, I hope you will accept it.' Lady Sussex, in reply, cannot promise much help, but suggests his selling some of his things, notably the silver porringer she had given to her god-son. She gives a lengthy account of her own straitened condition : ' Your word was security enofe to mee to

parforme what you desier ; but to my grife I may
truly assure you that my estate is falen so low, and
the unsartinty of itt and my life cuch haveinge nether
lese nor inheritance that any cecurity from mee cannot anyway bee considarable ; . . . my plat beinge all
gone but a very littill left ; and some of my gemes gon
to ; for this last year and halfe i disborst much more
then my cominges in ; my fiftes and twentyes part i
pade and ten ponde a wike for an extrordanry : . . .
contribusyons on both sides : . . . belive me uppon
my worde and truth i have tolde you nothinge but the
very truth of my fortune as now itt tis : . . . the hole
kaindome beinge as itt tis, wee cannot till how longe
wee may injoy anythinge : . . . and for my littill
rents that are due now i owe more then the com to ;
it trubles me hartily that i cannot assist you so fare
as i woulde do in this bisynes . . . for your sistir ;
how i may till you hade a thosonde [i.e. settled on her
so far as that she had £40 yearly interest paid her]
formerly if her name was pen ; it was the first i
partede with and afterwardes carye : . . . mony is so
hard a commodity to come by now that many cuffers
much ; i have in good faith but on cordiall [the
cypher word for £100] and a halfe left mee of that i
hade before you went ; and my pore sistir martens
children is in cuch want and right to mee daly and i
can do nothing for them, and some others as near to
me to ; and my brother Edword so unworthy and
naght, hath not nor will not part with a peny to any
since my mother debth ; now let me till you i thinke

you hade best let me put of the bason and euer and candillstikes and if god sende the times mende and that i have life i hope i may make itt up agane . . . and i will do my best to put of your blake things . . . the plate and blakes will fech near threecore i hope if i can get in my rents i may make it up a hondreth . . . i am resolvede to sell all i have before i will adfentir to boro agane.'

Ralph in reply writes that his sister is in such want of her dowry he must raise money however he can : ' rather than one soe neare me should want her portion and lose her perferment I must needes part with that you gave my Boy, which I have ever kept as an eminent testimony of your love and bounty, to myselfe and family. But now it must goe for I know not any other way. Therefore if my friend . . . sends for these things let them bee delivered into his owne hands, I beeseech you.'

In spite of her poverty Lady Sussex cannot help writing to Lady Verney : ' Swite madam if you make any stay in paris and see any prity thinges that is not to chargable fitt for my waringe beinge a wido send me worde ' ; and she seems also to have consoled herself with entertaining her friends, as she mentions having ' a great dell of compiny to dyne.' This was followed up the next year, 1646, by the reports of her marriage with Lord Warwick (Admiral of the Fleet under the Parliament) which reached Ralph from various quarters. Sir Roger Burgoyne writes to him : ' Certainly the match will go forward and I question not but that it is made known to you before this time from herself.'

Ralph in return thanks him for sending the news ; 'for whither it bee soe or noe, questionlesse she hath a greate interest in him wch may bee very beneficiall to mee ; I will thinke how to manage it to my most advantage, and shall be glad of your advise therein.' Sir Roger replies : ' S^r it is not for me to give you any direction to make a particular application to that pson which is to be married. I am confident the Lady will imploy hir utmost for to serve you for I understand as much by hir owne expression.'

At the same time Anne Lee writes to Lady Verney : 'my lady I presume you heer is to mary my Lord Worick . . . shee expectes to be very hapy. I wish it may prove so in conclusion, strange shanges in this world. my brother [i.e. Ralph] might do well to give good counsell but now it is to late. They are to mary within this fortnight. Pore Gorambery will be left wich troble me much, but if you wold com over agane I shold coumfor up myself.'

Ralph writes his congratulations to Lady Sussex thus : ' I canot prevaile with myselfe to bee any longer silent, espetially since divers of my freinds, and acquaintance (that well know how much duty and servise I owe your ladishipp) have been pleas'd to informe mee of your intended marrage. They say it is already concluded, and I know full well, that you doe nothing rashly (espetially in a matter of soe high concernement) which makes mee very confident the event will proove answerable to your expectation and my desire : the times I confesse at present are very sadd and miserable but I trust as you surpasse all others in goodnesse soe you may as far exceed them in happiness.'

A few months later Lady Warwick sends him the following account of her marriage and circumstances : 'I confes i have bene falinge in my lettirs ; yet i know you will not missintrept me nor belive it hath prosedede out of any want or lesinge of my truest respects ; indede i have hade so many distorbances bouth in my fortune by thes times, and of late my trublede thoughts for my one settlinge and change of my condisyon ; that hath made me unfite for any thinge ; my continuall trubles, wantinge a discret and healpful frinde as your noble father and selfe was ever to mee made mee thinke of marrige beinge unable to undorgoo what i fonde continully uppon mee ; i presume you have harde to whom i am wede ; and truly i hope itt will bee . . . for my happines ; my lorde is extreme kainde and i hope will continue so ; you as a frinde i have and must ever hily valy [highly value] ; i will now aquant you with what condisyons i made for myselfe, which was to keepe all my parsonal estate in my one pouer and a thord of my reveny that cam in clere ; and now i have tolde you my condisyons which i hope was not a mise all thinges considerde ; parpetuall compiny i have had since my change in my condisyon truly i have not

hade time for any thinge but now i am com into the
contrey my first lynes i derect to you . . . the blacke
bede and haninges your ante never sent for ; if you
woulde have me deliver them any wher i will or
keepe them with my one stofe which you desier i
will do . . . i shall ever have the same harte to you
and your i have hade ; and if ever i bee able make
good my promeses in all thinges. . . .' In spite of
these protestations, however, it would seem that her
friendship somewhat cooled after her marriage, and
there are but few letters from her to Ralph after this
date.   As the wife of one of the few Parliamentarian
Peers, and the Admiral of the Fleet, Lady Warwick
now played an important part in London Society,
after her days of obscurity at Gorhambury.   After
Lord Warwick's death in 1658, she married a
fourth husband, the Parliamentary General the Earl
of Manchester.

CHAPTER XII.

THE RICH 'WIDO.'

A Dialogue betweene Hope and Feare.

FEARE. Checke thy forward thoughts, and know
Hymen only joynes their hands ;
Who with even paces goe,
She in gold, he rich in lands . . .

HOPE. Parents' lawes must beare no weight
When they happinesse prevent.
And our sea is not so streight
But it roome hath for content.

HABINGTON, 1635.

THE youngest sister of Margaret, Lady Verney, another Margaret, had been left a widow in 1637, at five-and-twenty, with a large fortune by her husband, John Pulteney, of Misterton in Leicestershire. It was afterwards to go to his sisters and an infant nephew, but although this child had not the smallest right to anything during Mrs. Pulteney's life, the Court of Wards put in a claim of the Crown to a fourth of her jointure. Her petition against this great abuse was written for her by Ralph, but all that is asked of Lord Cottington, the Master, was that she be allowed to take a lease at least of the lands thus burdened.

The child, however, soon after died, Mrs. Pulteney's large jointure became free from any interfer-

ence, and the young widow was immediately beset by
a crowd of suitors. She seems to have been a clever
managing woman of the world, yet with a slight
varnish of the religious feeling which distinguished
both Dentons and Verneys. Her influence over Mr.
Pulteney had been very good, leading him away from
various dissipations in which he had indulged. 'She
deserved his estate for she saved his soul,' says one
letter. Although she consulted Sir Edmund from
time to time, Ralph, only a year younger than herself, was her mainstay. She sends him the various
love letters she receives, and appeals to him against
the reproaches of her mother when she refuses an
eligible offer. The pecuniary claims of each possible
husband are discussed one after the other with curious
directness and minuteness by her and her family. Sir
John Paulet (afterwards Lord Paulet) 'hath 2500
in demeanes, & £800 per annum was parsonage land,
& held of the Church, subject only to £300 of old
rent, & his mothers jointure of £100 p annum.'
Old Lady Denton objects to him because he does not
live in Bucks, but her daughter observes rather tartly
'it was knowne before ever he came to the howes
where his estate laye.' 'Good cusin,' she writes to
Ralph, 'I give you maney thankes for your care in
my bisnis, & for what peopel think, I care not . . . I
have writen to your father about Sir J. P. [Paulet].
pray axe my browther first of the pasiges that have
bin—for the man, my mother sayes she canot as far
as she sees Dislike him, & for my owne part I pray

god send me a good hus:, & I care not wher his land
lies. My lady Dencort [a sister of Lord Falkland]
writ to me very ernistly about her sun, that the mach
might goe forward, but i am soe much against it that
I will for no conditiones in the world here of it. My
Mother is for it, for shee heeres he hath a greater
estate than this [one], which is I beleve her reson ;
but for my part I thinke all the riches in the world
without content is nothing—for this liberty I will
take to myself, that is, to make choice of one as I
afecte, as for him I find I canot. As you have ever
bin carful of me, soe I dout not but you will continew
soe.' 'Suer I am not so fond as to be in love with
aney at tow days sight,' says the poor woman. 'I
hope god will give me power of myselfe yet. I shall
not setill my affections on aney till I see sum goodness in a man to induce me to it.'

Then comes a very fiery letter from the gentleman
himself, Francis Leeke, Lord Deincourt, showing the
style of wooing then affected by lovers to their ladies,
' the insupportable torments they endure for her
bewtie ' &c. ' Most honoured & virtuous Mistrisse,
since ye happy houre when first I see you my heart
hath still been contemplating upon yor bewties, & ye
only joy of my life consisteth in ye remembrance of
you & yor rare vertues. pardon therefore my bold-
ness in presenting you wi^t these lines w^h love commands me to send, & to lett you know both how
much I honour you, & y^t ye torments w^h I now suffer
for your bewtie are insupportable, if not revealed to

you, in whose power aloane it is to make me y^e
happyest or ye most unfortunatest man upon Earth,
for I vow to ye Sacred Heavens there is nothing in
this world y^t I desier mor than to be soe happy as to
be your servant, & I have A greate ambition y^t you
would please to honour me so farre as to lett me
receive some gratious lines from your faire hands, or
otherwise to admitt me to waite upon you, I should
be confident you would grant me these favours if my
lines might but be as pleasing unto you as I am perfectly y^{or} most loyall Servant.'

This ' mach ' was also set aside by the fair widow.
In the following year Lord Deincourt's courtship
was succeeded by that of Lord Howard of Ettrick, a
widower, with five children   Very full particulars of
his manors and lands within the counties of York and
Essex are forwarded for inspection : ' the manor of
Escrick containing by suretay four thousand acres—
rich grownes now out of lease & ready to be lett at
10^s the acre which a mounte to 2000 per annum.'

' Good Ralph,' writes old Lady Denton in March,
1639. ' For my lord Howard i knowe you my one
knoledge he is honorablye desendede, & upon report
is onest & worthye, but Ralphe you shall find by
your fathar's lettar howe i ame In gagede for a nothar
. . . Soe i beleve i ame bound in onystye to forbare
writinge to hur In any waye to prosed with my Lord
Ho & Ralphe i wil speake it to you I should nevar
ventar upon so many children as 5, althoughe the
ware wel provided for, for you know it is a grate

family . . . I will nether write anythinge against this match nor withe it . . . Noe man livinge coulde wright mor of any mane In the behalfe of my Lord Ho then my Ladye Hubbard did to me, but with all shee concluded his children was such an obstackle'—and so on.

Mrs. Pulteney's friends at last remonstrated with her on her carelessness concerning wealth, and she replies very sensibly, 'I am very willing to take your counsil in having richis enoufe, all ouer natewers is to apte to set ouer hartes on that which is worst for us, but I hope I shall never put my trust in uncertain richis. Some men will live beter with 500^{lb} per anam than sum will with fifteen if thay be roving feloes.'

Lord Howard's suit was urged by Lord Pembroke, whose opinion stood high both with Sir Edmund and his son, and a certain Lord Charles is mentioned, without a surname, who is also favoured by the Lord Chamberlain. 'I wish my Lord Howard's busines were at a nende, it is but a pore business,' says Lady Denton to Ralph. 'Sur Martaine Listar hath been with me & giveth much the best report that evar i hard. I pray God direct hur.' She adds, 'I have writ to her to come down with her brother, who will be for Lundon the end of this weeke, i feare al wil not be well els—i pray doe your best.'

Mrs. Pulteney had given some promise to the two suitors not to decide for any one during a given time, perhaps to prevent their quarrelling or in order to get rid of importunities, and this brought her into great

straits both with them and the Lord Chamberlain, as
each side considered that she was more or less pledged
to them, or at least that she would encourage no
other suitor. Suddenly the wilful widow took matters into her own hands, and in spite of all the per-
suasions and dissuasions, the recommendations and
warnings of her friends, she privately married a certain Honourable William Eure, son of Lord Eure, a
Roman Catholic, who immediately after the wedding
went off to join the king's army in the North.

Ralph was thunderstruck, and moreover alarmed
at the way in which the Lord Chamberlain, very
powerful in the days of Council-table Government,
would take this neglect of his advice and his wishes.
But what was much more serious to him and his
father was the fact that the selected spouse was a
Roman Catholic. Among the religious party to
which the Verneys belonged, this was looked upon
as a kind of infidelity and with a feeling almost of
horror as of apostacy to the great cause of religion.
The power of the Catholics at this time must be
remembered, and how the queen was straining every
nerve, with the assistance of the Pope's agent, to
obtain not only the remission of all penalties, but all
kinds of privileges for her co-religionists. Converts
had been made in great numbers among the gay
Court ladies or 'fantastic speculators, like Sir Kenelm
Digby,' and Henrietta Maria's power over her husband was sufficient to nullify the effect of any proclamations or acts which Charles might consent to

issue against them ; while Catholics and converts
filled the Court and were placed in great positions.
The tone of the remonstrance in ' Lycidas ' by ' the
pilot of the Galilean lake,' shows how deep was the
indignation excited by the proceedings of Laud,
whether tending consciously or not to Rome, and by
the ecclesiastical power he assumed—

> Besides what the grim wolf with privy paw
> Daily devours apace and nothing said.

Here is Ralph's letter to his father, then on the
Scotch expedition with the king, announcing the dreadful fact, April 1, 1639 : — ' Oh S^r shee is married, shee
is married ! and therefore now tis past recall. this
unlucky deed was donn before I mistrusted ever twas.
Her only aime now is to continue in your and her
mother's good oppinion, for I find her hart hardened
against any things the world or her other friends can
say. And since 'tis thus, let us endeavour (as much
as in us lieth) to preserve her (wilfully lost) reputation. I have advised her to goe downe and conceall
this, at least untell his returne from the North, and
then let him renue his sute and prevaile as uppon a
second pretention. This I conceive will bee the best
course to blind the world and protect her credit from
perpetuall shame.' He goes on to say how ' it afflicts
me to see on I loved soe well utterly ruined, but
since there is noe helpe . . . I would gladly doe
the best I could concerninge the carrage of the
businesse . . . that our friends in the country may
not have reason to lay the fault on us. . . . Had

this unfortunate businesse not been quite finished
before my cominge upp, I am confident I should
either have brake or at least protracted it, but twas
too late then (what hazard soever a man would
undergoe) to doe it ; those whome god hath joyned
togather tis not in our power to put asunder. . . .
I know you will beare to greate a share of the
affliction with him that will alwaies pray for the
preservation of her honour and your happy and
speedy returne. . . . I am so full with this businesse
that I cannot say how infinitely I am troubled for
the king's affaires. Most men are confident there
will bee no blowes. . . . God direct us to doe that
which is best, and grant that I may alwaies endeavour
to serve you as befitts your most obedient sonn.'

Sir Edmund fully shares his distress at the marriage. On receiving the news from Ralph he writes :
' I protest to God, when I redd your letter, a palsye
tooke my hands, soe that in five hours I could hold
noething steddyly.' In another letter : ' My soule
is greeved for her misfortune. . . . I praye deale
cleerely with her, and lett her preserve as much of
her discretion and reputation as shee can ; for, beleeve
mee, shee has made a large forfeit of them boath. . . .
This woman laye soe neare my heart that I shall
fiend her folly ther whilst I have an hower to live.'
A few weeks later he writes from Newcastle that
Mr. Eure has not come on with the army, ' but I
heare he has sould all his land, and means to settle
about lundon, wher hee is suer to have a ritch

widdow. I heare hee is a vast spender, and has a
father and a Brother to releeve that has not bredd to
eate ; hee sould his land for six thousand pownds.
all this layd togeather, God help someboddy.'

Old Lady Denton was not only furiously angry
at the match, but at its having been carried forwards
without her 'privity or permission,' and writes in
May to Ralph in the fiercest terms, as if he were
chiefly to blame. 'Your mother writes me word
about a samite [silk] gowne, i remembar i did here
tofore of such a thinge, but now i pray tel her if
she would provide me sack cloth and line y^t with
asshis, then i mought morne for the folie of my
wise disobedient children. i hear he is with out exception, only his religione—but that is such a cut to
me that y^t hath a most killed me. yf he had had
never a penye y^t should not a troblede me at all. i
heare he hath a 1000*l.* a yeare, and soe discret that
he will live better of that than sum will doe of to
thousant. Your house is ye common scare of towne
and cuntry howe he and shee hath foled you all, but
I know some of you knue of this, when ther was
helpe of yt. You say what God will must be. God
is not the othar [author] of any yll. the meanes was
nevar youused [used], becase she was kept from me.
Your father hath delt most noblye, onestlye, wisely
and lovingly with me and hur too. . . . I have not
youth and time to reveng, so I will betake me to
my beades and desire I may lyve to forgive and
forget injuries done me.'

Next comes Ralph's ' copy of a p^t of letter to my
father ' : ' Now S^r I must tell you the unhappy
woeman was married by a Popish Priest ; it seemes
you writ to her to know, and shee (beinge, as I
suppose, ashamed of soe foule an act), desired mee to
informe you of it.   She hath already in p^t taken care
for Pegg and I hope within a few weekes will finish
that worke.   poore woeman, she dares not make any
of her friendes acquainted with it, therfore you need
not take notise of it.   This unluckie businesse hath
made my grandmother infinitely offended with my
mother, my Wife and myselfe and indeed the whole
house, except yourselfe, for she often saith you
have dealt wisely and honestly and lovingly in this
businesse, but all the rest of her children are fooles,
and the night before I came from Hillesdon she told
me that (except you) wee had all dealt unfaithfully
with her.   Whilst she charged us with folly, I was
not much troubled at it (for I know myselfe much
guilty of that), but when she charged us all in
generall and mee in p^{r}ticular with unfaithfulnesse, I
could not but make some reply.'   He is afraid the
old lady will appeal to his father, and tells him the
words he used, how she ' might doe well never to
imploy those that had dealt treachoursly with her,
and that in castinge such false aspertions on her owne
children she did but defile her owne nest.'   He was
troubled that the censure should come from her 'that
had ever pretended soe much love to mee.   All this
was done in my aunt Isham's presence, and I am

glad it was soe, for many old people are apt to forget there owne words and mistake others,' with much more to the same purpose.

'Cosan Verney,' writes Aunt Isham herself to Ralph. 'Most of hur discose was off hur slfe, being ould and in trobles. You should not a rested hur wordes so soune out of hur mouth, and intarpating them to your owne sence, but a give hur leve to explane hur owne meneing, for she thinkes you, for all this, to be very true to youre frindes, and soe I end this discose to lett you knoe how well bisnes goe nowe my Brother Eure is come to his Wife: the party [her mother] is beter contented a great dell, and showes him more respecke then I thought she would a done . . . thus I rest youre loving Ante.' Then, comforting herself by enquiries as to the fashions worn in London, Mrs. Isham goes on : 'I pray send me word if wee bottone petticotes and wascotes wheare they must be Botend [buttoned].'

A letter, however, from the delinquent herself, in May, had shown that Lady Denton was beginning to soften. 'My mo' is in betir temper than shee was and is wiling as we should live here . . . but I must confec to you I like it not by aney meanes, nayther do I thinke as he will . . . I have writ to your father concerning it and what he sayth my mo' will be wiling to—As I have run all the hazard in my maching to him, so I desier to youse all the meanes I can to convert hime, for if I live neere London I can have

the best devines to my own house, and besides I intend to keepe on myselfe' [poor Mr. Eure !].   'You
know Mr. Ockly is but A crabid man and he may
dow him more hurt then good, and besids he is not
youst to disputations, for Mr. Sute told me of on,
I thinke he lives at Lambotte, he sayth he is yᵉ best
in ingland and hath bin youst to it.   Pray if you here
of are [e'er] A pritey hous as is fit for us, send me
word. he is wiling to live in London the next winter
but yᵗ I am uterly against, for he would be so con-
tinewaly amongst his own religion as I dow not like
that.   He did much desier to come for A wicke or
ten days and so, to A gon againe, but I intreated him
to the contrary, so I hope he will not, for my mo :
knows not that I am : and if he should com before he
comes home all togethur it must needs be discovred.
My intentions are to com to London as soon as he
returnes and thar to lye in the sitey privatly till I
can have A place to goe to and to discover yᵗ I am
maryed at the time of his coming home. . . . If I
could meet with A pretey hous I would willingly
have on in the privatest place I can, but neere A
church.'

Instead however of carrying out these admirable
plans of conversion, Margaret Eure, who loved her
husband, was not unnaturally brought over to his
faith, as was probably his intention and that of the
priest, who seemed to leave the rein on her neck and
later on drew it in much more tightly, for poor Ralph,
when in exile at Blois, complained that ' Misterton by

the instigation of her priest, has urged me harshlie, otherwise than I expected.'

Mr. Eure soon came from the king's camp at Berwick, and met his wife near London, where their marriage was declared.

Her sister, Mrs. Isham, writes for her, a few days before, ' she is veri sicke of a nagye [an ague] and she cannot rite hur slfe.   She wold have youre wife send downe hur Red Damaxe Peticote and Wascote ; ' and then come many injunctions concerning the fashions, the sleeves and the skirts : ' she wold have youre Wife by hur a blake taffity peticote and wascote, with a hansom lase and make get oup with haninges, sleves, and a rowne skrites and if they be worne. The resone as she maketh this hast is becase Sr Thomas Wanman hath spoke to hur to chrissen his Boye, and she wold wilingly be out of moring then ; and if shee should Die before she doth warit, yet would sarve to make a short moring Cloke for the Man you wot of,' meaning her husband, a somewhat grim jest for a newly-married wife.

She had in her widowed days given £900 to her god-daughter Margaret Verney. Ralph writes to her about the money ' which you were pleased to bestow upon my sister.' He has had it all engrossed and examined and sealed up by her brother Denton ; he causes soft wax to be put into the box that she might have no trouble, and adds a paper showing that ' you now alow her £20 per yeare be sides her diet which comes to £26 a yeare more, which would

be about the interest of the £900,' with a draft of a
paper saying that 'William Eure and Margarett his
wife appoint the profits of £900 to be yearly paid
unto my niece Mrs. Margaret Verney until the £900
shall be paid.' The bearer of the box is told to go
to Walden ' where my Lord Eure dwells. [He was
the only one of the old peers who afterwards accepted
a seat in Cromwell's House of Lords, consisting of
sixty members.] Enquire for Mrs. Margaret Eure,
Mr. W. Eure's wife—the letter and box are to be
given to her and if she cannot answer at once,
desire her to appoint any short day and you will
waite upon her again to see the writings sealed.' He
prudently adds that he will satisfy the Attorney and
his men for their pains.

Mr. Eure, though poor himself, seemed to have
behaved very well, and not objected to his wife's
large gift to her godchild, made in very different
circumstances. ' Swet cusen,' writes Mrs. Eure to
Ralph, ' I hope for al the bace reports of sum, as my
hus will proove himselfe an honist man, but if he
hath not y^t estate which he hath reported it to be, he
hath not deceived me, for I never inquired after it,
but I believe as it is full as good as he told you and
rather beter, but tis not y^t I stand uppon, for his
religion is now the thing I loocke after, which I hope
in time may be altred. I find no aversnes in him to
heare eyther me or aney as I shall bring, which I am
very joiful at, and his religion excepted I know few
like him. Since his coming up he spake to me con-

cerning Pegge. he told me as he thought as it was
my intention to dow sumthing for her, and desired
me to bestow that of her which I ever intend, and
desired me to dow it presantly, y^t it might be my one
[own] acte,' which sounds kind and wise on the part
of the newly married husband. ' I hope both you and
your wife hath seen him, for it was his great desier
to see you. . . . I reste your loving Ant.'

The god-daughter so kindly treated, now aged
sixteen, had a temper of her own, as appeared in after
life, and seems to have behaved with little loyalty to
her aunt. She was probably vexed and mortified at
the change in her position, and in the following year
it appears that she had spread evil reports concerning
her new uncle, till it required all Ralph's good management to set matters right with Mrs. Eure. He
wrote to his sister : ' I heare a greate noyse of a discourse beetweene you and my Lady Blanch Arundell's
woeman, (and I beeleeve your Aunt hath heard somethinge of it) in wch you spake liberally both of the
unhappynesse of your Aunt's marrage, and her discontents, and divers other things of that kind. I
woonder you should forfeit your discreation in this
way since you have had soe many warnings of it. If
it bee true, I must say you are not only ffoolish, but
ungratfull, for you above all others (haveinge received
soe many favours from that good Aunt of yours), have
most reason to conceall all things of that nature.
Till I heare your answere, I will not absolutely con-
demne you. . . . The perticulers of your discourse

I doe not at this present certainly know. . . . I pray
cleare your selfe to your Aunt, and tell her truly
what you then spake to the Gentlewoeman ; and in
all humble maner submit your selfe to her. By this
meanes it will appeare whither you are guilty or not.
If it bee falce, the injury will fall on them that first
raised it, but if it prove otherwise, I know nothinge
bad enough for you. I am in hast now, and can say
noe more, but wish this may prove a fable, for if it
should bee true, I must confesse I shall account my
selfe in nothinge more unhappy then in the title of
your Brother R. V.'

In April 1640 Sir John Lenthall wrote about
some business between Mrs. Eure and his wife which
he was arranging, ' I have appointed my cousin Eure
. . . about 2 of ye clocke in ye Inner Temple Church
[a curious place of meeting] where hee is very willinge to treate with Sir Alexander Denton [her eldest
brother] about ye businesse.'

Mrs. Eure lived much in Yorkshire, at the old
Lord Eure's, with her husband and her two little girls,
although she spent part of the year at her own home,
Misterton, in Leicestershire. Her account of the
utter disorganisation of country life during the civil
wars is as vivid for the districts in the neighbourhood
of York and Hull as are those of Lady Sussex for
St. Albans and Hertfordshire. Rents were not paid,
produce was not sold, tenants were not to be had
at any price ; and it must be remembered that the
writers were persons of large fortune, and that the

smaller landowners and those whom they employed must have suffered still more. It is often forgotten how it is only the larger owners and occupiers who employ labour, the smaller people do their own work, and the labourers are those who suffer on such occasions when there is no work and no money to pay for it.

In the spring of 1643 Mrs. Eure applies for a pass from the Parliament to go from Yorkshire to London 'that I may have liberty to wander up and downe.' She has many delays and disappointments, but 'longe loocket for comes at last.' She is in London in 1644 and finds her own people in dreadful trouble : her brother, Sir Alexander Denton, and his family, and Mrs. Isham and her husband are in the Tower, the men as close prisoners, the women sometimes in confinement, at other times voluntarily sharing in the troubles of husbands and brothers. Mrs. Eure writes to Sir Ralph from Tower Hill in April : 'I think Turkes could not be used worse—but all as they can doe to us, is but to make us suffer in this warlde—was left all as poore as Jobe, but with I hope the faith of Jobe, because ye Lorde gave us pashance to under goe that as we did suffer. Now I am come to towne to put ourselves into clothes.'

In the autumn of 1644, Colonel Eure was killed. Doll Leake refers to him as truly 'a gallant man, the whole nasion has a lose in him; he had but one fault,' that of his religion, which his wife's family could never forgive, though they had learnt to respect and love him. Lady Sussex writes to Sir Ralph in September :

' Your ante is i believe a very sad woman for the
lose of her fine husbande—i belive he hath not left
her so good a wido as he founde her.   She will have
an infinite want of you now, as i am suer i have, if
she be not changed in her religion she is happy.'

Mrs. Eure herself writes in November : ' Sweet
Nephew . . . I am now over run with miserys and
troubels, but the greatest misfortewn that could suer
hapen to me in this world was the Death of the
galentest man that ever I knew in my Life, but my
comfort is that he had time to prepare him selfe for
a beter world, which I am confident he will injoye, it
was my misfortewen to be from him at his death, and
as the currant of the times run it is a question
whether I shall see aney frend I have againe, for I
am now at Misterton and am ther like to contenew
for I have not wherewithall to visit a frend, but I
have one comfort left me yet which is tho I have not
a fortewne to my mind, yet I have brought my mind
to my fortewne, which is the greatest happiness I can
saye I do injoye.'

Sir Ralph replies full of sympathy, and offers her
the loan of the great black bed and hangings from
Claydon as the only consolation within his means.
This great black bed, with its impressive amplitude
of gloom, travels about the family whenever a death
occurs, till the very mention of it gives one a feeling
of suffocation !

Mrs. Eure was still a Roman Catholic ; she seems
to have been an amiable woman without much back-

bone, who required a man to manage her business for her, and her nephew, Harry Verney, much her own age, spent the next year with her, and talks in grand style about her affairs as if he was as important as herself in their settlement. 'We have just sold some land,' he writes, 'to him as will in herit her jointure after her death for two years purchase,' so depressed was the land market at that moment.

After about a year, however, consolation was at hand. Her brother, the Doctor, writes from Misterton, where he went to attend her in a serious illness, in September 1645 : 'My sister has relapsed into a bad jaundice. She remembers her service to you both. She is as ill in mind as in body, continues obstinate, but I hope the best, for I have great reason to believe she will quickly marry & (wi^{ch} is my comfort) to a P-testant this time. Take no notice of it, no not to Harry, to whom I daresay nothing is imparted for I had it sub sigillo. I would have sent you his name if I durst. Y^t marriage is intended is clear to Harry & to others, but to whom I p-sume is knowne only to me & one more of her friends. it is not so sure as I hope it will be shortly. Dear Raph, Vale.' The intended was the second son of Lord Sherard, and a Captain in the army of the Dutch States, and Ralph, in spite of his own poverty, inquires for how much he could buy the commission for his brother Edmund.

Two years after, Lady Verney writes that Mrs. Sherard ' is of our opinion now.' She is not in Lon-

don, because Captain Sherard is so fond of field sports
that he keeps her in Leicestershire, but a little later
in the year there is a long letter from her to Ralph,
lamenting over the death of her husband. She was
left with a baby Sherard and her two little Eure
daughters, afterwards co-heiresses of their grandfather, Lord Eure, whose sons had all died. His
estates, in Yorkshire and elsewhere, had been frittered
away at different times, although eventually Margaret
and Mary inherited 1,514*l.* a year each, 500*l.* per
annum of which was to be paid to their mother.
Mary was sent for education—French and music,
the ' gittar,' &c.—to Blois, where Sir Ralph and his
family were at that time in exile. ' Moll ' was a
lively, charming little girl, but very sickly and scro-
fulous ; being brought up thus with young Edmund
Verney, the heir of Claydon, under a governess—Luce
Sheppard, a sort of cousin—the boy fell, not unnaturally, in love with her—she ten, and he about fourteen
years old—and there are desperate love letters to her
when they both grew up. He never indeed seems
to have recovered her final refusal of him, although
they continued friends, and she married a Yorkshire
squire, Palmes, very inferior to the poor rejected
cousin.

Mrs. Eure always lived on most friendly terms
with her four Verney nephews, more like brothers
than her own, who, as often happens, seemed to
belong to an older generation. ' Mun ' comes and
stays with her for weeks at a time when the king's

army had ceased to exist, and London was too hot to hold such a strong Royalist. Henry, as we have seen, was at one time her right hand, and he was constantly backwards and forwards whenever he had no better place to go to. Even the scapegrace Tom was not quite out of the sunshine of her aunt-like regard, while she never ceased to consider Ralph and his wife her dearest friends, and she was almost as troublesome as Lady Sussex herself with commissions to him : ' for my dimone ringe, ther is seven ponde stons cut in the shape of yours & to littell ones, in the pendants are littall hanging stons without foyles,' which he was to have re-set for her—' Thirteen yardes of paudesoye, satteen, max mohayre, flowered sacsinet, striped goud stuffe for a gonne, scarlet taffety, & French Taby,' in one bill would make up a considerable number of fine gowns ; the cost of this particular envoy was £18 18s. 0d.

All the widows marry again, even when they have been much attached to their husbands, sometimes three and even four times, at the earliest convenient ' moment. Perhaps, in the troublous period of the Civil Wars, the protection of a man was very important, and they may have felt, though for different reasons, like a half-French lady friend of ours, who, when expostulated with for marrying after she was between fifty and sixty, replied, ' Dans ces temps de chemins-de-fer il faut absolument un mari.' Mrs. Eure's marriages at all events were very unworldly, and not like those of Lady Sussex with her three Earls.

CHAPTER XIII.

SIR EDMUND WITH THE KING IN THE SCOTCH WAR.

> ' Think you a little din can daunt mine ears ? . . .
> Have I not heard great ordnance in the field,
> And heaven's artillery thunder in the skies ?
> Have I not in the pitched battle heard
> Loud 'larums, neighing steeds, and trumpets' clang ?
> Tush ! tush ! fear boys with bugs.'—SHAKESPEARE.

THE king's assumption of absolute authority in ecclesiastical matters had provoked the strongest opposition in Scotland. Charles began to make preparations for war ; while at the same time he carried on negotiations with the Scotch concerning their grievances, he was himself to march with a considerable English army to the Border.

Lord Pembroke's summons, addressed 'to my very loveinge freind Sir Edmund Verney, knight, one of the gentlemen of his majesty's most honorable privy chamber in ordinary,' arrived on the 7th of February 1639. ' It having pleased the king's most excellent Majesty to resolve upon a royall journey to York,' all his sworn servants of the Chamber must attend him. His Majesty's royal pleasure is 'that, all occasions sett apart you be in readines in your owne person by the first of April next att the city of

Yorke, as a curassier in russett armes, with guilded studds or nayles and befittingly horsed, and your servants which shall wayt upon you horst in white armes, after the manner of a hargobusier, in good equipage.' If his necessary occasions in his Majesty's service will not permit, he is to send some gentleman of quality in his stead. The summons found Sir Edmund troubled in mind and infirm in body. Lady Sussex had written of him to Ralph a month before—'your good father mythought loked very sade hear this crismas. i fearede he hade been discontentede some way, but he tolde me it was not so, but that he was oftime in a grete dele of pane. i pray God he may get helpe or else it will shorten his time i doubt. . . . Let not your father know what i right i pray concerninge him.' Little as he sympathised with the objects of the expedition, Sir Edmund made his will and prepared to follow his master.

The will is dated the 20th of March 1639, and is witnessed by Tho. Isham ; Fran. Drake ; Geor. Elyott ; Robert Busby ; John Humfrir and Will. Roades. It is a touching document, showing both his earnest religious feeling and strong family affection :

' I, Sir Edmund Verney, . . . considering the frailty of mankind, ye certainty of death, and the uncertainty of ye time of death . . . bequeath my soul unto Almighty God my creator, and to his beloved son Jesus Christ, my only Lord, Savior and Redeemer, by and through whose only death

merits and passion I do assuredly trust to have sal-
vation and forgiveness of all my sins, and in due time
to be made an inheritor amongst the elect of his
heavenly kingdom. . . . My body I will shall be
interred in ye chancel of the Parish church of Middle
Claydon, with as little pomp and charges as my
executor conveniently may. . . .' He goes on to
give directions concerning ' such estate of goods and
chattels as it has pleased the Almighty to bless me
with in this transitory life. . . .' &c.

His trust in Ralph is entire : ' I constitute my
son Ralph my sole executor, having had experience
of his fidelitie unto me and of his love for his brothers
and sisters.' 20*l.* he leaves as a stock for the poor
people of the parish. Annuities of 40*l.* a year to his
sons Thomas and Henry ; to Edmund and each of
his daughters he leaves 5*l.*, they being provided for
by the profits of the Aulnage. ' To Doll Leake, my
niece, 20*l.* To John Rhodes my faithful servant and
bailiff at Claydon [whose descendants still live there]
an annuity of 5*l.*' To another servant the same.
To his daughter-in-law Mary, for whom his love was
great, 40*l.* for a ring, ' which I desire her to wear for
my sake.' To his mother 20*l.* ' To my dear and
beloved wife all such moneys as are in her custody
at the date of this my will ; ' half his linen, with the
use of half his plate and household stuff, which was
to be shared with Ralph, all his ' fuell of wood,
furze and cole at Claydon, the coach and four of the
coach horses with their harness and furniture'; ' stuff

for a mourning gown to the women and cloth for a mourning sute and cloak for the men legatees,' &c. &c.

He left London with the king about the 21st of March. The expedition was more like a progress than the opening of a campaign. Charles trusted to the reverence which his appearance would inspire, and as Clarendon observes, ' he more intended the Pomp of his Preparations than the strength of them,' seeming to think that a mere show of force was all that was required to make the Scots yield. The ' gay caval- cade ' which accompanied him was, however, not calculated to awe men who had taken up arms for what they believed to be a great cause, and when he rode into York on March 30 he was utterly astonished to find the state of things in Scotland so different from what he had been led to expect by his councillors, men who spoke smooth words without knowledge. The cry was that the king had been betrayed. Sir Edmund, writing to his son in the tenderest terms, the day after his arrival at York, says : ' Good Raphe, since Prince Henry's death I never knew soe much griefe as to part from you, and trewly because I saw you equally afflicted with it my sorrow was greater : but Raph wee cannott live always togeather. It cannott bee longe ere by cource of nature we must be severd ; and if that time be pre- vented [1] by accident yett wee must resolve to beare it with that patience and courage as becomes men and cristians ; and soe the great god of Heaven send uss

---

[1] ' Prevent us, O Lord, in all our doings.'

well to meete againe eyther in this woarld or in the next.

'The King has beene basly betrayd; all the party that hee hoped uppon all this while has basly left him; as we are this day informed : the two cassels of Edenbrough and Dunbarton are yeelded upp without one blowe; and yett they were boath provided soe well as they were impregnable soe long as they had vittle, which they wanted not.

'Dekeeth, a place of greate strength, wher the Crowne and Septer laye is yeelded to ; and the Covenanters has taken them awaye and a greate deale of Armes and munition to ; yett my lor Tresurer of Scottland undertooke to the King to keepe all that safe ; and all these are given upp without one blowe. Aberdine wee heare is yeelded upp to and noe blowe given ; and the King sent 4,000 of the choysest Armes hee had theather ; soe that now I am confident the show of making a party ther for the Kinge has beene only to gett Armes from uss, and to feede us with hopes till they were fully provided.

'My Lord Clifford sent woarde this morning to the King, that the inhabitants of Carlile had left the towne uppon a fright they tooke of the Highlanders coming suddenly uppon them, but hee has putt 300 men into the towne and they saye they are resolved to fight it out.   The Hilanders are in number 2,500 and 6 cannon as they heare ; we cannot heare wheather my lord of Essex bee in Barwick or not, by to-morrow wee shall know ; heere is this day gone

from this country 2,000 men to second him. My
lord Trequare is confined to his chamber ; wee expect
some others maye heare of it ; to that I will not
name, for the King has been basly betrayde by them
and that wee shall all smart for ; saye little of this to
the woemen least it fright them ; . . . . I heare
noething of my Armes.

'Comend mee to Honest Natt Hubbard and the
god of heaven bless you ; remember to see Gorham-
bery [i.e. Lady Sussex] as soone as you can ; if Nedd
Sidenham bee not on his waye, comend me to him
and acquaint him with what I have writt : tell him
and Charles Gawdy [they had married two sisters]
that I could wish they were boath heere, for the
King has but few about him, and that is a shame to
uss all at this time when beleeve mee the danger is
more then is apprehended, ther wher you are.

'I hope you have sent awaye my waggon. My
man Peeter and I are parted ; if hee comes to lundun
bee not deceaved by any false message ; write privatly
as much to Roades, the king goes to see the fortify-
cations at Hull on Thursday next.'

Meantime but little news had been received by
his anxious wife and family. Lady Verney was still
in London and wrote to her mother at Hillesdon,
April 6 : 'I should be glad that y^r newes of the
Scotish business were true, for here is none good.
Wee heare that they have turned all that are on the
King's side into England, and that they have stopped
all passages soe that the king can send no certain

intelligence of their proceedings ; all our frindes are gone out of towne and when my sister [just secretly married] is gon to I know not what to do, but my hope is that you wilbe so good as to send her to me again.'

Young Edmund and Dr. Denton were also with the army, the former having volunteered for the king's service, and the latter being appointed Court physician on the Scotch expedition. There is a paper of the Lord Treasurer showing that he is to be allowed his food and house-room and 6s. 8d. a day, though Sir Edmund sometimes writes of the king and the whole army being in the fields at night.

On April 25 he writes: 'I am now taking horse for Durham : my things are all gone & I must follow ; . . . Notwithstanding my haste I will give you some tutch of news. Yesterday the King received a letter from . . . the lords of the covenant ; I thinck ther was 20 of theyr hands to it ; my Lord of Essex sent it sealed upp as he receaved it to the king, but . . . they sent a coppy of it open ; to the intent if my lord made any scruple of receaving it, yet the messenger might read it to my Lord. . . . First they express great civillity to my lord ; and they seeme to wonder that a man soe well affected to the peace & wellfare of his country will appear in such a waye, as he does in this business ; and they wonder that ther is such unusuall preparations for warr in Ingland, . . . protesting that they never had a thought of offering the least iniury to this king-

dome, that they have often represented theyr greevances to his Ma^{ty} & by reason of some ill minded
men of theyr nation can obtaine noe answer. . . .
They have done nothing but what is warranted by
theyr laws & they conclude with a great desire of
Amity & peace with this kingdome, adding that
if they bee invaded they must & will defend themselves & ther lybertys as long as ther is a man living
amongst them. All thes hedds are in the letter : but
in my oppinion they are exprest with a great deale of
modesty, yett my lord Generall, (who is tender of
the honor of the King) thincks it full of insolence &
braving the King ; in breefe I feare it will rather
exasperate then mollify, and add fewell to that fyre
that raged inoughe before ; trewly I thinck it will
come to blowes, but you must not saye soe to your
mother.' He has not yet received his armour :
'I beleeve ther is never a long Gauntlett sent . . .
lett Hill make one with all the speede he can possibly ;
for it will kill a man to serve in a whole Curass. I
am resolved to use nothing but back, brest, and
Gauntlet ; if I had a Pott for the Hedd that were
Pistoll proofe it maye bee I would use it if it were
light ; but my whole Hellmett will bee of noe use to
mee at all.' He hopes 'there will be some shipps
coming dayly to Newcastle for coales, by some of
them you must send it with an extreordinary charge
to deliver it with all speede . . . Say noething of
this Gauntlett to y^{or} mother ; it maye give her cause-
less fears.' He thanks 'Mary, Nance, Doll, & honest

Natt for their kind letters but trewly I can write to none of them, my best love to them all. The Lord God of Heaven bless you. Your louing father.'

The number of horses required on a campaign, not only for Sir Edmund's own riding but for carrying the necessary equipments, was very difficult to supply. In one letter comes a sorry list. His nag Lipping is obliged to go into good grass and to be sold when he is fat. ' I praye lett the like bee done with the Bay Gellding I bought at Knights Bridg. I was extreamly cussend in that bargaine ; my Gelding Goodwin is here but I feare hee will never recover & one of my waggon Horses was spoyled by the waye heather & I am foarst to buy another.'

During April the king continued at York, but on the 29th he started north, sleeping at Raby Castle, which belonged to his treasurer of the household, Sir Henry Vane ; the next day he reached Durham, where he was received by Bishop Morton, and some enthusiasm was shown. Not long before he most unwisely tried to exact an oath from all persons in his service that they would fight in the king's cause, ' to the utmost of my power and hazard of my life,' and Lord Saye and Sele (who had married an aunt of Lady Verney) and Lord Brooke positively refused, whereupon the two Puritan lords were both imprisoned. The condition of the army was very bad, as the following letter from Sir Edmund shows. There was evidently little heart to fight the Scotch among the raw levies. A regular army will fight pretty

much as well against one foe as against another ;
professional feeling and force of habit carry the soldier
onwards without much caring what the cause may be,
but in the case of the untrained peasants whom Sir
Edmund describes, pressed by force at short notice,
ill-fed and ill-clothed, there was neither the enthusiasm
of Cromwell's troops in later years nor the *esprit de
corps* of an army as at present composed. He begins
by saying that he should not dare to write at all
except by private messenger, ' for I feare many of
my letters are not come to y^{or} hands, or if they have
yett I beleeve they have been opened, . . . for now
wee have gotten that curiosity here to examin who
sends news to lundon, . . . because I am confident
of this bearer, I will tell you trewly how I conceave
things goes here. Our Army is but weake ; our
Purce is weaker; and if wee fight with thes foarces &
early in the yeare wee shall have our throats cutt ;
and to delaye fighting longe wee cannott for want of
monny to keepe our Army togeather. my lord marshall [1] putts on the king to fight by all the wayes &
means he can possibly devise ; dayly urging the king
how nearly it concerns him in honor to punish the
rebells, telling that they are weake ; . . . then the
king is perswaded to it toe from Whithall [i.e. by
the queen] with all the industry that can be ima-
gind. the Catholiks makes a large contribution as
they pretend and indeed use all the meanes and
wayes they can to sett us by the Ears ; & I thinck

---

[1] Lord Arundel, commander-in-chief under the king.

they will not faile of theyr plott.   I dare saye ther
was never soe Raw, soe unskilfull & soe unwilling an
Army brought to fight.   My lord marshall himselfe
will, I dare saye, bee safe, & then he cares not what
becomes of the rest ; trewly here are manny brave
Gentlemen that for poynt of honor must runn such a
hazard as trewly would greeve any heart but his that
does it purposly to ruine them.   for my owne parte I
have lived till paine and trouble has made mee weary
to doe soe ; and the woarst that can come shall not
bee unwellcome to mee ; but it is a pitty to see what
men are like to bee slaughterd heere unless it shall
pleas god to putt it in the kings Hearte to increase his
Army or staye till thes may knowe what they doe ;
for as yett they are as like to kill theyr fellows as the
enemye.'   ' Heere has beene a whisper of an accomo-
dation betweene uss & the Scots, but I see noe hope
of it.'   He then writes about his money affairs and
says he is ' extream weary . . . & it is 3 of the clock
in the morning, att which time I am very sleepy ' ;
and then comes a postscript : ' My lord Saye is att
liberty & gone home ; ther was never soe weake a
thing done as the comittment of that man.'

Next comes a letter from Dr. Denton to Ralph,
alarming him about his father's ' warlike propensi-
ties ' : ' Ralph, wee have noe neede of foolinge, wee
have an enough of that here ; if the wisest were not
a little guilty of it, wee might bee happier then now
wee are likly to be.   Y^r ffather is as he useth to be
for matter of health, his wisdome I feare begins to

fayle him. I pray God the event doe not proove it
by exposinge to more daunger then he needes. my
iourney to Barwick hath not yett given mee leasure
to be sicke; when I goe that way againe I much
suspect my entertainment both for health and quiett-
nesse. I pray buy me Dr Read his treatise of wounds
and send it to me as soone as you can; it is a thinn
booke in 4°, & if it be only stitched it will be noe
more then 2 quire of paper. . . . when wee are over
past Newcastle, you must looke for noe more letters
from y^r assured lovinge uncle. . . . I comitt the dis-
tribution of love & service to y^r disposall.' The demand from the doctor for a treatise on wounds must
have been little reassuring to his friends at home. On
May 5 Sir Edmund writes: 'A little time now will
discover what I am unwilling to beleeve till I must
needes; but this daye I spake with an understanding
Scottshman & one that is affected the moderate waye;
hee is confident noething will sattisfye them but taking
awaye all Bishopps; & I dare saye the king will
never yeelde to that, soe wee must bee miserable; the
quorrell is allmost begun alreaddy for this daye news
is come that marquis Hamillton has taken fower
scotch shipps.' A few days later: 'My Lord Trequare & my lord Dyeale cam yesterday out of scottland; he tells the King (& hee desires his Ma^{sty} to putt
him in any Prison here & hange him if it be not trew
that hee sayes) that the Covenanters has 2000 as
good Hors as wee have any, & 2000 others that are
not soe good but yett very usefull & 40,000 foote

as good men as that nation can affoard, reddy at
five dayes warning, and therfore desires his Ma^sty
to goe with a foarce fitt to incounter this strength or
els all his men will be cutt in peeces. My Lord
Dyeale affirms the like uppon his life, but my
lord marshall sayes thes are but braggs & presses
the king extreamly to make haste to them; &
the king has given warning to march from hence
the next week. We shall march our whole Army
togeather in a Boddy with our cannon. Our Army
consists of 2000 Hors & 10,000 foote and that is the
most & more by some reasonable proportion boath of
Horse & foote that we shall have with us or that will
come to uss unless Marquiss Hamilltons foarces
comes to uss, our men are very rawe; our Armes of
all sorts naught, our vittle scarce & provision for
Horses woarce, and now you maye judg what case
wee are in; & all for want of monny to keepe uss
till wee maye bee better men or to bring more men
to us.'

Dr. Denton's alarming hints had borne fruit, and
Ralph replied immediately in great tribulation,
entreating him to do his best to keep Sir Edmund
back : ' Oh D^r if my father goes to the Borders he is
lost, I know his corrage will bee his distruction;
noe man did ever soe willfully ruine himselfe & his
posterity; god forgive him and grant me patience;
certainly his hart is more then stone, or else hee
could not soe soone forget both freinds & Wife &
children, & all to get (that which he can never loose)

honour, should hee spend all his time in contrivinge which way hee might make us most miserable, hee could not invent a readdier cource then this. Did he beget us to noe other end but to make us the sad spectacles of the world ? Will noething moove him ? Deare Dr : try, & try againe & set all his freinds uppon him, be more then earnest, night & Day perswade him, give him noe rest till hee hath yeelded to stay. I can say noe more, this greife 's to greate to bee expressed by your unhappy kinsman.'

By the same messenger he writes to his father in the same tone of passionate entreaty not to expose himself unnecessarily against the Scots. ' I find by Nat Hoberts letter that you meane (voluntarily) to attend my Lord Holland to the Borders (though many others stay with the Kinge, that have farr lesse reason) for S^r you know your yeares, your charge, your distracted fortune, your former life, were priviledge enough to keepe you Back, without the least staine to your reputation ; you may easily guesse how this afflicts mee, for if you goe, (knowinge your forwardness) I shall never thinke to see you more, but with griefe confesse that never man did more wilfully cast away himselfe.—Till now I never had the least reason to suspect your affection. But when I see you thus hastily ruñ to your owne ruine, and as it were purposely to loose that life that is soe much dearer to mee then my owne, how can I thinke you love mee ? hath the vaine hope of a little fadinge Honour swallowed up all your good nature ?

are your compassions quite shut up ? will neither
the numberlesse sights of your dearest freinds, nor
the uncessant cries of your forlorne widdow, nor the
mournfull groanes of your fatherlesse Brood prevaile
to stay you ? are you absolutely resolved by this on
act, to blot all your former ? and (by needlesse
hazardinge your selfe) expose your wife, and children
to perpetuall misery, and intaile afflictions uppon
your whole posterity.   I beseech you consider it and
bee not soe egere to make your selfe & us (your
unhappy children) the very objects of pitty it selfe,
pardon my boldnesse, it concerns mee neerly ; should
I now bee silent, perhapps heerafter 'twould bee too
late to speake, therfore let mee once more beseech
you to consider this seriously, and give not the world
soe just cause to account me your most unfortunate
sonne.'

In answer to these remonstrances Sir Edmund
replies quietly and affectionately : ' My designe of
goeing to the Borders with my lord of Holland had
only matter of kindness, none of danger in it.   yett
because it might seeme soe to my frends I was
desirous they might not know it, but that designe
was putt off and now wee are all goeing theather
wher I desire you to putt soe much trust in mee as
to beleeve I will not willfully thrust myself in
danger, nor will I thinck you could wish mee to
leave any thing undone when it falls to my turne to
bee in Action.   Raphe I thanck you for yor good
advice ; it has boath exprest yor Judgment & affec-

tion & I praye lett mee intreat you to beleeve I will neyther seeke my ruine nor auoyde any hazard when that little Honor I have lived in maye suffer by it, but trewly I thinck wee are not in much danger of fighting. . . .

'Comend me to Dr Cragg & tell him he is a churle for not wrighting all this while, I will never wright above a letter or two heerafter for uppon my credditt it is now almost three of the clock. . . . Comend mee to yor wife. . . . God bless you boath.'

He is afraid that many of his letters are 'gotten into ill hands . . . trewly I have never failed sending twice a weeke at least. . . . I shall not wright often now for we shall goe into the feeld presently, nay the King himself & all his Army after we go out of this towne [Newcastle] will lodg in the feelds every night & noe man must looke into a village.' He has received all his arms, 'but praye hast awaye my pott & take care itt bee wide inoughe for this is soe much to little that noe boddy but a madd man could have beene soe madd as to mistake soe grosly, therfore take care it bee wide inoughe now ; . . . this afternoone there is newes come for certaine that 2,000 Scotts are come within ten mile of Barwicke, they saye 8,000 more is coming after them & 2,000 more are gone to lye neare Carlile ; we shall soone have blowes now, but I beleeve it will be skirmishes with the Hors & noe Battle till towards the end of sumer, it is folly to thinck any longer of a peace, we

NAN UVEDALE
MRS HENSLOWE

Mrs Henslowe, dau: of Sir William Uvedale,
from a picture by Cornelius Jansen at Claydon House.

shall bee suddenly ingaged now.'   In the next letter :
' I have tryed my Arms & the Hedd peece is verry
much to little for mee ; if the Pott I expect dayly
from Hill [the Armourer] bee soe too I am undone ;
I praye send to him about it asssoone as you receive
this lēr ; this will come uppon noe part of my hedd
it is so very little ; the rest of my Armes are fitt. . . .
As I was thus farr in my lēr my lord chamberlaine
[Lord Pembroke] sent for mee and tould mee the
sadd   newes   of   sweete   Mʳˢ   Henslowes   Death
[daughter of his friend Sir William Uvedale] ; desire-
inge me to breake it to her father ; trewly I cannott
express my greefe for the loss of her ; shee was one
that I had an extraordinary esteeme for, & to whos
love I owe much ; I have now lost her, if shee had
lived a few weeks longer shee mought have lost
mee. . . . The God of Heaven bless you & yoʳˢ.'
Young Mistress Henslowe was only lately married,
and died with her first child.   There is a beautiful
Cornelius Jansen of her at Claydon in a shepherdess's
habit, and most living eyes.   Sir Edmund had
several affectionate friendships with ladies both old
and young.

　　Dr. Denton is extremely anxious to keep his
friends at home well frightened about Sir Edmund,
to whom he is sincerely attached.   In his next letter
he says that he will not thank Ralph for his book
until he sends him ' a paire of barbinge sissers ; . . .
yʳ father is yett well in body & att a good distance
from the borders. the King goeth towards Barwicke

on Thursday next & intends to intrench himselfe
wth in 5 or 6 miles of it, but on this side Tweede &
soe long as he keepes there I presume we shall be in
safety.' He hopes that the king will not fight this
summer, but will tempt the Scotch to bring out their
forces, and by that means exhaust them, 'but I feare
he will be cozened for I beeleeve that they be as
cunninge as they be wicked. The newes of theire
beinge 12,000 in a body wth in fore miles of Barwick
is false ; this is the best cordiall that I can send you
at this distance. Be confident that I will leave noe
stone unmoved that I conceave may knocke y^r ffathers
fightinge designes on the head & preserve him ; if I
can but keepe him from goinge out in parties, I hope
he will returne wth safety. I shall be very sensible
of any the least hazard that I shall thinke he may
be in & if all the witt & power that I have, or can
make, may prevent it, it shall be noe fault of y^r
assured lovinge uncle.'

There is a letter from Sir Edmund every few
days during this anxious time. On May 19 he
writes : ' Every hower now produces eyther something that is new or some alteration of our former
resolutions ; the King maks all the hast with this
little Army into the feeld that possibly hee can ;
. . . he has sent for 8,000 [1] men more with all
speede ; Lasly threatens to fight uss, but if hee comes
not quickly, he slipps a faire occation, for when we

---

[1] The levies ordered by the king were really 4,000 foot and 300
horse.

are intrencht and thes men come to uss wee shall not
much feare him which now wee doe, for if he bee
able to bring 10,000 men to uss any time thes twelve
dayes beleeve mee we are in verry ill case. My lord
of Holland is not yett come . . . we beleeve hee is
in Scottland; for hee was mett at Barwick, but
noeboddy heere seemes to know any such thing;
wee have had two of the coaldest dayes heere that
ever I felt, and I feare if it continues it will kill our
men that must lodg uppon the grownd without anything over them any time thes tenn dayes.'

Charles had lately issued a proclamation assuring
the Scotch that if they did not advance within ten
miles of the Border he would abstain from invading
Scotland; he negotiated with the Covenanting leaders
while at the same time he began to concentrate his
forces on Berwick.

Young Edmund writes from Mitford, in Northumberland, May 18, that the troops there are marching on Holy Island, the Marquis on one part, Lord
Dunluce with the Irish on another, and the main
body of the army on a third.

Sir Edmund enquires for the unfortunate steel
cap in every letter; Ralph had tried it on and found
it was too small, and ordered another. 'Raphe, as it
falls out I am verry sorry you were soe curious to
try the Pott, for an ill one had been better than none.
I doubt it maye come to late now, yett when it is
done send it awaye by the first shipp. . . . All the
Army except the privy chamber men, is marcht

awaye to the Rendezvous, which is within fower miles of Barwick ; to morrow the King removes and will bee ther the next daye if noething happens to change his resolution ; I am instantly goeing to view the grownd and place his tent reddy against he comes ; my lord of Holland has beene thes six dayes uppon the Border ; and till now the Scotts have not been seene in any great number, thoughe wee have often heard of great Armys coming towards uss.   He advertises the king now that ther are 1500 men come to the Borders allready and that they are informed ther is 15,000 foote and 4,000 Horse following them apace, . . . if this bee trew and that they make use of the advantage they have uss att, I doubt they will foarce uss to a dishonorable retraiet or els the kinge must hassard this Army which certainly he will not doe att this disadvantage ; but wee have had soe manny Alarms of greate Armys coming when ther was in trewthe noe such thing that wee beleeve this will proove a bragg too.   Within tenn or twelve dayes wee expect a great supply to our Army, and if they let uss aloane till they come to uss and that we are intrencht wee thinck they will not bee able to hurt uss and yet we shall always vex them . . . if ever they can make a foarce against uss it will bee now before wee intrench for I neyther thinck them fooles nor soe well natuerd as to suffer themselves to bee almost Blockt uppon all sides, if they can helpe it ; some are of oppinion that they are a little devided since the Proclamation ; for it is certaine the cove-

nanters has forbidden any man to read it uppon paine
of Death ; and this is conceaved stumbles manny
that are misled by an implicitt faith.' He then
describes a little encounter between ' some dussen
troopers of Mr. Goering ' with a party of the Scotch,
one of whom was killed ; ' this is the first bludd has
beene drawne in the busines, if more must bee lost in
this unhappy quarrell, I praye God it maye bee at
the same rate.'

Sir Edmund's next letter from the camp is
labelled ' Leslys pride.' They were now encamped
within two miles of Berwick, and had seen no enemy
as yett ; ' we heare lasly is within 12 miles . . . wee
fiend all the meaner sort of men uppon the scotch
Border well inclyned to the King and I beleeve when
time serves they will express it well ; but the Gentlemen are all covenanters, and I beleeve most men
are weary of the government ther now, for they lay
Heavy Burdens uppon the people. . . . in earnest
the King is most willing to suffer much rather then
have a warr, soe that I hope it will prove a peace.
Lasly has now the title of Soverain amonst them,
and the best lord amongst them sitt att a great distance below him, and under a lord noe man putts on
a Hatt in his presence ; all the Government of the
warr is comitted to him and of the state to, which is
to mee verry strange ; we heare the man is soe trans-
ported with this greatness that he gives offence to all
the Nobillity, and I beleeve they will desire a peace
to free themselves of him againe. I have beene heere

this three dayes in the camp ordering of things ther for the Kings coming tomorrow to lodg ther.'

On May 30 Charles took up his quarters in the encampment, about three miles from Berwick. The slight advantage gained by his adherents in Scotland at the ' Trot of Turriff' on May 14 had not been maintained, and. matters were looking badly for him. Some of his forces having crossed the border into Scotland, the Scotch held themselves at liberty to do the like; and when Lord Holland attempted to drive them from Kelso on June 3, he found them too strong to attack, and was forced ignominiously to retreat. Following on the discouragement produced by this failure came the advance of Leslie, the 'old little crooked soldier,' as he was called, who now marched to within twelve miles of the king, and encamped on the hill called Dumse Law with his army 12,000 strong. The king was so ill informed of their movements that the approach of the 'rebels' took him by surprise as he was about to go to supper, but he seemed to take it calmly : he took his 'perspective' and stood 'viewing and counting the tents a long while, and then said, "Come, let us go to supper, the number is not considerable." '

The situation was, however, an anxious one. The bad management of everything had dispirited the troops ; the biscuit was mouldy, there was no water within the camp, and provisions were scanty, while to add to their miseries the small-pox had

broken out. It was fortunate for the king that at
this juncture the Covenanters, who were no more
desirous to fight than the English, proposed to treat.
To save appearances, the king in reply insisted on his
proclamation, offering a pardon if they ' would return
to their obedience,' being read publicly in the
Scottish camp. This answer was sent by Sir
Edmund Verney, ' who was known,' says Baillie, ' to
be a lover of our nation and acceptable to the Scottish
people,' and therefore was an excellent ambassador
to choose. The result appears in the following letter
to his son from the camp late at night.

June 9.—' Raphe, I knowe you long to heare
what wee are doeing heere and I have as great a
desire still to informe you and therfore I faill not to
wright to you by every safe messenger if I have any
leysure for it. Wee are still at great quiett ; the
Scottish Army which is verry strong lyes now within
six miles of ours ; the lords of the covenant have
petitioned the King that they maye represent theyr
complaints and greevances by some of the Inglish
nobillity (for they saye theyr own country men has
beene falce to them and has misreported them and
theyre Actions to the King). His M^{sty} has assented
to thyr petition and has assigned six of our lords to
meete with as manny of theyrs att our lord Generalls
Tent in our campe ; they have petitioned for an
assurance under the King's hand, for theyr safe
returne, but hee refuses it and sayes they shall trust
to his woard ; this difficulty lyes yett in the waye,

but I assure myselfe ther will bee a waye found to sattisfye them in that, and I doubt not but wee shall have a treaty. . . . I hope it will be a good one. Uppon theyr petition to the Kinge I was sent by his M^{sty} with a message to them wherein thoughe I had a hard parte to playe yett I dare bouldly saye I handled the business soe that I begott this treaty ; otherwise wee had I doubt beene at blowes by this time ; but I praye take noe notice of this unless you heare it from others.' He ends with a pretty message to ' your good wife and give her my blessing, which I send her with as good a will as ever I askt any.' Sir John Temple describes that ' the Scots then assembled their cheife commanders, and gave way to Sir Edmund Verney to read it openly in the army.'

Sir Edmund writes on June 11 : ' This daye the lords on boath sides have had a meeting ; the King, contrary to expectation, went into the Tent to them as they begann to enter into theyr business, but I thinck it will not hurt the business ; the King heard them with patience, and answered with great modera-tion ; . . . the Scotts have a good Army, butt farr short of what they have bragd on, trewly I thinck wee shall have the better Army, for now our supplys are come to uss wee shall be able to make really 13,000 foote and 2200 Hors. They will have more foote but are weake in Horse, nor are they soe well Armed as wee, soe that I thinck they will hardly bee drawne to meete us in open feeld.'

Sir Edmund had been with Lord Holland in the

failure at Kelso, and Dr. Denton, writing on June 11
to alarm his friends, says : ' Raphe, the very next
day after I writt to you, y^r ffather was one of the
800 horsemen that were in a very faire way to be all
cutt off, for pistolls and carabins were all cocked,
swords drawne, and trumpetts goinge to mouth, which
had sounded had not some in the interim spied
forces in an ambush, wh^{ch} made them to make an
honourable retreat, since wh^{ch} time they have petitioned the Kinge ; your ffather hath caried messages
to and fro, and this day English and Scotch nobility
meete, and we are in great hope of an honorable
peace; if not your ffather, havinge quartered himselfe
with my L. of Holland, he will be almost in every
daunger, and now noe pswasions can remove him
thence, but I beleeve he will never stirr but wth my
L. . . . I am 14 miles from the campe with my L.
Chamberlaine, who hath had an agew, wh^{ch} left him
yesterday, and soe I hope to be att the campe againe
tomorrow.' Four days after Sir Edmund writes :
' everything is agreed on, and Monday appoynted
for a full conclution ; the King has promist them a
new assembly ; and to rattifye in parlament anything
that shall be agreed on in theyr assembly. They
insisted much uppon a rattification of theyr last
assembly, but the King would not yeeld to it ; more
particulars I have not time to send you, nor doe I
thinck yor curiosity is soe greate, but that the news
of peace will sattisfye it ; but now wee must travell
to Edenboroughe to the assembly and parlament ; soe

that thoughe wee have peace wee shall have noe quiett a great while. . . . I heare noething of my Pott from hill ; I will now keepe it to boyle my porrage in ' ; he does not forget the venison for one man and the protection for another—' I am suer y^r mother will easily excuse my not writing since I send soe good news of peace.' On June 18, 1639, peace was declared and the Treaty of Berwick signed.

There had been a quarrel between Lord Newcastle and Lord Holland in consequence of the former having considered himself insulted by being placed in the rear on one of the expeditions. He commanded a troop of volunteers which bore the prince's colours,[1] and to show his anger he had removed the colours from his flag-staff, and ridden sulkily back to the camp. Holland complained to the king, who took the part of Newcastle, and there the quarrel rested till the army was disbanded. Lord Newcastle then challenged Lord Holland, who chose Sir Edmund Verney as his second ; both time and place were settled for the duel, but the king, having heard of it, put Holland under arrest, and when Newcastle and his second, Francis Palmes, ' a man of known courage and metal,' presented themselves on the field, Sir Edmund came alone to explain ; Newcastle was soon afterwards also put into custody, and then the king made peace between the belligerents.

On June 17 Sir Edmund wrote to Ralph : ' Some

---

[1] Newcastle had been appointed governor to the Prince of Wales in the previous year.

are of oppinion that the King will shortly see lundon
and return heather againe ; others thincks his affaires
will keepe him heere, till his Scottish business be all
finisht, and that will not bee till the middle of
August.   I have a great desire to go to the Bathe
(for my payne troubles me much) ; . . . but till I
knowe how the King disposes of himselfe I can resolve of noething . . . farewell, yor lo : father.'

On June 21 : ' The King has stayed heere in the
feeld all this weeke to see his Army sent awaye. . . .
Assoone as I can find a resolution of his staye heere,
I purpos to aske leave to returne. . . . I praye wright
to Will Roads presently inquier out some grass for
geldings, for I have bought fifty Horses and Geldings
out of one Troope, and they will bee att Claydon
about Tenn dayes hence ; the Horses I will keep at
Howse till I can sell them.   I hope to see my frends
so shortly I will wright to none of them ; ' but he
asks Mary to ' choose him some patterns of cloath to
make me a sute of cloathes, for I shall have occation
to make some the next daye after I come to lundon.'
After he is gone, however, Dr. Denton writes an
alarming letter to Ralph, telling him that he has sent
his father safe to him, and intends to join him also at
the Bathe if he possibly can, but adds that ' one
Cunningham hath related to the Queene that all o^r
men runne away from Kelsay, of wch number yor
ffather was.   a relation so generall distastefull to all
that were there that he will be in noe quiett untill he
hath fought wth them all, and I know y^r ffathers

resolution is though not to seeke him yett to give Cunningham occasion enough to look after him ; verbum sapienti sat ; make what use of it you please, but not a word as from me.' Nothing more, however, turns up about Cunningham, and Sir Edmund was soon after at Bath. He was suffering much from sciatica, and the long journey, going round by London, must have been extremely trying. He was joined by his son Ralph, but the short time which he was able to be away from the king afforded him little chance of relief.

Exactly within a month he had returned to his duties at Berwick, whence he writes about ' warrants for Bucks, from Windsor in the great park,' and that he is ' sorry to hear the ill news of Harry Lee,' who is dying of small-pox, &c., &c. Young Edmund was sent to join the army in Flanders, and his father writes letters to Captain Apsly and Captain Homwood for the young soldier to take with him ; ' they will gett him assistance and directions what to do. He had best land at Flushing and soe goe directly to the Army.'

The extraordinary uncertainties of Charles's mind appear by the perpetual changes in his intentions ; no one knows what he is about to do, where he is going, or when ; but on July 28, a fortnight after Sir Edmund's return (so that the smallest consideration from the king might have saved him two long and painful journeys), he left Berwick for London, accompanied by Sir Edmund, riding the 260 miles in

four days. His army was disbanded ; he had found
his supporters in Scotland very half-hearted and his
opponents nearly unanimous ; but although he had
signed the peace, he intended as soon as he had
power, to enforce his canon and his ' Service-book,'
and the Covenanters, with a shrewd suspicion of his
intentions, kept together their principal soldiers.
There were great rejoicings in England for ' the
blesedness we heare of Pease,' as Lady Sussex writes ;
the Cavalier poets broke out into the most extrava-
gant congratulations ; Cowley wrote a pompous ode
on his Majesty's return out of Scotland :

> Welcome, great sir, with all the joy that's due
>   To the return of peace and you.
> Two greatest blessings which this age can know ;
> For that to thee, for thee to heaven we owe.
> Others by war their conquests gain,
> You like a god your ends obtain,
> Who, when rude chaos for his help did call,
> Spoke but the word, and sweetly ordered all. . . .
> . . . Again the northern hinds may sing and plough,
> And fear no harm but from the weather now.
> Again may tradesmen love their pain,
> By knowing now for whom they gain.
> The armour now may be hung up to sight,
> And only in their halls the children fright.

But the armour was scarce hung up before it was
taken down again ; and in a few months the war
with Scotland was renewed—'the second Bishop's
War,' as it was called.

Sir Edmund found much troublesome business
awaiting him in the south. He spent part of the
autumn at Bath, accompanied by Ralph, who was

very uneasy about him, returning to London in
November. The declaration of Mrs. Eure's marriage
gave him great pain. His wife was not well ; his
mother had been ill, and seemed to be rapidly failing,
though she survived both Sir Edmund and his wife ;
his mother-in-law, old Lady Denton, was much
troubled about her will and the disposal of her large
fortune of 10,000*l.* ; his brother-in-law, Sir Alexander Denton's affairs at Hillesden were unsettled ;
his friend, Lady Sussex, was in great sorrow, her
only son, Sir Harry Lee, having lately died. The
regulation of the hackney coaches was a troublesome
matter : 'the times are ill now for proclamations,'
and it was difficult without one to settle with the
fifty hackney coachmen. Tom Verney was for the
time disposed of at Barbados, but his father was not
without anxiety lest he should 'continue in his ould
cources.' Behind all private troubles lay the thought
of the probability of a renewal of the Scotch war,
which must have been as painful to Sir Edmund as
to his namesake son, who wrote in the winter from
Utrecht : 'I vow to you it is far from my desire [to
fight against the Scotch]. . . . I heare that the
King hath vast summes of mony given him by his
subjects, and that these forces are lyke to goe
against Scotland ; the former part I wish to be true,
but shall ever pray against the latter.'

So ended the year 1639.

CHAPTER XIV.

THE VERNEYS IN PARLIAMENT.

> ' Let this year bring
> To Charles our king,
> To Charles, who is th' example and the law,
> By whom the good are taught, not kept in awe.
> A session, too, *of such who can obey,*
> *As they were gathered to consult, not sway.*' [1]

THE Verneys were a very parliamentary family. Sir Ralph Verney, as before mentioned, was member for London in 1472, and from that time there was seldom wanting a representative of the name for the county of Bucks, or for one of its five boroughs, always on what would now be called the 'liberal' side in politics, as shown in the following table :

Edward VI. 1552.	Sir Edmund Verney for Buckinghamshire, and Francis Verney, Esq., for the town of Buckingham.
Philip and Mary 1556.	Sir Edmund Verney and Francis Verney, Esq., for Bucks.
James I. 1624.	Sir Edmund Verney (on his return with Prince Charles from Spain) for Buckingham.
Charles I. 1628.	Sir Edmund Verney (Knight Marshal) for Aylesbury.
Charles I. 1640.	Sir Edmund Verney for Wycombe, and Ralph Verney, Esq., for Aylesbury (the Short Parliament).

---

[1] 'A Cavalier's definition of the use of Parliament,' by Sir W. Davenant, Poet Laureate to Charles I.

Charles I. 1640. Sir Edmund Verney for Wycombe, and Sir Ralph
Verney for Aylesbury (the Long Parliament).

Charles II. 1680. Sir Ralph Verney, Bart., for Buckingham.

James II. 1685. Sir Ralph Verney for Buckingham.

William and Mary Sir Ralph Verney, Bart., for Buckingham (Con-
1688–89. vention Parliament).

Anne . . . 1710. Sir John Verney, Bart., for Buckinghamshire.

Anne . . . 1713. Sir John Verney, Lord Fermanagh, for Amersham.

George I. 1714. Viscount Fermanagh for Amersham. In his place
deceased, Ralph Verney, Viscount Fermanagh.

George I. 1722. Ralph Verney, Viscount Fermanagh, for Amersham.

George II. 1735. Ralph Verney, Viscount Fermanagh, for Wendover.

George II. 1747. Ralph Verney, 1st Earl Verney, for Wendover.

George II. 1754. Ralph Verney, 2nd Earl Verney, for Wendover.

George III. 1768. Ralph Verney, 2nd Earl Verney, for Buckinghamshire.

George III. 1790. Ralph Verney, 2nd Earl Verney, for Buckinghamshire. [The last male of the old family of
Verney.]

The present Sir Harry Verney has carried on the
parliamentary tradition. In the Reform Parliament
of 1832 and that of 1835 he represented Buckingham.
In 1837, 1857, 1859, 1865, 1868, and 1880 Sir Harry
again sat for the town. In the Parliament of 1847,
however, the Bucks farmers in the enlarged borough
refused to support him, believing that the repeal of
the corn laws, for which he declared he should vote,
would ruin them ; he therefore contested and sat for
Bedford, which had been lost to the Whigs by Lord
John Russell in 1837. In 1885 the borough of
Buckingham was disfranchised after a life of 340
years, its last member being a Verney, as was nearly
the first. The previous family of Verneys had represented Buckinghamshire in eighteen parliaments. So

long a connection is creditable both to electors and elected.

In the year 1640 matters had come to a crisis for the king ; the pacification of Berwick had merely been a truce ; he had exhausted all his expedients for raising money, even for the ordinary expenses of government, and was making most unpopular preparations for another campaign against the Scotch, who by March had reassembled their army. He found himself, after an interval of eleven years, obliged to summon a parliament, Strafford, who was in fact his prime minister, insisting on it, ' that he might leave his people without excuse, and justify himself to God.'

Ralph writes that he is going to Aylesbury, and again that he has been returned. On April 13 what is called the Short Parliament met, the father and son, Sir Edmund and Ralph, sitting together for the first time. Sir Edmund sat for Wycombe ; there was some trouble concerning his election, the choice of ' the Popular,' as they are called in a subsequent letter, not coinciding with that of the burgesses of the borough. No election committee was, however, nominated, such as on a subsequent occasion (mentioned by Ralph in his ' Notes ') sat to consider the election for Great Marlow, and after inquiry ordered a new writ to be issued—a fortunate decision, since at the second election Whitelock, author of the ' Memorials,' was returned. Lord Fermanagh sets down : ' Sir Edmund Verney and Thomas Lane were returned to serve Burgesses for ye towne of Wiccam in Com: Bucks by ye maior, Aldermen, Bayliffs and Burgesses being to ye number of 53, under ye towne seale, with 36 names inscribed to that indenture ; & 30 other inhabitants, not being Burgesses or free men, have returned Henry Bulstrode and Adrian Scrope, but not by ye sheriffe.' Sir Edmund's seat, however, does not seem to have been contested, and he sat without further question.

It is unfortunate that, as both Sir Edmund and his son were living in Covent Garden, and both the Lady Verneys were with their husbands, there were no letters between them. So little is known about the Short Parliament that Ralph's ' Notes ' would have been very valuable. There are no foul copies either of the letters which he wrote to Lady Sussex every few days, as she gratefully acknowledges ; they were probably destroyed as dangerous.

' It could never be hoped that more sober and dispassionate men would ever meet again in that place, or fewer who brought ill purposes with them,' is Clarendon's verdict on the members. They met, indeed, in a spirit determined to have their grievances redressed, but were ' favourably disposed towards the king's service.'

Charles offered to release his claim for ship-money on the receipt of twelve subsidies, but this the Commons indignantly refused ; if the right of taxation were inherent in the Crown, all other stipulations were vain. This was the great question which they

held must first be settled. They therefore declared
that the 'redress of grievances must precede supply,'
and the king's attempt to excite their indignation by
bringing forward an intercepted letter from the Scots
to the French king, 'inviting his help,' made no impression whatever ; it did not even delay the course
of the debate.

The sitting of April 16 was opened by Harbottle
Grimstone, an old friend of both Sir Edmund and
his son. That so moderate a man, full of respect for
the constitution, should have taken this prominent
part is evidence of the conservative spirit in which
the great leaders at first desired to conduct the
struggle. Pym followed next day with a calm, ar-
gumentative speech, beginning with the religious
questions. He declared that the new ceremonies
'had put upon the Churches a shape and face of
Popery,' and complained of 'the over-rigid prosecution of those who were scrupulous.' Only in the
second place came the political part, the 'insupportable grievances,' the tyrannical proceedings of the
Privy Council and Star Chamber, the monopolies, the
military charges, and the way in which the clergy
who had defended unconstitutional powers were
rewarded with preferment. The speech produced a
great effect, and there were cries of ' A good oration.'

A Committee of the whole House, with Grimstone
as chairman, sent for the records of the proceedings
in 1629 against Sir John Eliot, and a select Committee was appointed to consider the king's breach of

privilege in imprisoning him, as well as his two companions, who had only just been released after ten
years' captivity.

The feeling against the bishops rose high. In the
Upper House Bishop Hall was made to apologise for
having published a book, 'Episcopacy by Divine
Right,' and Sir Ralph's letters to Lady Barrymore
show that the feeling in the Commons was the same.
'The Bishops, for whose sakes all these troubles are
on us'; and again, in June 1841 : 'wee are soe bent
to remove the B^{pps} from the House of Peeres, that I
conceive if it bee denied, wee shall doe our best endeavours to abolish them utterly as the Scotts have
done.' Lady Brilliana Harley, whose husband was
Sir Edmund's colleague in the Long Parliament,
wrote about the same time : 'I am glad that the
Bischops begine to falle, and I hope it will be with
them as it was with Haman ; when he began to falle
he fell indeede.'

The king became alarmed, and finding the Commons still obdurate after he had by the advice of
Strafford come down to the Upper House, he roughly
dissolved the Parliament, which had only sat for
three weeks. 'Things must go worse before they go
better,' was the comment of Oliver St. John, but the
feeling in the country was one of exasperation. 'It
is impossible,' said Lord Northumberland, still on the
king's side, 'that things can long continue in this
condition ; so great a defection in the kingdom hath
not been known in the memory of man.'

Charles was thrown back upon his former expedients, and all in vain. The Scotch were advancing, while the army sent to oppose them was a mere mob. The feeling against the popish officers, who had been appointed in large numbers by the king, was very strong ; the men were heard to swear that they would murder them all, and whole regiments were in disorder. Lieutenant Eure, a Catholic, and probably a relation of Lord Eure, who refused to accompany his men to church, was murdered in Somersetshire.

There is an amusing letter from Edmund Verney in July 1640, about the way in which his men are mounting guard, upon the orthodoxy of their officers. ' My souldyers and I are now att one & indeede never had any greate difference above twice, the cheife of which I writt at large to my father the last weeke. For my goeing to church 3 times in a day it was true, but it was rather my own doings to give them satisfaction that I was noe papist then any compulsion of theires, but once that day I a little nodded at church, & had it been a minute longer truely I doe thinke I had been pulled by the nose, for the souldyers pointed extreamely at me, & the same day pulled up a Captaine of my lord Newport's regiment to the byshop's altar, but theire communion table, and made him receive, when scarce any of them would receive with him. Here is noe newes but that the county of Yorke takes this billetting of the souldyer upon them much to heart, and though they doe it upon a kind of

compulsion, yet are they resolv'd never to yeeld to it,
least the president of it might for ever be a prejudice
to theire posterity.'

Nothing could be worse than the state of the raw
levies of the king. On August 10 General Conway,
commander of the horse, received intelligence which
convinced him that an invasion was imminent. A
month before Sir Jacob Astley, whose duty it was to
receive the recruits at Selby, had written to him ' that
those expected had not come, & those that are come
have neither colours nor halbertes & want drums.'
He then went on to complain that he was ' to receive
all the arch knaves of the kingdom & to arm them at
Selby. Before I came some 500 of them beat the
officers & the boors & broke open the prisons. Two
days ago Colonel Lunsford's regiment fought with
their officers, & as they passed abused all the country.'
At length on August 20 the Scots moved forwards
across the Border with about 25,000 men, while the
king was utterly unprepared with either money or
troops. There had been several outbreaks among
the soldiers for want of pay, 3,000 of them were un-
armed, and there was such entire indifference among
the people to the approach of the Scots, whose mani-
festo declared that they would shed no blood and
take nothing, ' not a chicken nor a pot of ale without
paye for them,' that there was the utmost difficulty
in collecting a force to oppose them. The king in
despair summoned Strafford from Ireland to take the
command, but although Durham and Yorkshire at

length sent out their train-bands, there was no time
to organise them into an effective army.

A stand was made at Newcastle, which however
it was found impossible to defend, and Conway, who
attempted to stop the Scots in passing the ford of
the Tyne, was ignominiously defeated. The English
soldiers, 'altogether necessitous, the horse all cowardly,'
as Strafford declared, ' without heart or discipline,'
fled almost at the first onset at Newburn. After this
reverse Edmund Verney wrote from York : ' That we
were beaten you have heard, and for the circumstances
they are reported soe various that I know not which
to write to you for a trueth ; this is certaine, that if
Lasley had pursued his victory he had cutt us all of ;
buisnesses were very ill managed by some, for we had
neither cannon nor ammunition by us, but went on
lyke sheepe to the slaughter. I believe we shall have
peace, but if we have not I hope wee shall have better
doings, or else we are surely beaten againe, and then
I know not what part of the kingdome can or at
least will hinder theire march whither they please.'

Charles as a last resort summoned a great council
of the peers at York. But before they met he had
succumbed to the universal demand for a parliament.
On September 24 he announced to the assembled
peers his intention of summoning the Houses to
Westminster. On September 21 Edmund wrote : 'here
is noe newes since but that 16 of the Scotts horse are
slaine, and 34 taken prisoners, Edinburgh Castle is
given up upon condition of lyfe to the defendants &

the marching away with two peeces of the King's best
cannon, whether peace or warr it is yet uncertaine,
but I believe it will be knowne within this 8 or 10
dayes, for all depends on the Lords engaging or not
engaging themselves for money.'   Four days later he
writes again : ' The King doth soe much sympathise
with the Lords that he tells them if they will have
him disband his army tomorrow he will doe it, but as
God would have it they very nobly and most unanimously all cryed noe, but yet I feare twelve months
is the longest.'   On October 9 Edmund writes : ' For
newes, all that is now is of warr, for the Scotts, contrary to your opinion (I am sure) are very unreason-
able, they ask no lesse then 40,000*l.* for a month's
longer treaty, but wee have a company of noble lords
that vow to pay them in leaden coyne, but next week
I shall be able to give you a more certain information,
for the Scotch lords come to treat with the King and
ours on Monday next at Yorke.'

In fact, on October 7 Charles had proposed to
the Scotch Commissioners to come from Ripon,
where negotiations had been begun, to York, where
he himself was.   They flatly refused, the negotiations were resumed at Ripon, they consented on
October 21 to accept 850*l.* a day for two months, and
a cessation of arms was agreed upon.

On November 3 the Long Parliament met.
Both Sir Edmund and Ralph had been returned
apparently without opposition ; there are no details
given however, only young Edmund rejoices over

' the happiness which has attended you.' Ralph, who was soon afterwards knighted, was now twenty-seven years of age, and, except during the three weeks of the Short Parliament, he had had no experience of parliamentary life. It is always an epoch in a man's career when first he enters the walls of that great assembly, where the very heart of the nation may be felt to beat ; a proud moment when first he finds himself among the representatives chosen by the great English people to do the work of its government, and Ralph was one to experience this feeling in its full force. The importance of the right use of their power at this critical juncture, the momentous issues that hung upon their every decision, must have made it no light task for so conscientious a man to join in the deliberations of the House of Commons in the Long Parliament of 1640. There were only 460 members at this period, and young Edmund writing to his brother says : ' I commend my humble sute to you and the rest of the 460 Kings who sit at Westminster to have regard to the honour of us souldyers,' and see to giving them their long arrears of pay. In another letter he mentions ' the 460 tyrants who rule over us.'

An old print of this period represents the members with the broad felt hat and feather so associated with portraits of Charles himself—short cloaks, doublets, and hose, sitting on five rows of benches raised one above the other on each side of the floor of the House, as at present. The Speaker's chair, however, was a good way from the end, and there were seats behind him.

The chamber in which their deliberations took place was the same as that wherein Sir Ralph's successor, after 200 years, Sir Harry Verney, well remembers sitting in 1833-4 just before it was burnt down. ' Here for three centuries some of the most important business in the world was transacted.' It ran at right angles to Westminster Hall, and was as long as the hall was broad. Beneath it was a crypt with beautiful intersecting arches which survived the fire, and has been restored and richly decorated as a chapel. In the seventeenth century it formed one of the vaults where Guy Fawkes and his barrels of gunpowder were discovered. The House itself occupied the site of what is now called St. Stephen's Hall, but stretched further towards the river, where there was a large window at the east end looking out on the Thames. On February 17, 1641, a crowd of members rushed up to this window, having suddenly heard a rumour that Strafford would pass in a barge from the Tower to the House of Lords, ' but were disappointed, as the Lords had granted him another week.' [1]

There was an opening from the House into the Great Hall itself, which in those days shared in the excitement of what was going on within, and where members walked up and down in the intervals of the

[1] Sir Harry Verney remembers, in the year before the fire, the two front benches, Government and Opposition, with Lord Stanley at their head, followed by the rest of the House rushing to this window to look at the great boat race of the year.

debates. Through it the king passed on his way to apprehend the five members, and, as Sir Simon D'Ewes tells us, 'it struck such a fear and terrour into all those that kept shops in the said Hall, or near the gates thereof, as they instantly shut up their shops.'

The beautiful pointed arches and decorations of the old St. Stephen's Chapel, dating from the thirteenth century, which formed in fact the House itself, had been hidden after the Reformation by a flat ceiling eight or more feet under the old roof, and this space constituted what in later days was called 'the venti-lator,' with a large oval opening to the House below, round which the ladies sat and peered down on the heads of the members. It was the only 'Ladies' Gallery,' and I can remember being taken there as a child to listen to the debates, and seeing the Minis-terial and Opposition ladies keeping rigorously to their own sides of the hole. It was the best place for hear-ing in the House. There was also, in 1640, a rude gallery at the west end, afterwards done away with, into which members mounted by a ladder.

' There they sat, courtier and Puritan, the pick and choice of the gentlemen of England, by birth, by wealth, by talents the first assembly in the world,' says Forster. With the foremost of these on both sides Sir Edmund and his son were more or less intimate, and Buckinghamshire was represented by some of the best of them. There is a sheet of paper in the Claydon muniment-room whereon eleven of the names of its members are 'faire writ for sport'

by themselves, Hampden's firm round hand very
conspicuous among the signatures.

The business of the House began so early in
the day that it is difficult to understand how the
Ministers found time for their official work. Lord
Warwick, when begging for Ralph's presence at a
Committee on the Posts in which he had business,
apologises for asking him to be there by seven in the
morning; 'an unseasonable hour,' he calls it, as eight
was the usual hour of assembling. They seem generally to have stopped before their midday meal; but as
the times grew more and more anxious the sittings
grew later, and Lord Clarendon remarks upon 'the
House then keeping those disorderly hours and seldom
rising till after four of the clock in the afternoon.'

There is an appeal from the Speaker just before
the debate on the Grand Remonstrance, which, however, does not seem to have been much regarded,
'against the rush of members betwixt twelve and one
midday, such that he was feigne to tell them they
were unworthy to sit in this great and wise assembly
that would so rush forth to their dinners.'

Clarendon goes on to say that ' Mr. Pym's lodging
was in a little court behind Westminster Hall, where
he, Mr. Hambden, Sir Arthur Hazelrigg, &c., upon
a stock kept a table where they transacted much
business.' One day, when he had dined there with
Fiennes, they sent for their horses and rode together
in the fields between Westminster and Chelsea, which,
till about fifty years ago, were still known as 'the

Com Buckingham.

Mr. Henry Wilkinson.

Mr Thos Valentine.

Ed: Verney

fra. Denton

Ar: Goodwin

Ro Broke.

Bulstrode Whitelocke

Raphe Verney.

Jo Hampden   William Drake

Ed: Hounslow.

Peri: Hoby   Fran Drake

AUTOGRAPHS OF ELEVEN MEMBERS FOR BUCKS IN THE LONG PARLIAMENT
AND THE RETURNING OFFICERS.

Five Fields,' and very lonely ones too, as remembered
by Sir Harry Verney.

The difficulties of all artificial light made it almost
a necessity to confine the debates to daylight sittings.
On one occasion, in June 1641, when discussing the
army plot, 'it being dusk some members called for
candles ; the majority opposed the proposal, it being
so very late,' but they were brought in by a mistake
of the serjeant's. As he came in with them in his
hands (the number carried by one man must indeed
have been scanty for so large a chamber), he was commanded to withdraw, but two members seized them and
bore them triumphantly into the House. There was
a great uproar and the House adjourned. The next
day a serious debate took place, the culprits tried in
vain to excuse themselves, and by a majority of 189
to 172 it was determined that they should be committed to the Tower. They were then called to the
Bar, where, ' they kneeling all the while,' the Speaker
communicated to them the judgment of the House.
They were discharged only after six days' imprisonment. The discipline of the House was indeed stricter
than at present. How many weeks would a recalcitrant Home Ruler earn for himself nowadays ?

Sir Ralph, in his careful methodical way, at once
prepared to chronicle the proceedings. No record of
their debates was allowed by the Commons, and
D'Ewes and others mention the difficulties experi-
enced by any one who attempted to do so. On one
occasion Sir Harry Vane stopped an offender, saying

he ' remembered when noe man was allowed to take noates, and wishes it to be now forbidden.' Sir Ralph's notes are written in pencil on folded sheets of small foolscap paper, evidently held upon his knees and carried in his pocket. They are quoted as being full of interest by Hallam, Forster, and Gardiner. Sometimes, when the debate grew excited and members rose suddenly, the writing becomes illegible ; sometimes there are great jogs of the pencil as if someone in a full House pressed hastily against the writer's elbow when in the act of taking the note. Often he breaks off abruptly when the speaker became too rapid for him to follow. The passages relating to Resolutions of the House are full of erasures and alterations. Sometimes the confusion and irregularity of the note bears witness to the excitement of the House ; and the speeches are less frequently assigned to the speakers from a feeling of the danger of the times and the possible use which might be made of notes containing violent remarks.

The tremendous earnestness of the debates is extremely striking. Their subjects were matters of life and death to both sides, politically in this world, and concerning the chance of heaven and hell in the next.

There does not appear to have been the smallest interruption in the stern solemnity of the speakers, on the king's side as well as on the parliamentarian. There was no breathing time, as now, when frivolous questions will be asked and answered—when the members relax over the absurdities of one speaker or the insolence of another who, when called to order, takes pains to show his bad breeding by repeating his offence.

The only instance where the ghost of a smile could have been raised is treated in the severest style by Sir Ralph. A certain T. T., ' contrary to the custom of this House, doth seate and place himselfe neare the Speaker's chaire, where non but Privy Councillours and men of distinction are wont to sit, to the great scandall of the House. The said T. T., in a loud and violent manner, and contrary to the custom & usuage of Parliment, in the Speaker's [ear], at the putting of a question about the militia, on 3rd Jan. '41, standing neare the Speaker's chaire, cried " Baw ! " to the great terror and affrightment of the Speaker and of the members of the House of Comons, and contrary to his duty and the trust reposed in him by his country.' It does not appear, however, who this delinquent was or what punishment was inflicted for his crime.

Lady Sussex writes just after the meeting of Parliament : ' Now you will be taken up for your great affars. i pray God it may be a happy Parlyment to us all. When you have any idell time i pray let me have sometimes a lyne or to from you—and i will send you some bisket to put in your pokete and jhelly to comfort you up, as sone as my woman is in tune to make it.' The inconveniences of the House were so great and the hours so long that Lady

Sussex's pocket provisions were doubtless very welcome. When the jelly and cakes arrive, she says : ' You must remember let them be tosted.'

At the very outset of the Long Parliament the king met with a rebuff. He had desired to propose Sir Thomas Gardiner, Recorder of London, as Speaker ; but the City refused to elect him as one of their members, choosing to be represented by four Puritans. Lenthall was then selected by the House, and proved himself to be an ideal Speaker.

Lenthall's brother, Sir John, married a first cousin of Ralph's mother ; Sir Thomas Gardiner's son was about to marry his sister Cary ; indeed, the number of members with whom Ralph was connected by blood, marriage or friendship was curiously large. His uncle, Sir Alexander Denton, was M.P. for Buckingham ; Frank Drake for Amersham ; Nathaniel Fiennes, another cousin, for Banbury ; Hyde, his father's great friend ; Sir Roger Burgoyne, ' that trew friend,' and many of his country neighbours, including Chaloner the regicide, were all returned together ; the precincts of the House were almost a home to Ralph, who looked back to this time during the remainder of his long life with a sort of regretful affection.

The Houses at Westminster felt themselves strong in popular support, and behind public opinion was the Scotch army, ' a rod over the King,' as Strafford called it ; but they were conscious that their power might be short-lived. The Commons lost no time in turning to the examination of grievances. Harbottle Grimstone quoted a saying ' that the Judges have overthrown the law, and the Bishops the Gospel.' More than forty committees were appointed to examine into abuses ; Prynne was brought back from Jersey in triumph, ship-money was declared illegal, the farmers of the Customs were voted delinquents, and monopolies were finally abolished. Yet such was the awe inspired by Strafford and the fear of his influence, that measures against him were considered as important as the reform of abuses. He was not unprepared for the storm, and begged the king to dispense with his attendance. He would have felt safer either in Ireland or at the head of the army in Yorkshire, but the king, who wanted his advice, summoned him to London, promising him that he ' should not suffer in his person, honour or fortune.' Strafford obeyed ; on November 9 he reached London, and on the 11th he was impeached for high treason. Falkland alone urged delay and further investigation ; Pym feared he would procure a dissolution and accuse the parliamentary leaders of treason unless he were forestalled. The accusation was laid before the Lords, and the earl was committed to the Tower. The impeachment of Laud followed in December.

In January 1641 the Commons passed a Bill for Triennial Parliaments, by which, if the king failed to issue the writs, the returns were to be made without him ; to which the king replied that he would never delegate his authority to ' Sheriffs, Constables and I know not whom.'

Meanwhile, discontent in the army was daily rising. Edmund Verney wrote to his brother from North Stainely, near Ripon, on January 15 :

' Next Tuesday we have 6 weekes due to us and unlesse there bee some speedy course taken for the payments you may well expecte to heare that all our souldyers are in a mutiny to the ruine of the country, for they are notable sheepe stealers allready.'

In March he says : ' I beleeve you are buisyed in the parlyament and yet neglect the mayne busines of supplying the army, the effect of which with the terrible threatening musters may very well produce strange things, even not to be named. The horse have sent theire peremptory answere that they will not muster till they are payde ; if the foote doe the lyke, beleeve me it can tend to noe lesse than a generall mutiny. A worme will turne agayne if it be trod on. Souldiers are now used ass though it were sure there should never be farther use of them. Apes have bitts and bobs, but we have bobs without bits.[1] If it hold thus but a fortnight longer, you will have a letter in way of petition to redresse our greevances or to cashiere us. There are divers officers that owe ass much ass their pay comes to, and are put to such shifts, that it is hard to say whether it

---

[1] The expression ' to be treated like apes, with bobs and bits,' i.e. to be tantalised, occurs frequently in the letters ; ' bob ' seems to be a blow, and ' bit ' a bite of food.

goes hardest with them or the common souldyer. What foul dishonour is this to uss in our owne nation.'

On January 28, 1641, the accusation against Strafford was brought up by the committee appointed to prepare it ; on the 30th it passed the Commons and was laid before the Lords, but some weeks were allowed him for the preparation of his defence.

In February the Triennial Bill was sent up for the king's assent. He was reluctant to give it, but he was in need of money and feared that supplies would be refused unless he yielded. He therefore gave his consent in a speech to both Houses, in which he declared, ' You have taken the Government all in pieces, and I may say it is almost off the Hinges. A skilful Watchmaker to make clean his Watch, will take it asunder, and when it is put together it will go the better, so that he leave not out one Pin of it. Now as I have done all this on my part, you know what to do on yours.'

On March 22 the trial of Lord Strafford opened. Sir Ralph's notes begin the next day, and he follows carefully the details of the prosecution till he is called away to attend his mother's death-bed. On April 10 he is back in his place, when there was a violent disagreement between the Lords and Commons ; the latter withdrew in ' tumultuous confusion,' and Strafford could not hide his joy at the scene. The Commons having retired into their own House, the doors were shut, the key ' brought up,' and Pym produced the celebrated Minute of the

Committee of Eight, containing the speeches made before them by Strafford after the dissolution of the Short Parliament. They had been taken down by Sir Harry Vane, as secretary, and though the original report had been burnt by the king's order, a copy by a curious accident had come to light.

Young Sir Harry Vane was about to be married, and the title-deeds of the family estate were required for the settlements. His father, being absent from London, had entrusted certain keys to his son to enable him to examine his papers. Amongst these were found ' Notes taken at the Junto,' of which Sir Harry immediately took a copy and carried it to Pym with great expressions of a troubled mind, not knowing which way to steer, as indeed is not to be wondered at, for it was only by breach of trust that the paper had been seen at all. Now, however, that it appeared doubtful whether the Lords would find Strafford guilty of treason, the fresh evidence was invaluable, and strengthened by it his opponents introduced the Bill of Attainder, which passed the first reading that very day. On the 12th the Commons proceeded to the examination of Vane's secretary, Coggin, Sir Ralph's note on which is considered important by Mr. Bruce.

' Mr. Coggin saies there are 2 studdies in Sir H. Vane's house, the higher of which was comitted to his custody. In the higher was 2 Cabanetts, and in the lower, about September last, younge Sir H. V. came to him for a Cabanett, and perused it 2 or 3

daies.　Coggin had noe direction from old Sir H. V.
to open the studdy or cabinet.　Younge Sir H. V.
told him hee had the key of the black velvet cabinet,
and therefore hee bid him send it downe, and it was
donne accordingly. . . Hee told him, hee was to sort
some writings of his father's.'

The House sent a copy of Vane's Minute to the
Lords, who had been extremely irritated at the interruption of the trial by the Commons and the proposal of a Bill of Attainder. 'It is an unnatural
motion for the head to be governed by the tail,' said
one of them. 'We hate rebellion as much as treason ;
we will never suffer ourselves to be suppressed by a
popular faction.' Next day, however, the trial proceeded as before, and Sir Ralph goes on with his
record.

'My lord Straford did sum upp his evidence,'
going through each point one after another. 'Sir
H. Vaine's words swourne.　Hee spake dubiously, for
hee promised plainnesse, but spake but to the best of
his remembrance, and [yet] afterwards swore the
very words or to that effect.　But hee is a single
witnesse, and all the rest of the juncto remember noe
such thinge.' In fact, the examination of the other
councillors had proved little ; they could not remember that Strafford had ever proposed to bring
the Irish army to England.

'If,' as Strafford had said a little while before,
'words spoken to friends in familiar discourse, spoken
at one's table, in one's chamber, in one's sick bed . . .

shall be brought against a man as treason, this (under favour) takes away the comfort of all human society.'

'Fourteen yeares hee strived to proceed in *viis antiquis*. For his religeon, they have acquitted him. For subvertion of law, hee hopes to bee acquitted heere.'

On April 21 the Bill of Attainder passed its third reading. The Prince of Orange, a youth of fourteen, had just arrived in London for his betrothal with the king's eldest daughter Mary. It was believed that he had brought 200,000*l.* with him ; money had been found to pay the army in the north, rumours of plots were abroad, and it was evident that the prisoner's escape would be assisted or connived at by the king.

On the 29th 'the argument on behalf of the Commons before the Lords touching the matter of law,' i.e. the Bill of Attainder, was argued by St. John. Sir Ralph goes on : ' Wee met the lords in a Comittee of both Houses, and they cam without there robes, and Mr. St. John, the King's Solicitor, argued the poynt of law in his place about the midle of the house, and not at the barr, and hee was assisted by Mr. Manord and Mr. Glin. And my Lord Straford was present, but he was placed behind the barr, and not where hee was wount to sit, but Mr. Maxwell and the leiftenant of the Tower did stand before him, soe that he was not seene.' ' The King, prince, and Queen were present,' says Nalson.

On May 1 the king proceeded to the House of Lords, and declared to both Houses that 'he could

not in his conscience condemn the Earl of treason.'
This step created great indignation as an interference
with the freedom of debate. The belief that the
troops were about to be employed to release Strafford
and overawe the Parliament roused the feelings of
the people, large numbers of whom rushed to Westminster, wildly demanding 'justice on the great
delinquent.' The names of the members who had
voted against the attainder had been somehow procured, although the division lists were never published,
and the crowd posted them up at the corner of the
wall in Old Palace Yard, as 'Straffordians, betrayers
of their country,' thus bringing down violent popular
indignation on them. The list was inaccurate and
incomplete, that given by Sir Ralph was the first
complete one. Sir Edmund probably did not vote;
he would certainly not defend Strafford, to whom he
had been always opposed, neither could he vote
against the king while still in his service.

The crowd consisted by no means only of the
populace. About a week before a petition signed by
20,000 Londoners had called for the execution of
Strafford and the redress of grievances, and numbers
of merchants and shopkeepers now crowded round
the House, compulsorily idle from the interruption
to trade caused by the panic, and angry accordingly.
In the excitement the House with one accord drew
up a 'vow and protestation,' and the vehemence of
the whole proceeding appears in the disjointed, ill-
written state of Sir Ralph's notes.

Pym's speech on this occasion still showed his desire to avoid a breach with the king, and his argument was to the effect that ' being the King hath a tender conscience 'tis fit he should have good councelours about him.' Charles was still in theory supposed to be led astray by ' wicked counsels,' and the remedy was that he should change his minister. Marten followed, advising that they should unite themselves ' for the pure worshipp of God, the defence of the king and his subjects in all there legall rights.'

A committee was appointed and an oath drawn up, but altered again and again before it was deemed satisfactory. The final form given by Sir Ralph is, ' I, A. B., doe in the presence of Almighty God, promise vow and protest to maintaine and defend as farr as lawfully I may, with my life, power, and estate, the true reformed Protestant religeon, as expressed in the doctrine of the Church of England, against all popery and popish innovations within this relme ; . . . and according to the duty of my aleagence, his majestis royall person, honour and estate ; as also the power and priviledges of parliment ; the lawfull rights and liberties of the subject ; . . . and I will oppose by all good wayes and meanes . . . all such as shall . . . doe any thing to the contrary of any thinge in this present protestation contayned,' &c.

This protestation was taken by the Speaker first, and then by 368 members unanimously. Whilst

the Commons were thus occupied, the king, alarmed
by the crowds surrounding Whitehall, sent a message
to both Houses, calling upon them ' to take into consideration some speedy course to settle peace and
prevent these tumults.' Without taking any notice
the lower House appointed four members, Hollis
being one, to carry the protestation to the Lords.
The heads of his speech are given by Sir Ralph. The
king had attempted to seize the Tower, and the fear
of the army being brought down upon them filled
the minds of men. ' Two armies,' said Hollis (the
Scotch and the English), ' like vultures eate through
our sides. Winde and tyde are still against the parliment. Ill councells are like the strong east winde
that brings the locust.'

The danger to the Tower was averted by an order
from the Peers that the Lords Essex, Saye, and
Brooke should see that 500 men from the Tower
Hamlets were sent there to take possession.

The next day the Protestation was taken by all
the Protestant lords. A great concourse of men
again rushed down into Palace Yard calling for justice, they were armed with swords and clubs, and
were a rougher mob than that which had been seen
there the day before. In the afternoon, however,
they dispersed without doing any damage.

On May 5 Pym felt that it was time to disclose
part, if not all, that he had discovered concerning the
Army Plot, and the queen's intention of going to
Portsmouth, thence to summon a French force to the

help of the king. The excitement was great. It was resolved 'that this House doth declare, that if any shall councell, consent or assist the bringing of any forraing force into this kingdome, hee shall be declared a publique enimy to the kingdom, unless it bee by the command of the king, and consent of both houses of parliment.' Orders were given to the knights and burgesses to consider how their counties were provided with ammunition and arms, 'that they may be supplied.' Strict discipline was enforced on the members themselves. 'Every member of this house now in towne, shall bee heere to morrow at 8 a'clock, and those that offend heerein shall be proceeded against as for a contempt of this house.' 'If any man whisper, or stir out of his place when a message is deliveringe, or businesse of importance, to the disturbance of the house, Mr. Speaker shall present his name to the house to bee punished.' It is a hard measure, and one which would not now be endured.

The state of men's minds was such that when a board in the gallery cracked under the weight of two fat members, Sir John Wray called out that he smelt gunpowder. The memory of the attempt of Guy Fawkes was still vivid, the members rushed into the lobby and the strangers into Westminster Hall, before the alarm was found to be false. The City trainbands hearing the rumour, turned out to defend the House, and got as far as Covent Garden before they learnt the truth.

On Friday, May 7, ' an act to prevent the inconvenience that may happen by the untimely adjorninge, prorogueing or dissolvinge the present parliment . . . did passe this house,' Hyde and Falkland assenting to it as thoroughly as Pym and Hampden. Investigations of the Army Plot were being carried on, and Ralph notices a report by Pym of a conference with the lords under the heads of : ' 1. The running away [i.e. of Percy, Jermyn, and Suekling, charged with participation in the plot] confirmes [i.e. the truth of the disclosures respecting it]. 2. French forces designed for Porchmouth.' Thirdly, he mentions the various measures of defence to be taken : ' Secure the iles of Wight and Gersie and Gernsey, Hampsheire, Dorsetsheire, and trayned bands to bee in a readinesse,' &c.

Lady Sussex, thanking Sir Ralph as usual for his letters, says : ' it tis I confes to much after cuch tedious dayes as you have, to right cuch lettirs. This last wike it semes hath discoverde strange bissines ; God hath bine infinetly marsifull to this nasyone, in prefentinge still what hath bene intendede for our ruen's, & i hope will still so keepe us that the enimes to religon, & so to us, will never have power ; but that wee shall see the confusyon of many of them.'

The trial of Strafford had now lasted eighteen days, and on May 8 Sir Ralph records shortly that ' the Bill of Attainder passed [the third reading in the House of Lords].' Eighty peers had attended the trial, but only forty-five voted ; twenty-six for, nineteen against the conviction. He records on the same day : ' A conference about . . . the peace of the kingdom. . . . A conference to desier the Lords to move the king to give his answer to the bill of attainder with speed.' He also mentions that ' Lord Mandevill [Lord Kimbolton] gon to Porchmouth,' by order of the Commons, to secure the place. He was son of Lord Manchester, who was soon afterwards general of the parliamentary forces. The note proceeds : ' A proclamation for 5 that are fled [the courtiers concerned in the Army Plot]. The forces desierd, ordred to be in readinesse for the defence of the southerne parts,' against invasion by France.

At this point the 'Notes' end as far as Strafford is concerned, as Sir Ralph was only chronicling the proceedings of the House of Commons. It is here that we specially miss that ' wikely nues ' which Sir Ralph used to write to Lady Sussex, and for which she thanks him so cordially. That no copies of his letters can be found is a real loss, as they would have given the feeling day by day in Parliament and in the country concerning the struggle of the king to save Strafford, but it is evident that the danger of getting into trouble by observations and private letters, which were then continually opened, was always before the eyes of the writers. Even to his brothers Sir Ralph ventures on few political observations, and his letters to Lady Sussex were always sent by private hand.

On January 19 she had written : ' Yon great
lorde i hope will com to the honor of behedinge ; if
he scape he will do more ill than ever was don.
Your Parlyment makes many sade harts, i hope you
will make this a happy kaindom before you have
don ; i am very glad of your nues, for we have much
but littel true here ; ' and an allusion in another
letter—' I pray God your hoses may agree, and
that they may make an end of this great lorde '—
shows how strong was the popular feeling against
the earl.

That the technical proofs of Strafford's treason
were insufficient is evident, but it was surely well
said that ' the man who seeks to subvert the national
liberties must not escape because his offence hath not
been properly defined.' ' How many haires breadths
makes a tall man,' Sir Ralph quotes from Lord Falkland on April 15, ' & how many makes a little man,
noe man can well say ; yet wee know a tall man
when we see him from a low man, soe 'tis in this,
how many illegal acts makes a treason is not certainly well known but wee well know it when we
see it.' The House was convinced of the danger of
Strafford's very existence to all the objects which
they thought most important to gain both for Church
and State. ' That grand apostate to the Commonwealth must not expect to be pardoned in this world,
till he be dispatched to the other,' as even Digby
declared.

A final attempt at escape failed. It was afterwards known that Strafford had offered Balfour, Lieutenant of the Tower, 22,000*l*. and a good marriage for his son if he would connive at his flight ; but Balfour refused.

Menacing crowds continued to surround the houses of parliament and the palace at Whitehall, uttering violent cries for justice and calling for Strafford's death ; and at length, alarmed for the safety of the queen, and shaken by her tears and entreaties— for Henrietta Maria could see no reason for risking anything to save a man whom she disliked and feared —Charles basely surrendered his friend and counsellor in the face of his own assurances of safety ' on the faith of a king.'

His cowardly, shuffling letter to the Lords, with its most mean and impotent conclusion, ' If he must die, it were charity to reprieve him till Saturday,' marks the lowest ebb of Charles's career ; his courage —and his passive courage was great—never again gave way under his difficulties.

The great earl died as he had lived, nothing daunted. ' I dare look death in the face, and I hope the people too,' he answered proudly, when told of the jubilant crowds who would collect to see him die. ' I thank God I am not afraid of death, but do as cheerfully put off my doublet at this time as ever I did when 1 went to bed.' The feeling against him in the country was tremendous. ' I am glad justice is exicuted on my Lord Straford,' wrote Lady Brilliana Harley from Herefordshire, the best and kindest of women, but a strong parliamentarian—' whoo I think dyed like a Seneca, but not like one that had tasted the mistery of godlyness. . . . the wicked flowreschess but for a time in his life, nor in his death has peace.'

There was a great shout of joy on Tower Hill as the axe fell, bonfires blazed, and the triumphant cries of an immense multitude hailed the death of the chief support of the king and his party.